BORIS KAP

THREE IMMIGRATION

TRANSLATION FROM RUSSIAN
BY THE AUTHOR

I dedicate this book
To everyone
Who was dear to me and
Left behind unforgettable
Memory and pain of loss.
To everyone,
Who made my life
Worthy of their memory.

CONTENT

In the land of Israel

Coming down the plane, I inhaled the warm, moist air and set foot on the land of Israel.

I fell in love with this land a long time ago. It was in my thoughts and in my soul from the minute I decided to get permission to leave the Soviet Union. Finally, once the impossible and unlikely, it became a tangible reality.

Together with all the passengers, we headed towards the airport building. The happiness of the arrival was overshadowed by the bitterness of the loss, the feeling of which now manifested itself even stronger - here on the land of Israel were two of us, but had to be three.

Holding my daughter by the hand, I thought about her future in this country, where she will be surrounded by attention and care, and no one will ever hurt her because she was born Jewish.

We were taken to the hall, where among people coming to meet passengers, I immediately saw Matvey. Together with him, we were invited to the room where Matvey helped me understand the questions asked by the immigration officer. I realized that this is required by the procedure through which all immigrants pass. Then they gave my daughter and me, each separately, an Israeli identity card.

"Congratulations. Now you are Israelis," told us, smiling and shaking our hands, the immigration officer.

Matvey asked him to send to ulpan near Tel Aviv. There were no objections, and he gave us a referral to Netanya. Having received permission to take us to his home before the start of the studies in the ulpan, Matvey led us to the exit. We left the airport building and in his car soon were on the highway leading to Tel Aviv. Through the car windows, I looked with interest at everything that appeared in the field of my vision – the landscape of Israel.

After the last day's worries and experiences I went through, and the bitter minutes of separation from my parents and sister, it is difficult to put into words the feeling of these first hours on the land of Israel. The constant anxiety that haunted me and the tension disappeared. We are in our homeland.

We arrived into Tel Aviv, and the car soon stopped in front of a four-story new building.

"We at home," said Matvey with relief, tired of the long wait at the airport and paperwork.

The apartment was cool. The spacious living room was furnished with beautiful leather furniture. Sitting in comfortable chairs, we were finally able to move on with the conversation. Their family went to Israel two years ago. During this time, many events occurred in Minsk, which I did not mention in the letters, knowing that they are all checked, and I had no information about their life in Israel. Our conversation lasted until late in the evening.

The next day I wanted to see Tel Aviv. Matvey was at work. Rita wrote their address on a piece of paper, believing that, if we get lost, we will have to ask for help from passersby.

Having walked one block down the street, I noticed people in black suits, white shirts, and wide-brimmed black hats, and some of them had hats made of fur. It struck me that in such heat they could wear such warm hats. On the sidewalk, slowly paced men with lush beards. From the children's temples hung long hairsprings, as I saw it in the adults.

The heads of women were covered, and their long skirts resembled the female fashion of the last century. We walked the streets, and people looked similar.

In the evening, after returning from work, Matvey explained that their family lives in the area of religious Jews, known to everyone as Bnei Brak. Orthodox practices are jealously observed here. I was surprised to learn that the Orthodox do not recognize the Jewish state, and their children do not serve in the army.

Also, it is dangerous to drive on a Saturday in their area of residence - they can throw stones at the drivers.

Completely unfamiliar with religious issues, I was distressed by what I heard. I remembered my father's words before I left for Israel: "Among the Jews, there are also different people, and not with everyone possible to find a common language."

Probably, dad had in mind such religious fanatics. Dad was born before the revolution in a small Jewish town. He studied at the Jewish school, which was called - heder. His father and grandfather were religious people, like all the inhabitants of the town.

Matvey pleased us by saying that he decided to take a few days off, and since our arrival coincides with the beginning of the Jewish holidays, he will be able to show us a resort town on the Red Sea.

"Eilat is one of the most beautiful places in the south of the country, which we have not yet visited," he said.

The next day, in the company of his friends, our motorcade of three cars set off on a short trip through the Sinai desert to the Red Sea. Arriving in Eilat, we stayed at the apartment of Joseph Kushnir. The first time I had to meet him in Minsk when Matvey invited me to listen about the possibility of emigration to Israel.

Joseph greeted us joyfully and hospitably, saying that he really misses his friends who live far away, and he rarely succeeds in visiting them because of the great distance.

His bachelor and spacious three-room apartment in a new house with a small amount of furniture seemed empty. The air conditioner worked without shutting down, otherwise, as Joseph said, it would be impossible to live in this climate. Here, in Eilat, for the first time, I felt how hot and dry air instantly covered the whole body, as if I was immersed in water.

In the morning of the next day, the same motorcade of three cars departed to the sea. After a short trip, we found a beautiful place on the beach near the parking of our vehicles.

On the left side of our camping was visible Hotel "Eilat." Opposite us, on the other side of the bay, on the side of Jordan, was a ridge of mountain ranges of brown color and no sign of greenery. At the foot of the mountains at the mooring place, I could hardly distinguish a few ships.

I was told that along the coast and just a few kilometers from our parking area there are beautiful beaches with amazing under the water sea life with corals of all sorts of fantastic shapes and exotic fish.

We did not go there because men and women on that beach are not allowed to wear clothes. Nudists from all over the world come here, and they live in tents for months.

The temperature of the water in the sea all year round is kept at twenty-five degrees, and the beauty of the marine fauna gathers many lovers of scuba diving.

It was difficult for me to imagine how somebody can walk around in a public place naked, not feeling shame. This, of course, was my point of view. Continuing to think about nudists, I came to the conclusion that these people see a kind of freedom in nudity and, being in the company of their own kind, enjoy the realization that they are doing something that for others is unthinkable on the beach allotted especially for them. Naturally, this beach allows for young men to show not only their beautiful muscular body, and for women what they have tried to hide in other circumstances. I imagined what is happening to the parts of the body being blithely open when they run or play volleyball.

You can easily cover up physical defects with clothes, or show the difference in financial superiority. In nudity, - everyone is equal. There is neither poor nor rich. It turns out that they are the only equal society - like the natives in the jungle, but only in a developed nation.

Ruthless sunshine interrupted my thoughts, and I had to flee in the water.
Nearby, large boats slid with tourists. Through the transparent bottom, they could admire the fauna of the underwater world. The bright blue sky, turquoise water, white sand of the beach and hundreds of umbrellas with chairs in which the campers settled down - all this made on me an extraordinary pacifying impression.

After spending a few hours in the water and under the sun, our friendly company laid out the contents of the traveling refrigerators, and our stomachs received reinforcements.

Feeling that we were overheated in the sun, we agreed to return to the city and began to get ready for departure. Matvey, giving me the car keys, asked me to bring a bag from the trunk. I gave him the bag, and when he asked for his keys, I remembered that they were left at the bottom of the luggage chest, which I slammed. The car doors were closed. I was depressed and saddened by my inattention, mainly because we were left under the scorching rays of the sun.

Drivers gathered to discuss how to open the closed lid. We were exhausted from the heat, but no one could find a solution. Seeing our group, frolicking around the car, and realizing that we need help, one of the guests approached our company. Having learned what the matter was, he said that he would try to help us. Soon he came back holding a screwdriver. Seeing our questioning looks, he explained that he would open the trunk, but we would have to install a new lock. We had no other way out, and Matvey agreed. The luggage compartment was open. With relief, we loaded the things into the car and, tying the lid with the rope, returned to Joseph's apartment. It was the first and so unsuccessful, because of me, Matvey's trip in his new car.

We spent the rest of that day inside a chilled apartment. Only now I saw my red-skinned body, which burned when touched. My daughter had the same burns. The next day, seeing the blisters on the skin, there could be no question of going to the sea, and everyone decided to return to Tel Aviv since everyone's tan in our company turned into a sunburn.

Our trip to the sea, initially scheduled for three days, turned out to be short. The sun's rays have done their job - they punished us for our careless attitude to our health.

On the way back, the road did not seem as long as it was when we drove through the desert to Eilat. The lifeless, seemingly endless space of sand and stone hills was left behind, and when the Tel Aviv suburbs appeared in the distance, we felt more cheerful.

The War

Ulpan. The victory of Israel. Job seeking.
Family of Garik Schultz. Call-up in the army.
The story of getting an apartment.

The morning of the next day. The most important day of the year for the Jews has come - the Day of Judgment - when the fate of each Jew is decided, and his future is predicted.

We sat at home with the windows closed so that the neighbors could not see how we had breakfast. On this day, no one should eat and drink. But we, who grew up in a country where all religions were banned, did not realize how important this holiday is for us, the Jews. To watch TV is forbidden too. But Matthew decided to turn it on. After listening to the message, he turned to us. There was anxiety in his voice when he said that today the Arabs, without declaring war, attacked Israel. From the South, the Egyptian troops, after destroying Israel's first line of defense along the Suez Canal, are moving along the Sinai desert towards Tel Aviv, while Syria attacked Israel from the North.

We sat silently, trying to comprehend the terrible news. On the most sacred day for Jews, when the entire population of the country in the synagogues and prayers asks God for the forgiveness of the sins, on this very day, when Jews ask God to grant them life, the Arabs decided to take this life away from them. Rejoicing at their savage find, they presented a bloody surprise to the Jews of Israel. Stunned by the message, we sat at the TV all day.

The Arabs have once again proved their intransigence towards Israel. They could not forgive themselves for the three previous defeats and decided to destroy the state that provides a home to all Jews scattered around different countries.

And here again, without a declaration of war, a sneaky stab in the back. Matvey sat looking at the screen and listening. From time to time, he translated. It was clear that the country was in a critical situation.

There was heavy fighting, and at the same time, there was mobilization in the army. Israel suffered heavy losses and did not hide it.

Yesterday's day on the Red Sea, azure skies, hundreds of Israelis on the beach and a peaceful, friendly environment — all this, amid the message of the secret Arab's plan of attacking Israel, and the terrible losses that a country not prepared for such a turn of events, seemed non-believable. The desert, which we crossed yesterday morning, today turned into a sea of fire burning tanks and downed aircraft.

The next morning, Matvey took us to ulpan in Natanya and returned to work at the hospital, where the wounded soldiers had already begun to arrive.

Netanya turned out to be a cozy small town by the sea. We were shown an apartment which will be our home during a period of learning the language, classrooms, a dining room and was given a class schedule.

On the same day, we had lunch in the dining room. In the spacious hall, almost all the tables were occupied. Passing by, one could hear conversations in English, French, and Russian. At the table with us sat two women. One woman with her son, in the age of my daughter, and a single, middle-aged woman.

We introduced ourselves. Both women were older than me. A woman with a boy, a doctor of chemical sciences, came to Israel from Moscow; the second momen is a medical doctor from Lithuania. Both have relatives in Israel.

Judging by the remarks and muffled anxious voices - people discussed events in the war.

After lunch, we were all invited to a large room and the head of the ulpan, a tall old man, said that despite the in the country in the war, there would be no changes in the curriculum and activities.

After the meeting, I approached him and said that I would like to help the army with any work.
He smiled. "The biggest help is learning a language, without which help is useless."

Our teacher, a very young woman, led the lessons calm, but her face was sad – her husband was in combat.

A few days later, we learned that the advance of the Arab armies stopped and the situation on the front improved. Learning the language went well. I liked the program and the almost mathematical pattern of derived words.

I studied Hebrew with pleasure. I saw most of Americans experienced hardship while learning the language. I made friends with the family from New York, and we tried to talk in Hebrew using the standard phrases from the textbooks, holding them in front of us.

In our spare time, I often went with the daughter to the beach. Nearby were visible multistory unfinished buildings. They stood in anticipation of the workers, who at that time of the war were holding rifles, not construction tools. Next to the ulpan was a small farm of orange trees. Juicy, ripened fruits there was no one to collect. The owner of this farm was defending our country.

Every morning we came to the class to learn Hebrew, but we knew that on the battlefield, thousands of sons of Israel were fighting Arab armies.

Another alarming week has passed. When it was reported that the Israeli army had launched an offensive, the tense feeling, and and fear for the fate of the country disappeared.

In the next week, joyous news came about the crushing defeat of the Syrian and Egyptian armies.

Israeli troops crossed the Suez Canal and were in Egypt, forty kilometers from Cairo.

In anticipation of the complete defeat and the capitulation of Egypt, the United Nations announced the end of the war. In fact, this decision was made by the Soviet Union and America. The Soviet Union was furious. Despite the participation of their "military councils" and weapons, including the most modern aircraft and tanks provided by them to Egypt, Israel not only destroyed the Egyptian and Syrian troops but also captured many thousands of Egyptian soldiers, a large number of equipment and weapons.

Having won, Israel did not exult. He mourned and buried the fallen warriors. For all the time of the existence of Israel, this war was the most difficult and sorrowful. The battle took away the future from the youngest and most able-bodied people; in young men - learning, receiving a profession and creating a family; from the fathers were taken away the joy of seeing their children, rejoice at their success in life, see their wives and be their support at the right moment. Tens of thousands were injured and maimed.

It will take a long time before we hear joyful laughter and cheerful voices in the streets of Israel. Our teacher, the first time came to the class with a smile - her husband returned from the front unscathed.

After the war ended, Mark Gorfinkel, a medical doctor, came to visit me. We, old school friends, had something to remember and to talk about because we have not met for many years.

Matvey, my only relative in Israel, did not forget me either. During the free time of studies he was taking us in Tel Aviv, and we had the opportunity to know the city a little bit more.

The city did not look like I saw it at the arrival. Unfinished buildings, closed shops, sad faces of passers-by and tired faces of soldiers returning home, made it clear that the country would not come to its senses soon.

Returning to the ulpan, I heard about the terrorist attack near the hospital in Rehovot. There was an assembly point for soldiers waiting for buses in the morning for delivery to their units. A car drove up to the gathering place of the soldiers and exploded, scattering the soldiers' bodies over the whole area. This brutal act of terror shook me to the core.

Hundreds of maternal hearts will shrink from unspeakable pain. It was a reminder that Israel has enemies, both outside and inside.

Another month of study passed. The ulpan management began working on helping people to find jobs and to get housing.

Two American families have new cars. A family from Georgia bought a small truck. The owner of the vehicle, before the end of the ulpan, began to earn money on the transportation of baggage arriving from the Union.

In the family from Moldova, the dad-musician was invited to work in Jerusalem. A doctor from Lithuania, a neighbor at the table, also found a job. News about employment gave hope that all students of ulpan will safely arrange their lives. I was seriously studying Hebrew, realizing that I could get a job as an engineer only if I knew the language.

My daughter did not want to study hard. I did not insist, because I understood that she would have plenty of time for this at school. There were many children of her age in the ulpan, and she was playing with them after classes not far from our home.

I sat with the textbook. The girl came running and said that Sveta fell and hurt her leg. Seeing the daughter's leg, I was horrified: her knee was torn apart, the ligament was sticking out, and blood was flowing without stopping. I rushed home and, taking a towel, covered the wound with it than tightened my belt over her knee.

In the next house, where the American family lived, there was a car and I turned to them to help me take my daughter to the hospital, but the neighbor refused, explaining that for this I need to call an ambulance. My daughter lay on the ground with the profusely bleeding knee. There were no workers in the ulpan. I rushed to another neighbor, begging for help. He agreed. With my daughter in my arms, I got into the car.

At the hospital, she was immediately taken to the operating room. The doctor came out after the operation and said that she was lucky, he saved her knee, but maybe she would be a little bit limp. The leg was put in a cast, and we were taken back to the ulpan. It was already night. My daughter did not cry. She still was under stress from what had happened. Excited, I did not sleep, blaming myself for not being able to save my daughter from an accident. In the morning, I brought breakfast to her bed and decided to look at the place on the lawn where she was wounded. I saw a rusty metal pipe with torn edges and bloody grass.

Ulpan studies are over. Only a few families left. One of them was the family of a professor of psychology from America. I met them after the end of the war. One day, walking along the seashore, I saw him with two children who were busy in the sand, and a local guy threw pebbles at them. The professor asked him not to do this, but the guy did not pay attention.

I walked over to the bully and told him to get out right away. He realized that it was better to follow my advice. The professor thanked me for helping him out of an unpleasant situation and invited me to be his guest. Since then, my daughter and I sometimes visited them, checking our ability to communicate in Hebrew.

I learned that their family was left because the baggage with belongings and documents sent from America had not yet arrived. Without records, nowhere he was offered a job. I stayed because we had nowhere to go, and no one had a request for engineering work in my specialty.

Understanding my situation, the management of the ulpan gave me a small amount of money so that I could buy groceries and cook at home since the ulpan kitchen was already closed. For the first time, I had to learn to cook.

I remember how unusual it was for me to wash and clean raw chicken meat. With vegetables and potatoes, there was no problem. Oddly enough, everything was edible, and my daughter ate my soups and porridges with pleasure.

Every day I came to find out about a possible job offer, but for my engineering profession they, unfortunately, had nothing. About a month has passed. Ulpan for new immigrants has not functioned yet, but work has continued to assist those who need it.

Muscovite received an offer to work in a scientific institute and an apartment near Tel Aviv. Before leaving the ulpan, she came to say goodbye and said that her relative is the owner of a sugar factory in Gadera. He currently needs a mechanical engineer for the position of chief engineer of the plant. She told him about me, and he agreed to see me in his apartment in Tel Aviv.

I was incredibly surprised by her attention and was delighted with such a happy coincidence. She gave me the address, phone number, and asked to call. What I immediately did when she left.

On the phone, he spoke to me in Russian with an Israeli accent. I arrived at a specified time and was accepted by the owner. The apartment was warm. An elderly man, in his dressing-gown, said he was a little unwell, but he wanted to see me and talk in person after recommendation by his niece. After asking in detail about my work in Minsk and about my marital status, he paused and, unexpectedly for me, said that he is employing me for the job.

The next day, he called and said that because of a cold, he could not show me the plant personally, but the chief engineer who is leaving to work abroad agreed to show me the factory. I came to a meeting with a man whom I supposed to replace.

In an open-air Mercedes, we were on the spot an hour later. The plant was small. The chief engineer explained to me the entire production process, acquainted me with the equipment, the laboratory for checking the product quality, packaging, and a large repair shop. After introducing me to the production manager, he left.

After his departure, during the break, I was invited to the dining room. Then they began to acquaint with the team of the plant. The production manager said that according to my position, I would have a vehicle for official use. I will also be given a free apartment.

As if by the way, he touched upon problems that require urgent solutions. Having shown a gear about a meter in diameter with a broken tooth, he asked if it was possible to make a new one if there was no drawing for it. I explained that there is no problem. It is necessary to measure the available parameters, make the calculation and drawing of the wheel.

Continuing to show the plant, he suddenly asked. "Tell me how you might like to live in such a small town and work on such a small factory?"

I was unpleasantly surprised. Without answering, I left the factory and returned to the ulpan.

The next morning I was going to call the factory owner to discuss employment issues and to schedule the next meeting. I liked the plant, and from the engineering point of view, I did not see any difficulties.

But before I was going to call the owner of the factory, an employee of the ulpan appeared on the threshold of the apartment and happily announced that a design engineer was required at one of the factories in the Haifa area. I asked her to call and ask if this post really exists because I have very little money left to travel. Request confirmed, and I hit the road.

The name of the plant - Soltam - did not tell me anything. I was introduced to the head of the design bureau. His name was Mendel. After asking about my experience and reading my workbook, which had already been translated into English before departure, he suddenly offered to stay in the department for the day and draw a particular device. I agreed. He brought a drawing of a mechanism for an automatic feeding with details the machine and said that it needs to be redone to another part, the drawing of which was attached.

I was provided with a workplace and drawing tools. After reviewing the design, I get down to work.

It has been a long time since I held a pencil in my hand and sat in front of a blank sheet of drawing paper. I was deprived of creative work, which was a significant part of my life, during the long months of my wife's illness, preparing for departure, and then studying in an ulpan.

And here I am standing in front of the drawing board, feeling that my knowledge and experience can be useful to this plant. I forgot about the environment and looked up from the board only when I was invited to the dining room. On each table were tomatoes, cucumbers, peppers, and onions. I noticed how each of my design colleagues prepared a salad.

Participants of the last war, they only recently returned from the army. I was asked a few questions about my past and, having finished eating, we returned to the workplaces.

Several times one of the staff members approached the board and reviewed my work. By chance, I saw how, moving away from my drawing board, he looked towards the head of the bureau and nodded affirmatively. By the end of the day, I finished the work. After checking the drawings, the chief said that he was employing me and sent to the personnel department.

From the factory I was returning by bus delivering the factory workers. I arrived in Haifa, and from there, I got to the ulpan. I was so fascinated by the return to the drawing board, I did not even have time to think I had already been hired with a high position and, probably, even with a safe future. As if under hypnosis, I called the plant owner in Tel Aviv, thanked him for the position he offered, and politely declined the offer.

Years later, I realized that I had made a big mistake. I was inspired by the possibility to return to creative design work, where my experience and knowledge can be more useful.

The factory was in the Haifa area, and I wanted to find a home closer to my work. I went to Tel Aviv, where the department of absorption was in charge of housing allocation to new immigrants. Without any delay, I received an apartment in Kiryat Yam, not far from the factory of my employment. Happy with the success of having my own apartment, I immediately went to see it. According to the address recorded in given to me document, I found a house and saw someone already lives there.

I knocked on the door. A man appeared on the threshold. I showed him the document indicated that the apartment listed under my name. Without looking at it, he stated that this apartment was given to him and advised me to find out the error in the local municipality. A fat woman, resembling a market-place trader, who managed the distribution of apartments in Kiryat Yam, did not want to explain anything and sent me back to Tel Aviv.

I had to go back. I was told that in their documents not shown they had allocated this apartment to someone other than me, and it is necessary to find out how it happened.

Having learned about my housing problem, the professor from America suggested leaving my daughter temporarily in their family, as they recently moved to a large apartment in Tel Aviv. I was eternally grateful for their timely assistance.

Having solved the housing problem for my daughter, I went to visit my friend Garik Schultz in Haifa. He brought me to the balcony and showing on the folding bed said that I could be with them as much as I needed. Having arrived in Israel with the whole family two years ago, they were fluent in Hebrew and became familiar with the Israeli way of life. Both worked according to their profession. Garik worked as an electrical engineer, and his wife Zhanna was a nurse.

Having a temporary roof under my head, I was back to work. The factory, as I found out, was set up for the manufacture of shells and parts for tanks. It was also known for making stainless steel tableware, which, due to its excellent quality, was highly valued in the local market.

I liked everything; the department where I worked, the team, the people in the workshops, organized delivery to work by the transport of the enterprise, two meals a day, and the salary. It was so different from the country I left that I was overwhelmed with a sense of pride for our little Israel.

One month after starting work at the plant, I got drafted into the army for a three-month course of military training. The unit, for the most part, consisted of soldiers who were emigrants from the Soviet Union.

Our commander went through all wars Israel had to wage. A resident of the kibbutz, he spoke in a calm, not commanding voice. He taught us not only to shoot and throw grenades but also to be one team, where everyone performs the command and understands how best to carry it out, not exposing himself and his comrades to unnecessary danger.

He did not demand stretching before him, asked to call him only by his name and talked to us as equals, despite his high rank. During the breaks in the training, he found time to learn about who we are and where we are from, what our occupations and marital status.

Telling us about Israel, we going to defend, he warned us to be constantly vigilant even in every day of civic life, where we exposed to daily danger from Arabs, among whom there are many suicide bombers.

Standing at night on guard and looking into the silent night darkness, I thought about those who are now sleeping peacefully. I was proud of being a soldier at service to my new homeland.

After the daytime on the march under the scorching sun with a full combat load and heavy training, it was pleasant to take a shower and change clothes.

During the night marches, we often stopped for a rest. Taking off a heavy backpack and putting an M-16 next to me, I lay down on the back, gazing at the myriad of bright stars in the silence of the night. They sparkled peacefully against the black sky.

But there was no peaceful situation in the country, surrounded by millions of hating us, Arabs.

Why can't we live together peacefully under this sky and on this earth? Why do they hate us? Why do they want to kill us?

In the ghetto, I also asked my mother. "Why do they want to kill us? What have we done to them?"

"Because we are Jews," answered Mom.

That was over thirty years ago when the fascists of Nazi Germany were killing us, and now the Arabs fanatics want to kill us. How are they different from the Nazis? Why no one in the world wants to stop these fanatic killers? When will they realizes that no one can take from the Jews their original land?

After military training, I returned to the factory and felt that I had become a soldier, one of those who, if necessary, would defend the country.

Employees talked about household chores, needs, future plans, vacations, and home purchases. They returned from the battlefield, where they lost friends, saw death, were among the explosions of shells and burning tanks. And now, these people stood next to me at the drawing boards with a pencil in hand.

Drivers of tanks now seating behind the steering wheels of buses. Doctors returned to hospitals; builders returned to construction sites, moshavniks and kibbutzniks back to the harvest. The students returned to the universities continuing interrupted studies.

It was my country where every resident was also a warrior. Israel fascinated me not only with the blooming fruit trees, plantations of bananas and vast fields of ripening vegetables. Israel fascinated me not only with beautiful roads and transport communication. Israel fascinated me not only with modern high-rise buildings and cozy cafes - Israel fascinated me with people, who did all this and defended this beautiful country from destruction.

Even when my apartment was given, as a result of a scam deal, to someone else, it did not diminish my admiration for Israel.

At the factory, I met one of the workers who was also from Minsk. He invited me to meet his family, and after work we went together. He lived near the factory in a charming and green village called Tivon, built on a high and flat hill surrounded by the vegetable plantations, spread out on a vast plain.

They had a big apartment. Children already finished school, the wife did not work. I told them about myself and touched on the failure to get an apartment. They were surprised and asked why I did not do anything to return it. I explained that my visits to Tel Aviv did not change anything. They offered me to stay with them until the issue with the apartment is resolved because it was much closer to the plant from them than from the Hifa. Like in the Shultz family, there was a place for me on the balcony. Again a folding bed, but the view was astonishing, and the large pine branches descended directly to the terrace.

When I returned from work, Dina, the wife of my new acquaintance, said that she had a conversation with a neighbor who lived nearby in a separate house. She told him about my wanderings without an apartment. She also mentioned that I have been separated for half a year from my daughter, who is living now with not related family. The neighbor, the retired general, was outraged and wanted to see me immediately at his home. I told him the whole story and showed the document, where there was a stamp with the address of the apartment allocated to me.

With my document, Zeev, as he asked to call him, went personally to Tel Aviv and in the evening of the same day, when I returned from work, handed me my document with a new stamp of the selected apartment. I could not believe my eyes - it was the same address of the house in Kiryat Yam, just another apartment number.

The two-story house consisted of three entrances, where only one of them had flats occupied. I was the only inhabitant of the next entry on the first floor. All other apartments were still waiting for their future tenants. I was struck by the injustice of a swindler from Odessa, who, as I learned later, gave my apartment to an immigrant from Georgia for a bribe in the form of a carpet.

Finally, after so many wanderings, I got an apartment. I liked everything in it; a large living room, balcony with glass sliding doors, two bedrooms, shower, toilet and kitchen with gas stove. There was no refrigerator. The floor of the whole apartment, as everywhere in Israel, was covered with tiles.

In the nearest shop, I bought the most necessary things for cleaning the floor. Opening the glass door of the living room and the windows on the balcony, I took a full bucket of water and splashed it on the floor covering it with soap suds. With the mop drove all the water in the direction of the balcony and outside the flat. After rinsing the floor with clean water, I admired the sparkling plates in the living room. The same cleaning I carried out throughout the apartment.

Having received two metal beds with mattresses, bed accessories, a teapot, several mugs, forks, and knives, I closed the apartment and went to fetch my daughter. Immigrants from America, with their two own children, gave the shelter to my daughter, which, to my surprise, Matvey, her mother's brother, did not offer. Sincerely thanking the family of the professor for help, I left them my address and we went home.

Now I was able to bring the luggage from the port in Haifa. In the living room appeared furniture, and in the kitchen, there were dishes and pans.

Looking at the furniture that was broken in several places, I remembered how at Minsk customs, the worker with a cargo hoist fork pierced the box that contained the furniture and smiled, waiting for my reaction. Perhaps he did this without receiving a bribe from me, or maybe just for his own pleasure. I looked at all this indifferently. My thoughts were no longer with them.

First of all, I needed a refrigerator. Then I decided to buy a TV, tape recorder and radio. These goods were sold to us, the emigrants, for half the price.

My daughter continued studies at a local school. She had many new friends and, when I was at work, she spent time in their company. But from now, I had the responsibility to prepare food. For a long time, I did not need to cook since I had breakfast and lunch at work. I began to make breakfast for her again and in the fridge was her lunch.

To work, I was leaving home early. A bus was waiting for all the workers at the gathering place and was departing at seven in the morning. An hour later we were at our working places.

After breakfast, my daughter, with the key of the house around her neck, went to the school.

I did not have money to buy a car, and taking the advice of one of my new friends, went to see one religious person who lends money to Russian immigrants at a small percentage. To my surprise, without demanding any income statement and only asking where I work, he gave me to sign a paper indicating the amount I must return every month and gave me fifteen thousand shekels in cash. This amount was enough for the initial payment but allowed me to purchase a car. I chose Alfasud - the Italian brand - and, having signed a five-year contract with a monthly fee of almost half my salary, I arrived home. In my life, it was the first car I owned. I sat in the car studying the controls, opened the hood, examined the sparkling elements of the engine, checked the roomy trunk and satisfied with the feeling of ownership, returned to the apartment.

My first driving test, and the car learning, I did in our town. After driving a few kilometers, when I stopped the car on a red traffic light, the car engine suddenly switched off, and I could not start it. A policeman on a motorcycle stopped near and asked what had happened. I said that I do not know what the problem is and asked if he could help me find out the reason. Saying that it was not his duty, he advised to call for technical assistance. I picked up the front hood and looked at the engine compartment, not knowing where to start checking. Accidentally, I looked at the battery and noticed that one terminal has no contact. I sighed with relief. The dealer did not check the car properly. Correcting the clamp was no problem, I started the car and continued the drive around the town.

My first long trip by car I made to Tivon. I came to thank Zeev for his help in getting the apartment. Glad seeing my daughter and me, he asked a lot about my life in Minsk, my work, my parents, and how I managed to leave. Then looking at my daughter, Zeev said that our country created for children. Their future will be better than the one he had in his childhood when the Jewish state did not exist yet. Leaving Zeev, we went to see my new friends from Minsk and finding out that they were going to the airport the next day to meet their eldest son. I offered to take them in my car. They happily agreed, and I had an opportunity, on my turn, to thank them for participating in solving the problem with the housing.

The next trip was to the Shultz family. They greeted us warmly and were pleased to hear that the problem with the apartment was solved and I liked my work.

During the conversation, it turned out that they intend to settle in the new territory. I understood that it was the support for land development. For me, it was unexpected because they had a big apartment in Haifa and secure jobs. I also heard about several settlements created by religious Jews. I could understand them - they wanted to live among the same religious families. But for the Shultz family, I did not consider it reasonable. Listening to their arguments, I was convinced that they were quite seriously discussing future relocation. First, they will have to live in temporary homes. Later, on an allocated plot of land, they can build a house according to their project and resources. A group of ten families, all of them from Minsk, already formed. They would like to bring more people who share their idea of living in a small settlement in the company of a large family.

Towards the future settlement, the government has already begun to build a road and communications. When mobile homes are delivered there, they will start their life in the chosen location. Even spending a lot of time every day traveling to work and back home, did not diminish their desire to move. Before I left, they asked me to think well about the idea that we, former Minsk residents, can be together again.

I would be happy, but the thought that driving to work for more than two hours stopped me. I have a good job and a flat. We had enough wandered not having a home. My daughter attends a local school, and she has friends. I decided to postpone a relocation proposal.

All employees of the plant, on the holidays, received gifts. In spite, I was working only for several months; I got it too. It was a set of stainless steel pans. Also the fact that I received a gift after having an apartment said that it was taken into account. I would not dare to buy such an expensive set. I was sure, those involved in the distribution of gifts understood the needs of the new immigrants. I noticed that all the workers received various things, and everyone was satisfied.

Later, when I received gifts, I perceived it already as a norm, like it supposes to be. But my first gift made me excited.

I remembered another one gift. and I want to tell you about it.

As I said, gifts were always practical. The next gift was a picnic fridge. This happened after the purchase of the car and coincided with another Jewish holiday.

I do not think that it is necessary to mention that the holiday was Jewish, because in Israel there are no other holidays. In fact, sometimes immigrants celebrate the holidays of the countries from which they came, but it's nothing to do with the gifts that people receive at enterprises in Israel.

So, I got a fridge. Its place was in the luggage of the car - a permanent place. Under the sultry Israeli climate, it served as a reliable food keeper on every trip to the grocery store.

More than once, I had to accept invitations to the picnics with friends and acquaintances. Usually, we went to a wild place outside of the city. Each participant had its own fridge, the contents of which allowed him to eat and drink during the day and to share with others, as we did always.

We spent a day in discussions of world events and sharp criticism of our government rulers, and almost everyone had own opinion. We must not forget that there were several dozens of political parties in the country. Satisfied that they were able to express themselves, the picnic participants, finally decided to get some pleasure from nature and the coniferous air.

I did not take part in these discussions, because I did not understand anything in politics and, apart from work, I was not interested in anything. Those present at the picnic were in the country much longer than me. They understood and knew about politics more than I did. I did not agree with everyone but only listened. I saw that some of them did not like Israel.

I remember that in ulpan, one Muscovite did not want to study Hebrew, and from the very first days he began to look for an opportunity to leave for Germany. He, finally, leftand accepted to work at the news station called Freedom. He was over fifty, and his wife was no more than twenty-five. In Russia he was a lecturer at the institute, and his wife was his former student.

In another case, I had to get acquainted with another Moscovite. Then, I was still in the ulpan and looking for work. We met by chance. Very handsome and intelligent guy of my age. Mechanical engineer, he finished Bauman's Institute. Master of Sports in wrestling. It would seem that only one word – Bauman's - should have given him the way to any undertaking. To such specialists, as I understand it, should be given the best employment immediately. When I got to know him, he was unemployed for more than three months. First, he found a job at a small private factory. But when the owner told him that he did not agree with his calculation of the spring, the Muscovite was outraged by the stupidity of the employer and immediately left. He sold everything he had to survive. Recently, he sold his guitar to get food. He decided to go to America after receiving a letter from a friend in America who offered him a job. At the time we met, he already applied for a visa to America.

When he learned that we both were engaged in automation and individual production lines, he suddenly became interested and said that he could help me with his connections in America. He advised to follow his example and gave me his address where he would stop, his phone number and asked to keep in contact if I decide to go to America.

I could do it in Vienna. I had no desire to go to America because I saw myself only in Israel. Years later, I wanted to establish contact with him, but, unfortunately, I lost a notebook with his address.

After a year in Israel, two of my friends, Mark Gorfinkel and Fima Shalyutin, specialty doctors, left for Germany.

Now back to the story with the fridge. Before leaving the picnic place, we filled the refrigerators with empty dishes, uneaten leftovers, and rubbish - nothing allowed to stay in the forest. After the loading of folding chairs and tables, dishes, and refrigerators, people began to leave.

Arriving home, I opened the trunk and saw that my refrigerator was not in. Looked inside - nothing. Only then I remembered that when I was the reversing, before leaving the parking lot, I heard the sound of rustling and gnashing, but having decided that perhaps it was dry branches under the wheels of the car, I did not take into consideration and left.

Now, I realized that I forgot to put my refrigerator in the trunk, leaving it in the woods.

It was late in the evening, and to go back, I had no desire. I thought that in such a deserted place, no one would take my fridge, and I would get it the next day.

Unfortunately, when I returned, it was not there. Even if someone found it, who could know to whom it belongs.

Irreparable mistake

Casual meeting. My preparations for departure.
Tamara asks for a favor.
Delivery of documents in OVIR.
Tamara in Israel. Exposed deception.
The family falls apart.

Meanwhile, an event occurred that made my life full of misery. It changed the plans for the future. For many years, I regretted the mistake I had made out of kindness, or rather, because of my stupidity, when I left Minsk. Here is a brief story of my long tragedy.

One winter, like many workers in Russia provided by the enterprises with not expensive two weeks vacations, I was in the provincial holiday home.

I walked along the corridor with a partner; I shared the room. Suddenly, we heard someone trying to play the beginning of Beethoven's sonata "Elise." Walking into the hall, we saw a young girl. After the first chords, she was lost and started all over again. Seeing that she attracted attention with her play, the girl closed the lid of the piano and turned to us. My partner, a man of almost retirement age, began to wonder who she was, where she was from, and where she learned to play the piano. Tamara, as she introduced herself, said that she was finishing a medical school in Slonim, and playing the piano was her favorite hobby.

When Tamara started talking to me, asking where I came from and what my profession, my partner, referring to the late hour, apologized and left. Learning that I was from Minsk, she showed interest and said that she would like to get a job in Minsk, but she has no friends there. I gave Tamara my phone number and said if she will come to Minsk and have questions about finding a job, she may call me. I did not say to her that my wife was a doctor, but I thought, possibly she could help Tamara.

At the time of our conversation, a tall lieutenant appeared in the hall and headed towards us. She took his arm, and they left.

More than a year has passed. In my apartment rang the phone and I heard a female voice. "This is Tamara. Do you remember me?"

I was at home taking care of my wife, paralyzed after severe brain cancer surgery, and I had no desire to talk with Tamara. Having explained her my emotional condition, I hung up.

A year later, I buried my wife. Coming from work, stayed at home without a desire to communicate with people. My daughter after school sat down with homework. We had visited only by Oleg, Ida's elder brother, her cousin Nina and my parents.

One of these days Tamara called again. But I resolutely refused to talk to her. A month later, she called and said that she does not insist on the meeting, as she understood my grief, but she thought about my daughter and wanted to take her to the cinema and spend time with her.

My daughter, having finished her lessons, stayed with me at home. She did not have school friends and did not communicate with any of the children of her age. Thinking that because of me, she deprived of her interests, I agreed.

They spent almost half a day together, and when my daughter returned home, I saw her smiling. Tamara told me that after the movie, they went for a walk in the park and ate ice cream, and most importantly - they became good friends and agreed to meet more often. I thought that my depressed mood should not affect my daughter and, if she is feeling good in Tamara's company, let them sometimes spend time together.

During the period of growing tension at work and surveillance by the KGB, I was only concerned with departure to Israel.

Having received permission and wanting to leave my apartment to the parents, I began to work on solving this problem. Much time was also spent preparing the transfer of luggage.

When it was all over, I had only one week before my departure to Israel. Luggage sent. My apartment transferred to my parents, and they already lived there. I handed over all the documents to the OVIR and remained only with a passport, waiting for the receipt of the paper with the right to leave the country.

Tamara called and said that she would like to talk with me about something. We left the house and she, taking me by the arm, suddenly in a voice in which there were notes of co-feeling, said that I could no longer refuse a normal life and that I should think about the future.

"My future has already been decided," I replied. In a week, I am leaving with my daughter to Israel.

A smile disappeared from her face, and she fell silent, considering what she heard. Continuing to walk, she suddenly firmly said that, in that case, I must help her to leave the country. "It's impossible. You, Russian, will not be given permission to leave for Israel, especially since you have no one there."
"My father is a Jew, and all my relatives are Jews," she said.
I could not believe it, understanding what she wanted.

We continued our walk, and each of us was loaded with our own thoughts. Suddenly, Tamara joyfully shouted.
"I know what can be done! We can register a marriage, and after your departure, I can come to Israel on the basis that I am your wife."

"This is not only impossible, but also dangerous for me," I said, "because when I will hand over my passport, and they will see that I have a wife, I could be left in Minsk and deprived of my right to leave because I concealed the fact of the marriage registration."

The next day she came again and asked to help her. I saw that she did not understand my explanation, or she did not want to take it into consideration.
"I assure you that in OVIR everything is known about you. They would not even think of checking your passport. And I have the only way to leave the country legally. I am a nurse, and everywhere I can find a job," she said.

Her persistent and appealing voice had an effect, and I thought, "Why not help her to leave?"

We went and registered the marriage. Then Tamara asked me of another favor - to go together with her to her mother and introduce me, as her husband, so the mother would believe that she was married. We went.

Returning from the trip, I went to the OVIR to return the passport. The officer asked if I brought a certificate of renting an apartment and, without checking my passport, threw it into the drawer. Then he issued documents for me and my daughter with permission to leave the country. I left the building and walked without breathing, waiting to hear an officer's request to return. No one knew about the marriage. I was sure nobody would know about it because Tamara met none of my friends or my parents. I did not know how I was mistaken and how much misery this marriage brought in the life of my parents.

I was leaving the next day. At the station, I didn't get over the thought of how stupid I had been, and that I could be taken off the train at any moment. It seemed to me that the OVIR workers specially prepared this surprise to punish me and show to everyone who came to accompany me. When the train finally moved, I sighed with relief. I even felt satisfied that the trick with my passport was a success.

In Israel, it happened to meet women, but it suited me to say that I married and look for one who would attract me and take tender care of my daughter.

Tamara wrote letters, begging to send her the invitation which would allow her to apply for immigration. In each letter, she wrote that she could not live in Minsk, her thoughts only about us and, besides us, nothing else in her life, she wants to come to Israel and be a good mother to my daughter. In response, I wrote that we not right for each other, and she should arrange her life and not think about leaving for Israel. But letters with asking to save her life continued to come. In one of the letters, she wrote that she would commit suicide if I do not send her invitation to join me.

Her perseverance, with assurances of devotion to my daughter and a desire to devote her life to taking care of the two of us, led me sending her a desired invitation.

"Even if I meet a woman in Israel," I thought, "can I be sure that we will have a good relationship and my daughter will be fine. With Tamara, there could be no doubt - they were best friends. And if it is good for my daughter, then it will suit me too."

In Israel, one of my friend's wife was Russian. Both are engineers and worked. Their family environment was warm, full of care and support for each other, and their two boys were already at school and spoke fluent Hebrew.

I sent the invitation to Tamara, and a month later, she flew to Israel.

The meeting at the airport made a strange impression on me. Tamara did not rush to me with joy, as usual do people who have not seen each other for a long time.

Sluggish and indifferent, with a face that does not express any emotion, she handed me a suitcase and followed me to the car. On the way home, she was silent. I thought that this was due to the long flight and decided to give her a little rest.

Seeing my daughter, she greeted her coldly, took a shower, and went to bed. The day before her arrival, I bought a lot of berries and fruits in the market. The refrigerator was filled with dairy and meat products.

In the morning, she glanced at a juicy set of fruits, furniture in the living room, kitchen, and asked what plans I had. At work, I was given two days of vacation, so I decided to devote this day to her acquaintance with our city.

Next to our house was a small grocery store. The owners, two Georgians, gave me all the necessary products in credit and I paid them at the end of the month when I received my salary.

"It is very convenient, and you do not need to go anywhere. Choose any products you need, and I will pay later," I explained to Tamara.

I always liked to walk the streets of our area. High-rise buildings emerged at such fast pace - like mushrooms after rain. The tenants were mostly Russian-speaking immigrants, but there were many families from Europe and India. The immigrants from Arab countries who arrived in Israel in the fifties lived on the outskirts of the city in old houses, envying the "Russians."

The city center was far away, and I decided to walk to the sea - the beach sands were visible from the windows of our apartment. Despite the end of summer, the sun was not going to give a break from the heat and the moist air. The sea was stormy. The strong wind threw hot grains of sand into our faces. Such a walk could not bring pleasure, and we returned home.

Tamara still was not talkative. None of my friends and acquaintances, especially my parents, as I thought, Tamara could not know, since our marriage was a secret. Therefore, I did not ask her about them. I wanted to know about her personal life in Minsk. But she left this topic and started telling how in OVIR she was offered any help and an apartment if she would refuse to leave for Israel. She was persuaded almost to the very moment of departure, saying that she, Russian, had nothing to do in Israel.

Unfortunately, I did not receive letters from my parents, and they did not receive any of mines. Only later, I realized that it was the revenge of the KGB for the fact that I was able to deceive them with a passport. My punishment was cruel. I paid the price for this stamp with seventeen years not being able to correspond with my parents.

Weekends I began to devote to Tamara so that she had an idea about this small country, she was dreaming, and of which I was proud and loved with my whole soul. We traveled to Haifa, Tel Aviv, and Jerusalem. I wanted to show her the country where lived the girl, whom Tamara, as she wrote in the letters, wanted to be as her mother. Now she has this opportunity, and I am glad that my daughter would not be left alone when I am at work. Tamara will take care of her, and my daughter will have a woman, her best friend, to whom she can talk about what she's too shy to talk about with her dad.

In the meantime, at work, I was offered the position as a chief of the primary production department. I agreed, especially since the salary was significantly higher. Under my supervision were two departments - mechanical and foundry. In the latter, one of the casting furnaces worked twenty-four hours a day. The total number of employees - more than two hundred, including eleven supervisors and a personal secretary.

I left for work in a car sent for me at six in the morning and returned at nine or ten in the evening. I saw my daughter on weekends, because in the morning when I was leaving, and in the evening, when I was returning, she was sleeping. Once I asked her about how she and Tamara spend time together. She looked down and said that Tamara does not talk to her, but only said what must be done at home and Tamara was always dissatisfied with her work.

I noticed that my daughter at the table does not finish her meals. I decided to talk with her in private. I thought perhaps she does not like the way Tamara cooks food, but my daughter almost crying said that the food is stuck in her throat when Tamara gaze at her while she is eating. I could not imagine that. Perhaps, it only seems to my daughter; they were such great friends. I decided not to talk about that with Tamara, considering she was in Israel for a little more than a month and life it is not easy for her without friends and knowledge of the language. As time went, I felt tensions at home, and I did not understand what the matter was.

Only now I paid attention that Tamara never speaks to my daughter in my presence. But I explained it to myself that at home we were alltogether only on weekends which I tried to use for traveling around the country. The car allowed freedom in choosing a route and convenience that public transport did not provide. But my daughter began to refuse to participate in the trips and said she would spend time with her friends from school. I agreed, considering that she was bored sitting in the backseat in a car, and she was more interested in being with her peers.

One day, returning from work, I saw my daughter's tear-stained face. Through tears, she told me that Tamara beat her up. I looked at Tamara. Full of determination, in a stern and cold voice, she said.

"I concluded that your wife and you, both of you, could not bring up your daughter and teach her the rules of good behavior. Your daughter is disobedient and disrespectful. It is necessary to remove her from our home and send her to the place where she will learn good manners."

I did not understand what had happened to me, but I remember that everything went cold in me and, instead of words, I hit her. She fell to the floor and did not move. She could not come to her senses for a long time. I picked her up and laid on the bed in the bedroom. When an hour later I looked into the bedroom, she angrily threw in my face – "Dirty Jew!"

From that moment on, she ceased to exist for me.

Only now I imagined how she hated my daughter and me, and how she tried to hide it. But I didn't understand how this woman could hate a girl who was lost her mother and who had not known tender attention for many years. I could not believe that Tamara was a monster. She wanted to tear my daughter from her father - the only person left in her life.

I lay all night on the couch and could not sleep from the horror of what I heard. I blamed myself for believing this woman, to whom I had no feelings. I frankly wrote about this in letters, trying to explain that we have nothing in common. I blamed myself for not believing a daughter who saw and felt something that I could not even imagine.

I blamed myself for believing this woman who deceived me. I blamed myself for being a fool and sending her the invitation. I blamed myself for not understanding her real intentions - to use me only to be able to go abroad.

Now that I saw her real face, I did not know what to do. Another person in my place would simply open the door and throw her out of the house, having solved this problem forever. But even now, when she became a nothing to me, I refused to do it. She did not know the language, she did not have money to exist on her own, and besides, she was already pregnant. About this joyful event for me, she told me a few days ago. And now my thoughts were with that child whom I wanted to raise on this earth, and whose childhood I wanted to see happy and free. I thought and could not imagine how we, from this day completely strangers, can live together under the same roof, sharing only the apartment and a kitchen.

Daughter after school spent time at the home of school friends. I had a feeling of guilt. Having a home, my daughter does not want to be in it when I'm at work.

With the birth of my son, I had to assist with childcare. She took my daughter's room for her son, although it was enough place for two of them in her bedroom. She put my daughter's bed on the balcony. I did not mind - it was already warm and the balcony was insulated.

I visited General Zeev in Tivon and said that I would like to give my son a name that would reflect his connection with Israel.

He thought a little and suggested the name Amichai, explaining that in abbreviation it means - Am Israel Chai, and in the translation from Hebrew - the People of Israel Live.

I really liked this rare name, and I invited him to the Brit Mila ceremony at the hospital where my son was born.

The son was a calm boy, never cried, he ate well and slept. Holding him in my hands, I admired his curious eyes and the smile that appeared on his face, and his blond hair.

I pressed this innocent creature to my chest, trying to escape the thoughts that he got the genes of his mother too.
Once Orit, name given to my daughter in ulpan, came up to look at her brother. I let her to hold him. Suddenly, Tamara, who wolked into the room, snatched the baby out of my daughter's hands and told her not to dare to touch him. I thought it is good that my baby son doesn't understand it now.

Once a neighbor came to visit me. He also had a child of the same age as Ami. We sometimes met and talked. He worked as a turner at the factory. His wife did not work.

I understood that he had come to talk about something important. And I was not mistaken; he decided to quit his job and open a store in one of the new high-rise buildings. He had already spoken to the city administration and received permission. The store will sell the products of the first necessity, including dairy, sausage, bakery, alcohol, vegetables, and others. In Israel, such small shops called "makolets." He is confident in successful trading because it will be only the second such store in our district, which is built up with multi-story houses with a population of many thousands.

But to open a business he needs money - a sum of 90,000 shekels. He offered that both of us would sell our cars, and the remaining amount to borrow in the bank. Since our wives do not work, they can cooperate with the supervision of children, when one of them works in the store. He proposes to own the shop jointly and divide the income equally. We will not need our cars, because all products will be delivered by suppliers.

He wanted to share his business with me, because he has no relatives, and we have known each other for a long time, and he trusts me. Also, the business will require many hours of work in the store, and it will be very tough for him alone, especially if it is necessary to leave the shop for urgent matters.

His proposal was resonable, but not in my circumstances.He did not know anything about my relationship with Tamara and my plans for the future. I politely refused, saying that I do not want to sell my car, and I don't have other funds to contribute. He asked me to think about this opportunity and his proposal.

A few months later he opened his shop. Business flourished. A year later, he bought himself a new car, and then another year later he opened a second store with a partner.

Tamara knew that she has no return to our family life and made an attempt to find a job. She never learned the language, but she managed to find a job to care for people in the home for the elderly and disabled. Most of the sick people knew Russian. She hated the job, realizing whose pots she had to carry out, but she had to bear it.

For our son, we found a nanny. In the neighboring, next to our house lived a family of immigrants from Tunisia, and they gladly agreed to look after him. Ami already walked and even began to speak. His first words were in Hebrew. It turns out that two female students in the nanny's family regularly taught him Hebrew.

After a year of working with the elderly and learning Hebrew, enough for communication, Tamara managed to get a job at the Haifa hospital. She chose to work at night so that we would not have to stay at home together. In the morning, coming home from work, she took her son to the nanny and went to bed, and when I returned from work, she was no longer at home.

On my days off, I took my son by the hand and we walked along quiet streets and talked. He asked me a lot of questions, each of which began with the word "Why?" It was painful for me to think that we would have to depart.

My daughter was already almost homeless for several years and sometimes even stayed overnight in the family of her school friend from India. They became her second family.

Tamara has a man with whom she spent those days when she did not work in the hospital.

I realized that I could not sacrifice more the life of my daughter and my own. Amichai was looked after by the nanny. Tamara has a well-paid job. To live together and hate each other was wrong for all of us, especially for my son who will soon begin to understand what happened and it can hurt him.

I had not many opportunities for getting out of the situation. I could not keep a separate apartment, given the continued payment of the car. To deprive Tamara of the home and make her wander with her son was unacceptable for me. There was only one option - to leave her everything and go abroad. I had these thoughts when the son was born, but then I could not do it because she did not have a job and no knowledge of Hebrew. Now the situation was completely different. I leave to her the furnished apartment and a car. A great nanny takes care of her son, and her work gives her independence.

It was bitter to think that I have to leave the country that accepted me, gave me secure job and a roof over my head.

I traveled it along and across from the northern border with Livnom to the southern border with Egypt. In Israel, I felt like an equal person and was happy.

During regular army mobilizations, I patrolled the Jordanian border, guarded the holy tomb of our ancestor Abraham and patrolled the streets of hostile Hebron, stood at the pilgrimage site of Jesus Christ's birthplace in Beit Lekhem, served on the border with Lebanon and Golan Heights. I saw Israel and fell in love with this country with its rare forests, cold rivers in the North and small resort towns with a dry and sultry climate in the South.

I plunged into the atmosphere of never falling asleep Tel Aviv. Wandered through the sacred streets of Jerusalem, where the old city's stones retained the smell of the centuries. I stood at the holy Wailing Wall, bathed in the Dead Sea and toured the ancient fortress Masada - a symbol of Jewish courage and bravery.

My thoughts about broken family life and the search for a way out of the situation led me to see the Shultz family and discuss the possibility to join them in Ariel.

To dispel my doubts, I went on a visit. Leaving behind my town, reached the main highway Haifa - Tel Aviv and two hours later passed through Petah Tikva, behind which was a beautiful asphalt road. On both sides of the way, there were small Arab settlements. Their houses behind high concrete walls reminded me of miniature medieval fortresses, but without towers. On the tops of the walls stuck out the glass fragments. Along the road - the pillars of power. Fresh asphalt and new posts made it clear that it was laid recently. It twisted between the hills with olive trees and grazing sheep.

Half an hour later, I drove up to a high hill surrounded by a barbed-wire fence. At the gate stood a soldier. Having learned that I would like to see Shulz family, he showed me the direction to their house.

The winding road led me up to the top of a hill, where on a rocky, bulldozed surface were rectangular houses – blocks with flat roofs. They looked like metal containers for sea transport, but they were made of cement.

There were about a dozen of them. The Shultz family had two such blocs joint together because they had a large family. Naturally, they were glad to see me.

Bearing in mind my thoughts about the possibility of relocation, I began asking about life in the settlement. They told me about themselves and their friends, with whom they share the burden and joy of the settlement life. The silence, the fantastic view of the endless hills from the windows of the house during the day, the night sky flickering with a myriad of stars, fresh and clean air - were a contrast against the backdrop of the scorching sun of the coastal cities of Israel.

The first dozen of families, connected by common ideas, hopes and plans for the future, was one large family. Everyone was always ready to help and pay attention when needed. They did not pass over the conversation the life's difficulties. First of all, the problem with a long drive to work was not solved. Riding in the car took more than two hours and was very exhausting after a busy day. Finding a job near the settlement was not possible. Food products need to be delivered from far because there was no shop in the vicinity. The nearest school was in Petah Tikva, an hour drive, and so the medical services.

After the visit, I was convinced that my initial decision was correct. In my case, moving to settlement meant replacing some problems with others.

The thought that Tamara created a situation in which I have no place in this country made me suffer. Because of this woman, I have to part with my son, with my white-haired boy, with whom we walked through the streets of our city, visiting friends and acquaintances. I held his little hand and answered his many questions, but to my own question, "What should I do?" I was not able to answer.

Trip to South Africa

Johannesburg. Lucky employment.
The Israeli businessman.
Miss Kay. Spinal injury.
Return to Israel.

The life in the split family became unbearable. Having arranged my daughter in a kibbutz, where she found a family atmosphere and was provided with everything necessary, including continuing school, I packed a suitcase, and kissing my son, went to the airport. The plane took me to Johannesburg.

The purpose of the trip - to familiarize with the living conditions in the country with a significant Jewish population. I was interested in the opportunity to get a job and, most importantly, to provide my daughter with living conditions, which she was deprived of because of my unforgivable mistake.

In Johannesburg, I phoned a relative of the family, which took care of me in Tiwon. I was in correspondence with him shortly before departure. From his letters, I learned that the opportunity to find a job exists, and getting a legal right to reside in the country is not easy, but possible. A taxi took me to a hotel on a quiet street, not far from the center of the district. After paying for the weekly stay, I left the hotel and decided to see the sparkling with lights city.

Slowly walking along the main street, I was browsing the windows displays of shops and looking at passing by people. In one of the cafes, I saw players bent over the chessboard. For me, a chessplayer, it was my first pleasant impression. Seeing a sport club and swimming pool on the opposite side of the street gave me indication that my previous year's sports activity could be continued.

Having passed quite a bit, I heard a conversation in Hebrew and stopped by the open terrace. On a vertical skewer, I saw frying meat, pita heated on a hot stove, smell of falafel. Seating in high chairs at a long counter, sipping a cold beer and talking were Israelis. I sat down, ordered a pita with a kebab, a beer, and enjoyed the small piece of Israel on the foreign country. Listening to Hebrew, for a moment, I forgot that I am in Africa.

The next morning I began a search for an agency that can provide information on the availability of vacancies for design engineers at the city's enterprises.

I am again on the same street, that day before was flooded in the evening with advertising lights, and now, in the morning, waking up from the late night. In the cafe, which seemed was not closed from yesterday night, people were having the morning breakfast. Continuing to walk, I saw the sign of the agency I was looking for. In a small room, at a large table littered with numerous papers, sat a middle-aged man. Glancing at me, he pointed to a chair and asked what I was looking for. In my rudimentary English, I began to explain. To my surprise, he understood what I mean. Having opened his notebook, he calls somebody on the phone and after hanging up says that he has such a job and they are waiting for me to come for the interview. Then he wrote on the paper the address, phone number, and the name of the employer.

I traveled a long time before I found the given address in an industrial area on the outskirts of the city. Mr. Logan, the owner of the factory, of medium height and business appearance Englishman, puffing a cigar, began to ask me about my work experience. Realizing that my English would not allow him to determine my capabilities, he took one of the many photographs lying on his desk and handed it to me. I saw a simple vibrator setup with a grid but did not know for what type of products it was used for. He asked if I could design the same, only with other parameters. "Yes, I do," I said. He called his secretary and told her to fill in all the necessary papers for my application for work. Then, showing me the room where were the desktops with the drawing boards, he said that I could start work tomorrow.

I thanked and returned to the hotel. Inspired by the success, I went to a Greek restaurant called the Three Sisters. The sign said that for the specified price you can eat anything without restriction. Having paid, I found myself in a large self-service hall, lined with tables, on which one could choose any dish. I looked at the diversity of meat, fish, vegetable dishes and soups, at the tables filled with cakes and could not believe that everything that was exposed could be tested by a person, not to mention the eating.

Walking through the city after such a plentiful meal was already a necessity, which made me walk for a long time. Continuing my acquaintance with the city, I paid attention to the absence of the Negro population among pedestrians, although I saw them cleaning the hotel and side streets, where they took out the garbage from shops, restaurants, institutions, and houses.

My first working day began with an introduction to the drawings that were already on my desk. After explaining to me which parts were patented by him and I should not change them, Mr. Logan went to his office, and I set to work. By the end of the day, the assembly drawing was ready. Mr. Logan was surprised to see the finished work. I noticed on his face a feeling of satisfaction that he was not mistaken in me. Thanking for the job, he said that he assigned me a salary of eight hundred rands per month.

I did not know it is much or little, but I understood that it would be sufficient for my needs. Based on the price index, I knew that it was about one thousand two hundred dollars. On the same day, I moved to a decent hotel, where for one hundred and sixty rands, I had a room with a bath and three meals a day. Public transport practically did not exist in the city, where everyone had a car.

Wishing not to lose a lot of time traveling to work, I accepted the offer of an employee in the office to use one of his cars for two hundred rands per month. The car was old, and I had to pay a lot for gas. But I had freedom of movement and the possibility to visit places in the city and suburbs. Unlike Israel, the movement of transport was, as in England - left-sided. It didn't give me any inconvenience, and I drove confidently from the first trip.

The hotel owners, Mr. Katz, and his wife kept the facilities of their business perfectly clean. Service in the dining room was exceptional, and everyone could order any dish of choice, and anyone could have more if the meal were desired. There were no restrictions on fruits and juices.

The local people of the city, mostly single women and men of different ages due to certain circumstances, they chose to live in this hotel, having solved the problem with cooking and housing. Almost everyone worked. It was evident that they feel at the hotel like at home. Here, in the hotel, they clothes were washed, shirts and suits ironed. At the table they were sitting in suits, puffing cigars after a hearty lunch and reading a newspaper.

Once, on a Sunday morning, during breakfast, a man, a little older than me, sat down at my table. Having made an order to the waiter who came up, he asked me how long I had been at this hotel. Hearing from me that I had been here only one week and came from Israel, his face broke into a smile. By my accent, he realized that I was from Russia and introduced himself - Shmuel. Also Israeli. Arrived in Johannesburg on business matters. I was pleased to switch to Hebrew, and after breakfast, he offered to walk and sit in a cafe where the owner is his friend - an Israeli. I was delighted. So there will be another thread that connects me with my country. A small cafe was located on the main street. My new acquaintance said that he comes here to drink a cup of real Turkish coffee. Continuing our conversation and answering his questions, I told him about the reason for my arrival in South Africa, and mentioned my daughter, whom I temporarily arranged for a kibbutz and about my plans to move here, if I can get a residence permit. After hearing a brief history of my family life, he said that we have a similar fate. He also does not live with his wife, but with the only difference that he did not leave his wife, but his wife left him. Having paid for the coffee with a credit card, he explained that he never holds money in his pocket and always pays with this plastic, saying it's so more convenient and safer. We departed. He went to buy a gift for his daughter, and I continued my Sunday walk. Seeing the synagogue, I decided to come inside. In a large hall with high ceilings, a small group of elderly people sat at the table with the opened books. Seeing me, one of those sitting approached me. Looking at me carefully and holding out the kipa, he said that a Jew cannot be in the synagogue with his head uncovered.

He invited me to sit down and said that he did not see me in their synagogue. When he learned that I was from Israel, his face was kind and he wanted to know where and when I came to Israel.

Hearing that I am from Minsk, nodded his head. Oh ... yes, Minsk is known to all. Inquiring if I had any relatives in Johannesburg, and hearing that there was no one, he thought for a minute. Then he said that he would try to help me. He knows one woman, and if he is not mistaken, she also from Minsk and speaks Russian. She lives near the synagogue. Thanking for the participation and help, I returned to the hotel.

When I called her that day, I introduced myself and explained who gave me her phone number. She invited me to visit and gave her address. It was not far from the hotel, and I went on foot. Her house was located on a quiet street next to a large park. I was met by a woman, possibly in her late seventies with a stout body, a big head, and intelligent, curious eyes.

She invited me into a room full of old furniture and asked if I would like to have tea. I have not refused. On the sound of a little bell - a maid appeared. After accepting the order, she left, and Miss Kay, as she asked to call her, began to ask me about my past and present.

Then she told me about herself. Parents came from Russia to Africa when she was still a young girl. The family settled in Rhodesia, where she married and lived most of her life. Her husband was a successful businessman. Her only son, David, was educated in Johannesburg and remained here to work. After the death of her husband, she left Rhodesia, to stay closer to her son. To keep herself busy, she began to buy houses, repair and rent them out. Besides this house, she has three more. She bought them for nothing when people, frightened by the Negro riot against the government, hastily began to sell homes and leave the country. Now, these houses have risen in price, and she is pleased that she has invested her money in the property. At parting, she said she would be glad to see me and help in anything if she could.

She was my only contact among the local Jewish community, and I began to visit her on weekends. Almost always, she was at home, and I saw that my visits entertained her gray days. Our conversations, she kept formal. Ringing the bell, she asked the servant to bring two cups of tea. Once I came at the time of her lunch. Continue her meal, she said that, unfortunately, because I did not inform her about my arrival, her servant did not make another one stake. I apologized for not calling her and said that I had my lunch already.

On one of the Jewish holidays, she invited me to visit her son. I put on a newly purchased suit and came with a bunch of flowers. At the big round table, we were already expected and everybody in her family looked at me with interest.

I was asked many questions which I was already able to answer briefly in my improved English. They knew a lot about Israel, so they wanted to know about lifethe life in Russia, as they called the Soviet Union. The dinner was a little formal, but it was interesting to see the Jewish family in the country, which I was looking to make my home. It was the first family I met outside of my hotel.

At work, I was doing well. Mr. Logan was pleased with my work and, trying to use me, generally, in the development of projects, hired a young guy to help me for detailing the design. The guy was a university student and worked to earn money for paying off his studies. He was from a poor Jewish family. We often talked, and I noticed that he was very liberal and sympathetic towards the situation of the black population in the country. Seeing that I showed a genuine interest in what he tells me about black people in the country, he decided to show me the outskirts of the city. Seeing living quarters made rusted sheet metal and old plywood, I could not believe that such housing still exists in such a developed and prosperous country. To which he calmly replied that about two million Negroes live in such huts in a village near Johannesburg. They come to work in the city by trains and buses, and at the end of the day they leave, because they are not allowed to stay in the city. If one of them is found on the streets of the town after working hours, he is arrested and then the owner of the company where he works have to pay a hefty fine.

His story showed me the other side of the medal of this country, which for the majority of the white population was the land of wealth and abundance.

Unexpectedly, my boss invited me to dinner. In his car, we arrived at a club, of which not everyone can be a member, as he said. The atmosphere in the club resembled a picture of old England. An ancient building with servants in gloves and tuxedos, heavy curtains on high windows, wood-lined walls, leather armchairs. There was an English composure, of which Mr. Logan himself was a part. We went to the buffet where he ordered us steak and salad. There were not many people. I felt a fragrant smell of tobacco smokers at the next table and I drew attention to the accent of their speech, similar to the pronunciation of my boss. Judging by the way he exchanged greetings with visitors, many people knew him here. On the way back to work, he told me that he visited his club very often, as it helps to establish contacts in the business.

Over time, my English became much better, and I began to feel freer in conversations. I was often invited to various families, where I was asked about my past, and I, in turn, was interested in the life of my new acquaintances. Most of them had their own businesses - manufacturing enterprises, or private ownership of residential buildings and land; all kinds of shops and cafes. Most doctors, lawyers, and other professionals had a private practice.

Many were educated at universities, but business, inherited from their parents, was the only kind of income and activity.

In conversations with them, I learned that in almost every family, the history of the business began from the time when their parents came to this country, fleeing pogroms in Russia or Poland. The descendants proudly talked about how their parents, not having money, began to build a life from anew.

Now I saw in front of me happy families, happy wives and happy children who did not know what poverty is about.

Those who were next to me in the hotel, as I understood, did not seem to be rich people, they were lonely due to divorce or widowers. They had temporarily arranged care, meals, and company of their own kind.

One of them, a man of my age, suggested that I spend the day on a guided tour organized by a society of Jewish singles, about whose existence I knew nothing. We left in the rented bus out of the city, and a few hours later we were in a beautiful valley surrounded by wooded hills. At the foot of one of the mountains, I saw a large two-story house with terraces. In front of the house was a swimming pool, and a little further away - a tennis court.

Our company went straight to the building, where breakfast was already prepared for us at the buffet.

I drew attention to the fact that in this excursion, of so-called loners, only I was a loner - all the rest were already in pairs and talked to each other like people who know each other for a long time. My hotel acquaintance, whose partner was an amazingly beautiful woman, much younger than him, began to acquaint me with a company. Soon I was involved in a general conversation.

After breakfast, part of the group went to the pool, and the rest stretched out on the green grass cut and exposed their bodies to the rays of the sun. One of the women, probably twenty years younger than me, entered into a conversation with me. She came from England. Alone. Beautiful face, but very fat. I politely answered her questions but did not express a desire to continue the conversation. She felt this, leaving me alone and returned to her friends.

Then, another women, the only one who did not want to sunbathe and stayed in pants and blouse, approached me shortly and introduced herself - Dorit. Painted blonde with so much makeup on her face that from a distance she could be given not more than thirty. Now I saw a woman about five years older than me. She was so thin that even clothes could not hide it. It was clear why she was embarrassed to sunbathe. Smiling with brightly painted lips and with an English accent, pronouncing my name with an emphasis on the first syllable, she, having learned briefly about my profession, family, my work and that I live in a hotel, suggested that I move in with her. She has a free room, for which she will take a small fee, and I will always have meals because she cooks all the time. Then, without waiting for my answer, she suggested to visit me in the hotel and take me to show her house.

I agreed, considering that the homely atmosphere should be more comfortable compared to a hotel.

The following Sunday, I stood at the entrance of the hotel. A German "beetle" stopped in front of me. From the open window of the car, waved Dorit inviting me to get in.

As if apologizing for such an old car, she jokingly said that her vehicle already had a Bar Mitzvah, making clear that it was over thirteen years old. I paid tribute to her humor, seeing that there is a need for additional income behind it, not to mention buying a new car.

The house outside was not in a better condition than her car. We went into a fairly spacious living room, and she introduced me to her son, a boy of twelve. After going around the house, she invited me to the kitchen, where the table had already been served and lunch was ready. It is necessary to pay tribute to her cooking, but I noted to myself that in the hotel the meals were not worse, and maybe even a better and more abundant. Dorit, probably, has already prepared her son for the fact that they will have a guest and he looked at me inquisitively, but without any kindness.

Compared to the hotel, my room seemed rather spacious. We returned to the living room. A bottle of cognac and two glasses appeared on the coffee table. Putting the record disc on the turntable, she sat on the sofa next to me and lit a cigarette. The room was filled with the sounds of my beloved Chopin. Spilling cognac in two glasses, she took a sip and said that this drink and music gave her the greatest pleasure she could give herself at the end of the day.

She was the private secretary of the owner of a large legal company. The position is responsible and requires a knowledge of the business specifics. She was coming home tired, and there was time for relaxation with a glass of cognac and music before bedtime.

We agreed that I would pay her three hundred rands a month, which was twice as much for the hotel. I moved into to her house the next day.

A few days later she said that we were invited to her brother for lunch. I have not refused. Brother had a psychiatric practice with an office in his home. We arrived ahead of time, and I saw in the waiting room of his office a middle-aged man who, after greeting Dorit, complained to her that he had of menopause period. Deciding he was joking, I laughed. But Dorit assured him that the doctor would help him. We went to the living room, where Dorit told me that this was her brother's patient. He is gay and considers himself a woman. I never met gays and now was confused by my laughing.

Soon in the living room walked in a tall guy. We met. Sam, he said, holding out his hand. First, Dorit asked about the health of his mother, then how long he was going to stay with his parents. When her nephew answered the questions and left, she told me that he was a talented musician and came from England to see his parents.

After finishing the reception, her brother came to us. Tall, with a broad forehead, a shaggy head, large horn-rimmed glasses, behind which large brown eyes, enlarged by thick lenses, were carefully and thoughtfully looking at me.

It seemed to me that expression of his face had an imprint of the hidden anxiety and detachment from what is happening around. We went to the dining room, where his wife, woman with a pretty and friendly face pointed me to a chair near her and Dorit. I found myself sitting opposite the doctor. When the whole family was at the table, the maid started pouring out the soup. It was thick as sour cream and wiped. I began to eat and, fearing to dirty the tablecloth from the soup stuck to the bottom of the spoon, I cleaned the bottom of the spoon on the edge of the plate. Suddenly, I heard the doctor spoke loudly and excitedly. "Stop that stupid way of wiping your spoon on the edge of a plate. I can't stand it. Everyone eats soup fine."

There was silence at the table. Dorit was silent too. I did not mind, realizing that his remark surprised not only me alone. Then was served the second course.

After dinner, the doctor's wife apologized that she needed to leave our company. After her departure, Dorit's brother approached me and asked a few questions concerning my family situation, specialty and status in the country, trying to smooth over the unpleasant impression that he made on me with his remark at the table. But his face remained thoughtful and sad.

Returning home, Dorit told me about the family tragedy. The brother's wife is in the last stage of the cancer disease. The son flew in to say goodbye to his mother, and her brother himself does not understand what is happening around him.

On weekends, Dorit asked me to help in the house where men's hands were needed. At first, she asked me to bring in the order the garden, where the territory was cluttered up and needed cleaning. Next time she asked me to repair the fence around the house. The area was not very big, but there was a lot of work. It was necessary to separate the old one, put new pillars, and assemble again. She also asked to clean the chimney, but here I could not help.

Every evening, I was invited to talk over a glass of cognac and listen to classical music. But I had my contacts and friends, and I could not always accept her invitations. Often, I did not come to sleep.

At the table while eating, Dorit began to make remarks that I often did not come to dinner and did not pay enough attention to her. Even her son once said at dinner time, "Mom, I see that Boris annoys you." In the evening of the same day, sitting with a glass of cognac in her hand and with a cigarette in the other one, she turned to me, "How do you see yourself in my house, a lodger, or think about our more serious relationship?"
"Only a lodger," I replied.

A few more weeks passed. Her brother's wife passed away, and Dorit was at her brother's house for about a week. Returning, she said that her brother wants to see me.

When we met, her brother directly asked if I liked his sister. I said that she could not count on me in her plans for the future. But my answer did not satisfy him. The doctor understood that the reason was something else.
"What don't you like about her?"
"She drinks cognac every day," I replied, dodging the root cause. I could not tell him that I just did not like her.
"Does it bother you?"
"Yes," I replied.
"Then why do you live with her? Go away."

When I returned home, Dorit asked me the same question, and I answered the same way I responded to her brother.
"Then I don't need you here," she said.

The next day, when she went to work, I put my things in a suitcase and returned to the hotel.

Taking into cosideration that my visa stay in the country ends in one month, I told about that to my employer. He immediately issued the necessary documents and sent them to the appropriate department in Pretoria, assuring me that he really needed me and he would do everything possible that I could get a residence permit.

I continued to work. Having a lot of free time, I decided to remember my old days and went to a sports club. After an eight-year break, I had to start with small loads, but, not thinking, I took on my shoulders the weight I used to many years ago. Feeling sudden pain in the back, left the exercising, and went to sauna. Going home, I felt some kind of strange feeling in my spine. There was no pain.

The next morning, after breakfast, I left the hotel. I took a few steps and felt an unimaginable pain piercing my spine. I stopped, feeling that my face was covered with drops of sweat. Had tried to move, but my right leg did not obey me and, in order not to fall, I clung to the wall of the building with my hands. Pulling up the leg and holding the wall, I began to move to the entrance of the hotel, which was very close. Then I took the elevator to my room and called friends. I told them about the injury and asked for the phone number of the doctor who could visit me at the hotel. I called the doctor and explained that I was not able to move. Two hours later, there was a knock at the door, and a doctor stood on the threshold.

After inspection, he said that I had a severe spinal injury. The shifted disk presses on the nerve. Recommended complete rest on the bed without a soft mattress. After prescribing pain pills, he advised wating a few days before deciding to go to the hospital. He explained that they could hold me the hospital for up to two weeks on a spinal stretch, and when they remove it, everything can return to its former state. He advised taking hot baths to reduce pain. In his opinion, the muscles of the body themselves can correct the damage.

I did everything he advised. I lay on a wooden door, which they brought me on order of the hotel owner, and took painkillers every four hours. The pain did not subside. I lay in a bath with hot water for a long time, but as soon as I got out of the tub, the pain resumed. In this state, I spent a few days. I fell asleep only for a few hours - that's all that pills allowed.

Shmuel's visit made me happy. Arriving and learning about what happened to me, he immediately came to visit me. He said that he has suffered from back pain for many years. He can advise a specialist who treated him successfully, and he is sure I could be cured, but my treatment will cost me one thousand and a five hundred rands. For me, it was excluded - I did not have that kind of money. To get away from the pain, I called my friends and asked me to bring me a book by Ilf and Petrov, "Twelve Chairs," which I had seen at their home. A hot bath and the book distracted from the pain. A week later, I was able to walk to the elevator and down to the dining room. Then I went to see a massage therapist. It helped for half an hour. It was impossible to sit - the pain increased. A few days later, I got into the car, and through the pain, drove to work. Passed one week.

Work distracted, but the pain continued to bother me. There was no response to the submitted documents. I didn't want to lose the right to legal emigration, so I told my employer that I had to leave the country. In no case did he want me to leave, assuring me that he would do everything possible and would even go to Pretoria to get permission for my legal residence. I believed him. He was a man of his word. During the check of the factory for the presence of illegal immigrants, I saw how he gave an envelope with a bribe to the inspector. This showed me that he really wants me to work with him, and he believes in me. I felt guilty when, resisting his request, I began to prepare for departure.
This was my ill-conceived decision, or rather a big mistake, but this I realized it when I returned to Israel.

I had no money for a ticket because I spent all my savings on the services of doctors, massage therapists, and medicines. Shmuel lent me money to buy a ticket, and I promised to repay him a debt in Israel. He gave me his address. Already saying goodbye, he asked if I had a car and what brand. When he learned that the car was only four years old, he said that he wants to buy a car for his wife in Israel. I promised to bring the car to his house so that he could be convinced of its excellent condition and care, but he could only get it when I receive the documents for legal emigration.
I came to Shmuel when I was ready to leave Israel after receiving from South African Embassy document of the permanent residence.

The car was repainted entirely, and I made full maintenance check up - it was done in gratitude for the help with the ticket and a moral support during my spine problem.

Shmuel went out to look at the car, but refused to buy, saying that there is no need for that anymore and did not explained the reason. This was our last meeting. After returning to South Africa, I never had to meet with him.

I had only a few days before my departure and I had to give the car for half the market price to one of the Russian dealers.

Return

Visiting my daughter in the kibbutz.
Meeting with Shultz family.
Confirmation of the permanent residence.
Tamara's blackmail. Farewell dinner.
Daughter's escape before departure.
Heart attack.

At the airport Lod I was met by Garik Schultz. Already sitting in the car, he suggested me to stay with his family, explaining that Tamara had a man in her life with whom she is in a relationship already for a long time. I explained to him that I could not wander anymore, as it was years ago before I got my apartment, and if I could endure the home situation for four years, I could suffer a few more months. Besides, I must receive documents for legal residence in Africa, and they will be delivered to my official address in Israel.

We met with Tamara as strangers, realizing that with this situation both of us would have to, if not agree, then at least reconcile. My son grew up, he was already almost four years old. I could not lift him with my arms because of the pain in the spine. He did not see me around for a lomg time and looked at me with a curious gaze as if he wanted to ask something and did not dare.

Limping, since I could not heal the spinal injury, I went with him for a walk. He spoke with me in Hebrew as any natinve sabra (sabra, it is one who born in Israel). I was happy - my son real Israeli. I looked at my boy, and I felt apain that I have to leave him here, and I do not know when I can see him again. We were already walking towards the house, when, Ami, pointing to the other side of the iron railroad, said that uncle Misha lives there. I understood who he is talking about was, but that was already indifferent to me.

The next day I went to Kibbutz Alonim, where I, not without difficulty, managed to arrange my daughter before leaving to

South Africa. She looked good. Tanned, with a smile that I had not seen on her face for a long time, she rushed to meet me. She was happy here. The elderly were sad when they found out that I was taking Oritr back, and asked to leave her on a kibbutz, where everyone likes her for her calm temper and hard work.

We sat in their little house, and they told me that Orit is very good at school and that she has many friends. I spent in the kibbutz all day. My daughter showed me all the housekeeping, and I saw that she felt here, at home. At the end of the day, I brought a letter to the kibbutz administration, stating that I was taking my daughter home. Thanked for the help and shelter. My daughter was sad as well that she has to return to the house, which caused her terrible feelings, but I explained to her that this was only for a short time. Having received the documents, we will immediately leave to South Africa.

Taking her from the kibbutz, I involuntarily put her in the same conditions from which I wanted to protect her before leaving for Africa. But I was comforted by the fact that I would now spend more time with her and hoped that I would not have to wait long.

Remembering the last conversation with Shultz family about the settlement, I wanted to see how they settled at a new place.

Their apartment was deprived of the comfort that they had in Haifa, but it was bigger. Most importantly, everyone's mood was optimistic.

The settlers continue to live in temporary homes. The state pays the cost of electricity, water, and gas. When they would build houses on their designated home lots for their projects, they will not have these benefits.

Construction of private houses is expected soon, but meantime at the moment it is necessary to take a loan from a bank to pay construction costs.

Currently, the whole family is engaged in exciting and creative work - planning the rooms of their future home.

There are many unresolved issues, one of which is finding a job closer to their new home. Zhanna got a job as a nurse in their settlement, and Garik has to drive to Haifa - more than two hours one way. Every family in the community is experiencing the problem with exhausting commuting. Children need to be taken to school, and they have to buy food on the way home from work.

They told me about the sad tragedy - the death of one of Minsk dwellers. Like all of the rest, he had to drive to work a few hours. Returning home late at night, he fell asleep at the wheel of a car and crashed, leaving his wife and two small children.

Silence, the pacifying view of the surrounding hills, bright stars in the dark sky is a reward for patience and temporary inconveniences that migrants have to experience daily.

I was returning home with bitter thoughts that, for me personally, such a life is unacceptable. I paid tribute to their patriotism and dedication to the idea, to their patience in overcoming the difficulties, and the constant protection at night from a possible terrorist attack.

But living in my own country behind barbed wire was not only an inconvenience for me. I didn't want to find myself again behind the barbed wire of the ghetto, even if it was created voluntarily for the best of reasons.

I am a soldier, and I agree to protect my country everywhere and always, and I want to live on land that for centuries belonged to the Jews, as a free man. We must put behind the fence those who threaten us. I want to walk on our land without fear for my life.

With all my pride for Israel and for the achievements that the country has achieved in all areas of life, I could not agree with the government's policy, which, for political reasons, did not want to ensure the security of Israeli citizens by necessary measures.

I remember myself sitting on an open transporter while patrolling the streets of Hebron. The Arabs threw stones at us, and we had no right to shoot these killers. We were an unanswered target for the Arab villains, whom our inaction incited to terror, knowing that they would not be punished.

I thought it was the humiliation of our army. The murderers were protected by the law of Israel, and the soldiers of Israel had no such protection.

Continuing to reflect on what I saw, and realizing how difficult it is for them to come to a new place, I envied their courage and perseverance. They were real people that Israel could be proud of, and their children, with whom they build the future, will be proud of them too.

Given the uncertainty of the time spent in Israel in anticipation of documents, I began to look for work. Not far from Kiryat Yam I saw a two-story modern building.

In the office on the second floor, a middle-aged woman asked me about the reason for my visit. I explained that I am a design engineer, and I am looking for a job.
"You're lucky," she said with an English accent, "the director urgently needs an engineer for a new project.

Returned a few minutes later she said that the owner of the business wants to see me.

In the office, furnished with modern furniture, a large man in large horn-rimmed glasses sat at the table. Learning that I was working as a designer at Soltam, he said that I would be the right person for the future project and immediately went with me to the design department.

In a large bright room, there were six drawing stands with tables. Two of them were free, the rest occupied by two young women and two men. Pointing at one of the free once, the owner said that this would be my workplace. Then turning to the workers, introduced me as a new designer. Without delay, he took me to the workshop and presented to the shop manager. The young and smiling man shook my hand. I paid attention to the fact that there were only few metal-cutting machines in the workshop, but many welding installations of the most modern models. The wide and clean passage inside the spacious shop had access to the outside factory yard. We returned to the office. My new boss looked at me with a smile and said that before telling me about my future project, he wants to give me some information materials for familiarization. "You can take them home to read or read them at your workplace."

I decided to stay and to read in the office. One of the books was in Russian. Now I understand why he was smiling. All the others - in English.
"You have to do the translation to get to know the content," he said, "get yourself a dictionary."

I said nothing because I didn't want him to know that I know English.

Then he came with me to his secretary's office and spoke to her in proper English. "Employ this guy from tomorrow. It seems to me that he can do this simple work. His salary will be like everyone else's."

He left, and his assistant began to fill out a questionnaire. Having signed the document, I returned to my desk. The salary was low, but it suited me considering that I saw myself anyway only temporary at this place. I started to knowwho my colleagues are. The young Israelis, a young man, and a girl were students of a technical college and worked to earn money for their studies. A Russian man of my age and a Russian woman, as I understood looking at their drawings, were designers without work experience. Later, I helped them in their work, and they listened to my advice. Seeing the work of two others, I came to the conclusion that there could be no exciting development works at this plant. That I was mistaken, I understood later.

The student turned out to be very friendly and talkative. He told me that the owner of the plant is a retired colonel. Engineer. He served in the Navy. His business provided with a stock of small orders from the Ministry of Defense, in which he has connections. The job assignment he gives to each person personally. If he doesn't like something, he can raise his voice. I was surprised that this student knows so many details which he could not receive personally from the owner of the plant, judging by the way he described it to me our boss.

Russian designers turned out to be uncommunicative, and I returned to my workplace.
I sat down for the books received from the "boss," as the student called him. I opened the first page, went into the material, and forgot about the environment.
Suddenly, I heard the student's voice. "Boris, we have to go home."
I took one of the books home and left the rest at work. From this day on, these books have become my companions. They opened for me the science of using solar energy.

Since childhood, we used a magnifying glass - we called it "incendiary" because we could burn holes in the piece of wood or set fire to dry branches.

I was surprised to read about the use of solar energy in ancient times and even unusual architectural solutions for the buildings in the past.

The supply of apartments with hot water in Israel was solved – each residence had its own solar water heater.

The books given to me for review, described how to attain high temperatures with spherical or parabolic concentrators.

A few days later, the Boss invited me for a conversation to his office and told me why he became interested in solar heaters. One of the well-known Israeli cotton processing companies needed a lot of steam, which was used to clean the cotton. The process of producing the steam required large amounts of electrical energy.

The company appealed to the research institute with a request to solve the problem by using solar energy. My "boss," having contacts at the institute, offered to develop a model of a water heater at his factory.

The task set before me became now clear, but I had no idea about the possibility of using solar heaters to achieve high water temperature and turn it into steam.

I needed to study technical literature, do calculations, and design a solar energy collector.

After reviewing the material provided, I came to the conclusion that the production of a spherical collector of solar rays is more suitable for a model. The calculations showed that half a hemisphere with a diameter of two meters would create in the center of the sphere a concentration of sunlight that would allow a temperature sufficient to produce steam.

Having needed parameters, I started with designing the whole system. Soon, the ready drawings went to the shop. Time passed and I saw my design in the finished shape. The spherical surface was lined with aluminum sheets having an almost mirror quality surface. In the focal point of the sphere on three pillars was fixed a device in which the water was heated to a high temperature, turning into steam in the outlet. The hemisphere with the apparatus was mounted on a frame, which allowed turning the hemisphere vertically and horizontally. The hub of the beams was rotated by two hydraulic cylinders, which were regulated by a sensitive four-diode sensor, the circuit of which I found in the literature.

So was carried out continuous monitoring of the spherical surface following the movement of the sun. The cylinders were driven by the pressure of water from the domestic water supply.

The finished installation was taken from the workshop and installed outside, directing the sphere to the sun's rays. When at the output of the apparatus appeared the stream of steam, the owner rubbed his hands with pleasure and shook my hand.

The next day, a group of three people appeared at the plant. The "boss" asked not me, but his engineer-consultant, whom he invited for a purpose to explain the work of the apparatus and the sun tracking system. From this event, I still have a photo where I see myself in the company of unknown people.

Later, a student told me that one of the men was the minister of industry, and the other was the director of a research institute.
A few days later, I asked my employer "What will we do after the test?"
"Nothing. What was necessary to do, I already did."
Another week has passed. My abandoned installation stood alone among the waste products at the factory yard.

A student who knew everything said that our "boss" after the test demonstration received one million shekels from the state for the manufacture of a solar concentrator. Now I understood the meaning of his words "I did it already.

During the lunch break, I went to a nearby store, bought dozen of sausages, and invited the staff to share the snack. We sat in the yard of the factory. Having one of the sausages, I looked at my solar collector. Suddenly, just pampering, I put a few sausages in a glass flask in which there was an apparatus for heating the water. Literally, in no time sausages increased in volume, roasted and burst. My colleagues I and enjoyed tested sausages.

But the roasted sausages brought me to a new idea. If the owner does not want to use my design for continuing development, then why not come up with a useful use of this device for cooking food and boiling water in places where there is no electricity or fuel.

However, the next task distracted me. It was necessary to design a frame with cells for launching rockets from the navy speedboats. It should be made of aluminum for minimum weight. I was given all the parameters. When I finished the design, it was necessary to test the structure for the strength of the main components. But the frame turned out to be so crusial that a consulting engineer was called for such responsible work.

He checked more than two hundred welding joints on the computer, and the "boss" brought me a long ribbon of calculations, where the red marks show the frame points that needed to be strengthened. They turned out to be only a half dozen. All the rest of the frame equipment was done in an enterprise where I was not invited.

The owner of the plant went on vacation for a long time, leaving me some simple work.

The idea of using a spherical collector of sunlight did not go out of my head.

I imagined my installation on a smaller scale and saw an inverted umbrella, the inner surface of which is made of aluminum foil, and in the focus of the sphere can be placed, for example, a vessel for boiling water, or the same sausages. In Israel, where campfires are not everywhere possible, such gadget could be useful. Israelis like to go out on the weekends to the forest areas. I made drawings of parts that can be made of plastic. This made it possible to get perfectly regular spherical shape of the reflective surface. The "umbrella" could be folded and opened like ribs of the fan, which have a reflective surface.

When the owner returned from vacation, I didn't say anything to him about the idea to make a smaller size collector, realizing that he was making money more securely.

Before leaving Israel, I tried to talk about my idea to the owners of several enterprises. Nobody was interested. Later, in South Africa, I made several attempts - the same result. The drawings of this gadget I keep until today in a folder with the rest of my unfulfilled ideas and patents.

Time passed. I have long ago paid off the debt for a ticket and patiently waited for the residence permit from Africa being sure mister Logan would keep his word. Feeling my inevitable departure would take me from the country for a long time, I started visiting many of my friends, and showing to Orit the historical sites we did not visit before.

I was glad to see new buildings and new roads. We wandered along the Tel Aviv embankment and visited Yad Vashem in Jerusalem, went to the Dead Sea, and drove along the twisted road to the city of arts and artists - Safed. This was my farewell to what I loved and what I am leaving behind.

Finally, I received a letter from the Embassy of South Africa with an invitation to come to Tel Aviv to receive documents for permanent residence. Congratulated as a legal resident and future citizen of South Africa, I also was told that I have two months to prepare for departure.

After receiving the documents, I informed Tamara, saying that the apartment, the furniture and a car I am leaving to her; my daughter and I are flying to South Africa in a few days. She listened to my announcement calmly and then said with a smile.

"You will not go anywhere, because I, through my lawyer, imposed a ban on your leaving the country. If you want to leave, then you will have to take the son and me with you, because I do not want to live in this foreign country."

I did not expect such a turn of events. Tamara again confirmed my suspicions that she came to Israel using a passport scam and my stupidity. Now she is blackmailing me so that she can leave Israel. It was a cruel blasphemy - to deprive me of the ability to live in Israel, and now she is using me again, to go to South Africa.

I was so astounded with her Jesuit nature that I could not come to my senses for a while. I calmed down and thought that there is no return to the past. Staying in Israel means staying in the same apartment with her, which is unthinkable. Leaving with her will allow me to see my son. But to protect my daughter from further contact with this terrible woman, I set my own conditions - on arrival to Africa we live separately and are officially divorced. She agreed.

In principle, I did not need any divorce, because she was not my wife in Minsk and, according to the law of Israel, she was not considered to be my wife either. I made this decision so that I did not have problems with her in South Africa.

I returned to the Embassy with the request to add a wife and son. They did not object, and in a week time, I received additional documents.

Seeing documents for a permanent residence for her and her son in South Africa, Tamara instantly transformed and began to talk with me as if we were the closest people. The tone of her conversation changed, she smiled while talking to me and began to discuss the departure with me, as if this was our ordinary family matter. Then, unexpectedly, she offered to arrange a farewell dinner and invite all those close "to us," as she put it.

Separately from Tamara, I decided to visit all my close friends before leaving Israel and invited them to the dinner at our place.

A large table was set up with plentiful food and drink. Matvey and Rita came from Jerusalem. Garik Schultz and his wife came from Ariel. Friends I had to work together, and close neighbors gathered at the table. Meals with food and alcohol have created a warm feeling, and I answered many questions related to life in South Africa.

We sat till late, and the guests began to gather home, wishing us the best in our new country. It was already dark when I went to see them off. Returning home, I wanted to help clean the table, but suddenly I felt that I was losing my balance and falling. All the objects in front of my eyes began to spin, and I began to lose consciousness. I tried to get up and turned to the door, saying to Tamara that I am going to the hospital.

Reaching the car, I found that I was not able to open the eyes. Tamara sat behind the wheel. On the way to the hospital, I almost lost consciousness and vomiting did not stop.

Tamara brought me to the hospital where she worked. In the waiting room, I was not able to answer questions. I was unconscious. I do not know how long I stayed in such a state, but I remember that when I opened my eyes, the ceiling was turning and vomiting was returning. As the doctors told me later, I only came to my senses on the third day. When I asked what happened to me, the doctor said that the cause of my condition was incomprehensible to them. Such a case they have not yet seen. He said that when I was brought to the hospital, I was very drunk. My wife told them that at home there was a dinner with friends, and I consumed a lot of alcohol, so I was not given any medicine except for intravenous infusion. The following days brought no improvement. I tried to sit up in bed, but the dizziness made me lie down, and I could not open my eyes. When I started to sit down and eat, the doctors removed the IV drip, and after a few days I was discharged from the hospital. Tamara met me coldly. Her hated look made me suddenly understand the cause of my incomprehensible state.

"Did she want to poison me?" I thought.

It is quite possible because she already has a permit to live in South Africa, and inviting friends and drinking with abundant food is the most powerful alibi in the case of a successful poisoning. Just the dose of the poison apparently was not enough.

Having lost many days to recover, I began to plan a departure. One neighbor's family, after my return from the hospital, again started a conversation about the transfer of my apartment to their son. They had a small business - a sewing workshop. Their son was the main pillar of the company. Having married recently, he and his wife lived in the same apartment with the parents.

Not knowing about the problems in the family with Tamara, and I am leaving the country only with my daughter, they thought that we were going all together. I did not want to explain to them why I can not help them with the flat transfer and did not give them an answer. But now everything has changed and I answered positively.

I could not sell the apartment because it belonged to the state. But it was possible to transfer to somebody else with the consent of the residential department of the city

Neighbors began to engage in paperwork. A few days later, the apartment already belonged to their son.

Having decided not to waste time, I sold the car and some things that we could not take with us. I left to the newlyweds as a gift all the furniture, a TV with all electronic gadgets, a refrigerator and all the appliances in the kitchen.

Money received from the sale of the car, I divided equally, and I explained to Tamara that the amount she got, with modest use, would be enough for the necessary expenses for at list six months.

Tickets have been purchased. Having packed the bags, I suddenly realized that I had not seen my daughter all day. I went to check with the neighbors, where Orit used to spend all her days. They told me that she called someone on the phone and left their house in the afternoon. I travel across the city, but I have not seen her anywhere. I called the police, and they instantly appeared on the threshold of the apartment. I said that the whole family was leaving abroad tomorrow, but my daughter did not come home, and I do not know where she is. I gave them all the data and photos and said that she was with her neighbors all days. They took the addresses of neighbors, my acquaintances, and friends and went out, assuring that they would find my daughter, if not today, then in few days.

When they left, I suddenly felt a sharp pain in my chest and I experienced difficulty in breathing. I lie down on the sofa. The pain did not stop, and my head was spinning. Neighbors came to see me, Tamara called my friends, and Garik Schultz arrived late in the evening. They sat next to me, recommending to go with them to the hospital for inspection. Without knowing what happened with Orit, I refused. Nobody left and sat next to me all night.

Early in the morning, the police arrived with my daughter. They found her in the kibbutz where she stayed when I left for Africa. She took refuge there, not wanting to leave. It was her protest against my decision to take Tamara with me.

I looked at my daughter, but could not speak - the pain did not let me go. I was not angry because I understood why she did it and considered only myself guilty. Only now, when my daughter was next to me, I agreed with friends to go to the hospital.

In the emergency room, doctors determined that I have a heart attack and immediately took the necessary measures. Seeing that the treatment began to help, doctors said that I would have to stay in the hospital until the end of the procedure.

I refused treatment, explained the reason for the refusal, took upon myself all the responsibility for not wanting to stay in the hospital, signed the necessary forms of documents, and returned home.

On the same day, the guy to whom I gave our apartment, put our belongings in his car and drove us to the airport.

The beginning of the second immigration

Formal divorce. Responsibility for two families.
Miss Kay. Esther.
Brothers Maurice and Sidney Siff.
The "Chicken"'s millionaire.
Rola.
A religious cheater.

During the flight, I suddenly felt worse. The pain rose to the throat. I took out a piece of paper, wrote a phone number, the address of my friends and gave it to my daughter.
"If anything happens to me, phone to these people, and they will take care of you. Put my wallet in your bag and do not lose it."

After a few hours of flight, noticed that the pain in the chest subsided and it was easier to breathe. It was a positive sign and I hoped to withstand the flight.

After landing in Johannesburg, I felt much better. After leaving the plane and entering the airport, we went to receive the baggage. I noticed that I breathe easily, and there is no pain. On the taxi we arrived to the same hotel where I stayed before departure. Having provided everyone with food and a roof over my head, I needed a rest. It was necessary to concentrate the thoughts on how to settle our split family.

Called Mr. Logan. He was delighted with my arrival and wanted to know when I could start work. Upon learning that I was not alone, but returned with my family, he gave me a week for sorting out all matters.

For Tamara and my son, I found a furnished apartment. Orit and I stayed at the hotel, where she had a separate room. Tamara said that she needed a carpet and a sewing machine in her apartment. Without arguing, I bought these things from my money.

A few days later, I filed for divorce. Because we did not have any joint property and housing, the divorce did not present any difficulties, and after two weeks, it was formalized. Orit went to school, where according her age and school documents from Israel, she was accepted to the appropriate class. I bought myself an old car but Mr. Logan did not approve of the purchase. "Based on your earnings," he said, "you could afford to buy a new car.

I had to appreciate his advice in a few days. During the trip to work, I heard the rumble of metal, and the car stopped. The driveshaft came off and fell to the ground. All day spent in the repair shop. A month later broke off the bracket mounting exhaust pipe.

I decide not to buy ane new car for a reason. I needed to maintain two separate hotel rooms, pay for Tamara's apartment and, supply them with food. I placed my son in kindergarten, believing that it would allow him to communicate with children, thus helping him to learn a new language faster. English, Tamara did not know, and she could not find a job. The situation was the same as in Israel, with the only difference that she was with her son now and lived alone in her apartment.

After the official divorce, Tamara was against my desire to see my son. So, missing him a lot, I visited the kindergarten and watched from behind the fence how my son stood alone on the side looking at the children playing. My heart sank with pity. When I was delivering the next batch of products to Tamara, she told me that she needed money, because of the amount of money we shared in Israel, nothing left. It was not clear to me what she could spend such an amount of money on, getting full support from me. Having opened the door of her refrigerator, I saw one sausage on empty shelves. My anger had no bounds.

The next day I met one of her new friends, who said that Tamara invited her with other new acquaintances, and treated them with testy beef chops. It was the meat, a box of which, along with the rest of the products, I brought her a few days ago. I usually brought large quantities of food so that she would have enough of them for a long time. Now I saw that she was doing this to upset me, causing damage to herself and her son. But I had no choice. I could not allow my son to remain hungry and continued to supply them with food.

My salary was not enough to support two families, and I was looking for a way out of the situation. An unexpected conversation with my employer made me decide to look for another job. Mr. Logan invited me to his office and, having asked me about how I got settled in and got used to life in the country, he turned to the subject of his business. He told me the story of starting his company from nothing and the years spent on making the business a success. The company is small, but it has regular orders, and the firm brings a steady income. Because I know all about the production and I can make a decision on my own if necessary, he decided to transfer the management of his company to me.

"After twenty years of hard work, I want to rest. If you accept my offer, I will be sure my business will be in good hands."

When I mentioned the subject of the salary, he said that I am the most highly paid employee, but his budget does not allow him to increase my salary. I thanked him for believing in me and my abilities and for everything he did for me. However, because I need to provide for two families, and I do not have enough money, I have to look for a better paying job.

I expected his indignation. On the contrary, he said that he regretted that he could not offer me a higher salary and asked me to consult with him to help me avoid an error that I can make without knowing the market and people well. I was sorry that my personal problem forced me to part with this decent gentleman.

I started looking for a better paying job. A few days later, I signed an annual contract with a German company that manufactures large cranes.

The design bureau was located in the city center. My income has doubled.

After consulting with my daughter, I decided to rent a separate apartment, where we will have two bedrooms and a kitchen. Since I started working, we only had dinner at the hotel. The breakfast and lunch, for which I paid, was lost. I was leaving to work early and so my daughter to school. The convenience of the hotel consisted of meals we did not have to cook, changing the bed and do the cleaning. I wanted my daughter to have the feeling of her room, her apartment, which she had been deprived of for many years; so that she learns to cook, clean the apartment, become a little housewife, such as her mother was.

After arriving in South Africa, I was able to spend more time with her than in Israel. Together we traveled the whole city, which I knew well. Visited former and new friends. Mostly these were the same immigrants as ourselves, and they lived in the same area where we lived. Among them, my daughter had new friends, and when I was busy at work, she spent time in their company.

Due to the lack of her language knowledge, Orit experienced difficulties in the studies, and spending free time among Russian-speaking immigrants, naturally, did not contribute to better results in the school. After only two years of school in Minsk, she had to learn Hebrew in Israel, which she knew well. In South Africa, becoming a high school student, she began to learn another language. It was difficult for her to learn all school subjects in a language she did not know. She was not to be blamed. I just hoped that life in a new country and time would heal the she experienced in the recent past, and she would become as cheerful and happy as her peers-friends.

I managed to see my son several times, and once Tamara even asked me to take him with me.

 I was delighted. At home, I cooked him a delicious dinner, and then we sat together and talked. Suddenly, my son burst into tears and said that he wanted to be with me too. Touched by his confession, I said that I would never leave him, and I will always be his dad. I tried to explain to him that I could not live with his mom because we are entirely alien people. He could not understand why dad and mom are strangers when I am his dad, and she is his mom. I decided to calm him down.
"You do not have to be upset, because now you have two houses - one house with your mother and the other house with your father. You can always come to dad when he wants. He thought and lowered his head. When I brought him home late in the evening, he suddenly pressed himself against me and kissed me tightly." I was going home and cried.

After returning to Africa, busy with the affairs of the family, I had not seen Miss Kay for a long time and decided to visit her. Arrived, as usual, without a prior call. She was at home and was delighted to see me and my daughter, whom she knew about on my previous visit to Africa. Putting a fruit platter on the table, she began to ask me about our life, about the place we live, about my work. She was surprised to learn that I had to take my wife and son with me. She approved my divorce and noticed that I have to think about my personal life too. A few days later she called and said that she wanted to introduce me to one woman, and asked me to come because she could tell me more about this woman.

Esther, the name of the woman, was the daughter of a well-known family in the Jewish community. She received a university education, read a lot, understood the art, and played the guitar. She fell in love with an Israeli, whom she married and had two children. But the husband turned out to be a fraud, did not work, and was a drug addict. Esther, ashamed of her mistake, hid her personal tragedy from the parents. When her father learned about her husband, he went to the police, and they sent this rogue out of the country within twenty-four hours. The mother of this woman was the sister of Saul Kerzner, a famous tycoon and owner of the largest casino in Africa called Sun City, located in Botswana, a small country bordering South Africa.

A week later, I received an invitation from Esther for dinner. She lived in a small two-story house with a servant and two children. The maid led me to the dining room filled with bright light, and the table already set for dinner. A slim, thin woman with brown eyes rose to me and with a sweet smile extended her hand to me.

"Esther," she said and introduced the children.

She sat opposite me with the children. Each of their requests began with the words: "Can I," or "please." After dinner, she sent the children to sleep, and, inviting me to sit next to her on the sofa in the living room, she asked me to tell about myself. When I finished my story, she suddenly pressed herself against me, clasped my head in her hands and gently kissed me.

In the morning, when I returned home, she called me and said that she was already missing me and wants to see me again. I was delighted with such a stunning admission. We started dating.

One day she invited me to dinner at a cafe that her children liked, and I asked her to one of the events at Rolla's home, which my yoga teacher arranged for those who attended her classes.

When she saw Esther, Rolla was amazed and asked how I managed to get to know her.

At one of our meetings, Esther said she was going to rest in Switzerland and asked if I wanted to join her. I did not immediately realize what to say to her, but I realized that she absolutely did not understand the difference in my and her financial capabilities. I said that the management at work won't allow me at this time to take a vacation.

Her gentle nature, kindness, and immediacy attracted me so much that I decided to find out how she sees our relationship in the future. My question surprised her, and after an embarrassing silence, she said that she had not thought about it.

After a few days, she called me and said that her mother wanted to talk to me and invited me to her dinner next Sunday. It was the day I spent with my son, and I took him with me. Esther, with the children, was already there.

Her mother was sitting at the table in a wheelchair. She didn't ask me anything. After serving the dishes on the table, she turned to me and said that she knew Miss Kay. Nevertheless, she wonders why Miss Kay decided to introduce me to her daughter. In such a big city, she could find me other women who would suit me more than her daughter. Esther sat with her head down and was silent. I did not answer, put my fork on the plate, rose from the table, took my son by the hand and, without saying goodbye, left their home.

I imagined this invitation quite differently than what it turned out to be in reality. The humiliating remark Ester's mother could only afford with me, the immigrant. When I came to Esther's home, she refused to accept me. Our relationship ended.

After the sanctions imposed by America on the government of South Africa, which carried out the policy of apartheid, many foreign firms closed their enterprises, and local companies lost their orders. American banks have ceased to operate in the country and soon began unprecedented unemployment. The first to suffer were the Negro population. They supplied the unskilled labor.

After a while, my working contrast with the German firm ended. I had to pay for high earnings with long hours of the working day. During the lunch break, I used to have smoked ham sandwiches and sausages, and also I became a lover of fresh white buns with jam. The sitting at work and abundant nutrition did not benefit me. I gained weight. The jacket on me was not fastened. Despite a decent salary, I did not have savings. The money went to the support of two families.

Having lost the job, I bought products with the last money, divided equally, and brought Tamara her part. Having said that I had no more money left, I made her understand that she should be frugal with the food.

Fortunately, a week later, I found work in a large factory, which was owned by two brothers - Maurice and Sydney Siff, former emigrants from Lithuania. Both were already over seventy. The eldest of them, Maurice, told me how they came to Africa, having only tools. They went from home to home, inserted locks in the doors, repaired furniture, repaired electrical appliances, and did all kinds of work that house owners needed. With the savings, they opened their own workshop, bought a few machines, welding equipment, and hired workers. Appeared orders. Then they bought a small factory and additional equipment. During World War II their company received a request from the state for the manufacture items for the army. This allowed them in a few years to become the owners of a vast enterprise. They became millionaires.

I had a small salary, but as an engineer, I had a company car and a problem with transport was solved. Then, a base for the table was welded from the waste of the profile iron, on top of which a wooden door was laid. It turned out to be my working desk. It was placed in a vast empty hall on the second floor.

After reviewing the plant, I was surprised to what extent machinery and equipment were outdated. The territory of the plant occupied a whole block a long the road and had many buildings with work shops. A separate workshop for the manufacture of stamps - was the only one where I saw the precise equipment.

As Maurice explained my responsibilities, my job was to improve the production and quality of the products. Based on what I saw, my first suggestion would be to get rid of all the old equipment that was as old as the owners themselves. I was not going to even hint about it to him, being sure that I would insult proud Maurice and his business. Every morning, sitting on his moped, he circled his property.

On the eve of one of the Jewish holidays, I received an invitation from Maurice for dinner, as is usually done by wealthy people when they invite poor Jews to their house to celebrate such events.
I arrived with my daughter on time. Maurice met us and acquainted with everyone present. His family gathered at the table, where his daughter's husband, a dentist, amused us with witty jokes and anecdotes. Naturally, I was asked about my life and immigration to Israel.

Getting acquainted with the production of the enterprise, equipment, and working conditions, I saw an open field of activity in any workshop. I came to Maurice with suggestions that could increase the production of products and improve their quality. To my surprise, he was not interested. I began to doubt that he took me to work because of the need. "Most likely, because of charity," I thought. He probably did not forget his young years and wanderings in the search for a living, and this left him with a sense of understanding of those who find themselves in the same position.

But I continued to create projects, make sketches and calculations. Maurice often came to my workplace - the largest office in the world because my desk stood alone at the window of a completely empty workshop fifty meters long - and looked at my sketches with suggestions. Noticing that I was doing calculations on one side of the paper, he advised me to use the back side of the paper too. I took his remark as a rich man's oddity, but when the next day he brought me a stack of printed sheets of paper and asked to use the other side for my sketches, I compared this with my desk, which was made of waste metal, and came to the conclusion that it would not be easy for me to do something useful for his business.

I was not mistaken. Passing by one welding device and seeing how four black workers hold metal sheets in their hands, and the fifth strengthens them with welding, I suggested making a device which could replace the job of four workers. Maurice replied that he pays very little to the workers, which is covered by the sale price of the product, and my device will cost him a lot of money. I continued to carry out his instructions, and when I addressed the chief engineer of the plant with one of my proposals, he said that only Maurice could make the decision. Now it became clear that I submit only to the owner of the enterprise and I can hardly bring any benefit to productivity on the factory.

During this period, when I lost interest in my work, I had a new acquaintance. His name was Misha, and he was from Belarus. He was also an immigrant, the owner of a cafe, where, along with selling cornmeal, bread, and beverages to the Negro population, he also sold them fried chicken. Misha lived not far from me and invited to his home to talk about his business. He told about his plans to increase income and wanted to show his cafe. We arrived at the central bus station, located next to the railway.

From here, at the end of the working day, the blacks, exhausted by hard work, bought food to feed their families.

Entering the room, I saw the dirt on the floor and felt the smell of burnt oil. In the room-refrigerator, there were hundreds of chickens on the shelves, and a large chicken grill stood next to this room. I paid attention that the grill was made in America. Misha said that this grill is the basis of the entire business and brings him high income. But the demand for grilled chicken is much more than he can do for sale. Misha wanted to know if I could design a grill that could be made at a local factory. He promised to pay off my work on the project and the manufacture of the grill. I was interested.

I bought a drawing board, the same brand as I used to work on it in Minsk. Coming from work, I was busy with the project until late at night. Three weeks later I finished the assembly drawing. The design of my grill completely differed from the American. I came to show the work to my customer. Misha looked at the drawings, listened to my explanations, but I saw his eyes gliding over the paper without interest. He invited me to stay with them for dinner.

While his wife was setting the table, he led me into the next room, filled with household items. Everything was new, in the original packaging: a refrigerator, a gas stove, a washing machine, a vacuum cleaner, beds, desks, wardrobes, etc. Seeing my surprised face, he proudly said that he was preparing to move to Israel, where he has many relatives. When I was asked when he was going to leave, he replied that he had not yet decided. Meantime, he hopes to increase his income, mainly by selling chickens in bigger quantities.

"I," he said with a grin, "managed to make enough money never to work again."

Moreover, he is going to help his relatives in Israel. Yes, I thought, his business is not a laughing matter - the hens made him a millionaire.

I remember a bucket with dirty cloth in it next to the mop in the corridor. The bucket was full of money from the day's sale. Misha said that in the case of the robbery, nobody would think to look into the dirty bucket.

Two weeks later, having finished the project, I came to show him the drawings. I was sure he would have been delighted. He received me coldly and without the previous hospitality. I put the drawings on the table an offered to explain the new method of grilling. Suddenly, he said that he does not believe in my ability to design a device I did not have previous experience. Then he added that he would not invest money in the grill that, as he thinks, is not reliable.

I folded my drawings and left. The mood was terrible. On Sunday, as usual, I went to yoga at Rola's house, which I visited every week. Her home has always been open for everybody at any day and any time. People were coming here not only for yoga. Here people were met with the warmth and understanding. Rola was a person to whom peole enrtusted the secrets of their own life and listened to her advice.

To understand why she has had such respect and popularity, I have to bring up the past of this an extraordinary woman.

She was born in a very wealthy family with property in many parts of the city. Her father even called some streets by the names of his children. I personally saw one of them with the name "Rola". In her youth, she left to Palestine and took an active part in the struggle against the British rule. She personally knew Menachem Begin and all leaders of the Jewish resistance.

Returning to Africa, she fell in love for a man who wasn't Jewish. Her angry father derived her from the inheritance.

She left Africa and traveled with her husband to Europe. She was not happy with the marriage, left her husband and went to India, where she spent many years, devouring herself to Indian culture and yoga. Rola returned to Africa already in old age and bought a small house, which became the place where she gave yoga lessons in to provide herself with a minimum income. Her brother and sister, having father's inheritance, lived on large estates with numerous servants, and did not want to recognize their poor sister.

The oldest Rola's daughter, a very energetic blonde, lived in Los Angeles. She taught in elite circles the rules of nutrition for weight loss and was a private trainer for those who wanted to strengthen their body and unburden one's heart. She often came to visit her mother and always with a new partner, twice younger of her age. All her partners were handsome with developed muscles. They smiled politely and rarely talked.

Successful, as she said, in business, the daughter asked mather for the "plastic" - so she called a credit card. Making it sound like something insignificant, and disappeared with her temporary lover, as they all were, for the whole day. She spent time visiting restaurants and returning home with shopping bags. I looked at Rola, at the extinct look of the eyes that were always kind and attentive, and realized how ashamed she was for her daughter, who was taking mother's earned money.

After yoga session, we gathered in the dining room, where a samovar and delicious buns of jam were waiting for us. We liked to sit with Rola at the table and to have a conversation in which she skillfully touched on topics of interest to those present. We sat, pacified by meditation and exercise, and felt like at home. Yes, it was really a house where we came at any time, and we were always met by her inquisitive and intelligent eyes, reading our thoughts. People brought their problems, joys, successes, and disappointments here because there was always a person for them with useful advice and the right decision.

Looking at me, she asked if I would like to share something that makes me sad. She knew everything about my personal life, as well as about the life of everyone who came to her house. I started telling her about my work on the project and how it ended. She listened carefully. Apparently, one of her clients had a husband who, besides the business of importing goods, also had a cafe.

I knew this woman, she was irregular, but she came, most likely, to talk in private with Role about home affairs. A few days later, Rola called me and said that we were invited by this woman to the dinner. As far as I understood, the owner of the house already knew about the matter we were invited, because after the lavish meal he invited me to his office and asked to tell about the grill. Having dwelt on the features and advantages of my design in comparison to the American one, I began to explain about possibilities in using it in small food shops.

Judging by his questions, he was interested. Robert, the owner of the house, had not one, but five cafes. Then, in my presence, he called a friend, the owner of a big enterprise, and offered to go with him into the business. After a lengthy telephone conversation, they came to an agreement to finance the production. I was asked to make a detailed description of the new product and to head the grill fabrication on the premises which they will find. I could not believe that my disappointment would be replaced by such an unexpected success. I took up the job.

A few days later, Robert's wife calls me. She says that her husband came to a conclusion - having two businesses, it will be difficult for him to take on another one. I decided to hear it from her husband by myself. He accepted me and began with an apology that he did not consider the amount of time and work that needed to be given to a new matter. Asking about his partner, I heard that he came to the same conclusion.

Seeing my disappointment, Robert advised me to submit an application for an invention so that no one could take this idea away from me. I agreed with the concept of patenting but made him understand that I do not have now such ability. He understood what I mean, brought a checkbook and wrote me a check for five hundred rands. This amount was sufficient to patent my product, which I received two months later.

Meanwhile, Tamara found a partner in life, and I had a hope that my financial support she would not need anymore. Unfortunately, a few months later, her Polish partner was killed in some kind of brawl. Tamara was able to prove that she was his wife and received a decent compensation, about which she did not tell me. But a little time passed, and I learned that lost Polish partner was replaced by his friend. Chris, the new husband, was an electronics specialist and had a well-paid job. My financial support was over.

Wanting to see my son's stepfather, I came to check them out. Chris met me, unfriendly. My son was delighted with my arrival. I decided to talk with them about a permanent day I will spend with my son together. Ami showed me his room. His bed was a large mattress on the floor, a bookshelf, a small writing desk, including a large white dog that lay on the mattress as if it belonged to him personally.

I left their house understanding that there was a person in the house who would not allow them to be in need, and judging by the smell from the kitchen where the meat was frying on the pan, I could not worry about my son now.

Since then, we spent every Sunday together, and Ami had the opportunity to see his older sister. Orit was already a ninth grade student. With a mixed sense of relation and regret, she looked at her blond brother, she was separated from by the efforts of his mother. My meetings with my son also carried the imprint of a past. The first two years, I had to see him only occasionally, while the delivery of food products. He could not say the word "dad" for so long that I saw his difficulty to pronounce this word when he wanted to ask me something or say something. In subsequent meetings, we already talked a lot and I learned what my son's interests are, what he likes to do and who his friends are.

Maurice rarely visited me, and I was not quite sure whether he remembered me.

Coming to work, I began to use my office for making drawings and parts of the grill. After obtaining the patent, I needed to make a prototype. My attempt to get Maurice himself interested in my product ended in failure. Even though the plant, based on the available equipment and the availability of free space, was suitable for this purpose, he did not want to hear about the introduction of a new product into production.

I began, from time to time, to bring to Ari, the manager of the workshop, drawings of small parts that do not require much time for manufacturing. He never asked about my projects, because he often had to do small jobs for me before. He did not suspect that I was making parts for my grill. Ari, an Israeli, worked at the plant for more than ten years. From the first days of our acquaintance, we became friends, and he introduced me to Izya Gillis, a very friendly and hospitable Lithuanian immigrant, who bought a house with a pool and a site of land where he grew vegetables in the garden and planted fruit trees. In Lithuania, Izya, without having higher education, made money and quite successfully. This allowed his family not to deny themselves anything.

However, his family life was unsuccessful. His wife left for Israel with their son. There were a lot of women in Vilnius, for whom a stocky and strong man with friendly smiling blue eyes was desirable, and if one takes into account his money, he is also a big bait. But only one of them, a young and attractive Lithuanian woman, succeeded, having given him a son, to marry him. When his underground business began to experience difficulties, he decided to leave Lithuania. He chose not to go to Israel because of problems that might have arisen with his second wife and son, who were not considered Jews in Israel. Friends advised him to go to South Africa. The market for houses on sale was in his favor, and he immediately bought the house and a car. For a long time, he did not need to work. Brought money allowed to support the family, but came time to think about earnings. Without a profession, he, no longer young, but a strong man, could not find work for a long time. When I met him, he was already working. When I learned that he was engaged in repairing dies in a small enterprise, I didn't believe it, but I soon became convinced. I came to his factory and saw him in a dirty working apron. He was busy with one of the dies arrived for repair. His hands, which held money all his life, now held a hammer. It was the end of the working day. Having changed clothes, he left with me outside. I could not resist and asked how he managed to find a job, which requires specialists in the manufacture of dies. His answer surprised me: he told the plant manager that he had once worked on dies, but had forgotten a little and, if given a chance, he would restore his knowledge. One of the workers was attached to him for help, who explained to Izya what a die was about and began to show the simple operation - disassembly. And for several years now he has been "restoring his past experience," which he never had, and is sitting on a firs part of the process - disassembly. Personally, I saw his hands, covered with grease, and became full of respect for him.

After completing a dental assistant course, his wife found a job. Dentist became her lover, and she moved into his house, taking her son wih. Izya stayed in the house alone.

On Sundays, my son, I and Ari, who introduced me to Izya, came to visit him and stayed for the whole day. Izya fried the chicken, then he brought a salad from his garden, the seeds of which were from Lithuania, fresh green onions, radishes, and we sat at the table. I must say that Izya's culinary skills were excellent. Then, we spent the whole day by the pool, which the owner of the house kept absolutely clean. Ami spent a lot of time in the water. Tanned and refreshed, I brought him home in the evening, and we parted until the next meeting.

At work, I was busy with my personal project. I saw that Maurice seemed to be tormented, not knowing what to do with me. After my conversation with him about my invention, he began to appear in my workplace more often than usual, asking what I am doing. I understood that, sooner or later, I would have to leave this enterprise and tried to concentrate all my time on making a prototype of my grill. I was hoping for success and saw new opportunities in the future.

Once, at my desk appeared a man, whom I did not meet at the factory. Almost my height, a little younger than me, a friendly face framed a neatly trimmed beard. On the chest, in wide-open collar of his shirt, was the golden Star of David on a golden chain. He held out a hand with a solid gold bracelet on it and introduced himself - Sol Katz. Works in the supply department.

After shaking his hand, I saw that he came not only to meet me, so I asked how I could help him. Smiling, he replied that he had come to talk not about plant matters, but about a personal one. Since this business is not related to production, he believes that it is better to talk about it at home.

He lived in an area where, mainly, religious Jews lived, as he was. In the spacious room where we sat, there was a large grand piano and heavy leather furniture. His wife, a pretty blonde, in a long skirt, much younger than her husband, brought two glasses of orange juice and went out, leaving us alone.

Before moving on to his business, Sol began asking about my personal life and the circumstances that brought me to the country. I and answered very briefly, wanting to know what this meeting is about.

He admitted that the work at the plant does not suit him, and he thinks about his own business, but he needs the help of an engineer in the implementation of his ideas. Then he got to the point. He paid attention that in all cafes where juices are sold, a thick mass of pulp, which contains many useful vitamins, remains to lie on the bottom of the container. The useful pulp with vitamins in the buyer's cup remains very small.

He would like to make such juice dispenser, in which this thick mass was distributed evenly in the whole volume. In this case, the quality of the juice is preserved when it is sold to the buyer. In the future, he would like to set up the manufacture of such devices and to sell them. When I asked how he would finance the production, he said that he got a legacy from his father, which allowed him and his entire family to have a steady income. Therefore, for the manufacture of the prototype and other expenses, he will allocate his own money, but for the business, he has the support of his uncle, his namesake Sol Krock, who promised to give him a million rands, in case he proves that his idea is feasible. I used to hear the name of Soli Krock, even during my first visit to Africa. Krock and his brother owned one of the largest pharmaceutical companies.

He was considered one of the wealthiest businessman in Johannesburg, buying factories and enterprises in bankraptcy when inflation began in the country.

As always, when the task itself attracts all my attention, I begin to think about it, forgetting to ask what the compensation is for my time and work. I started from acquainting myself with the juice dispensers, which I saw in the café. But only now I noticed that a layer of pulp stays at the bottom.

A few days later, I found a straightforward solution, having designed a container that, swaying, continually shakes up the whole mass of juice.

I showed the drawing to Sol and explained that a small electric motor through the gearbox and lever rotates the container with juice, preventing the thick mass from accumulating at the bottom, and the oscillation frequency can be smoothly changed by changing the number of revolutions of the engine. Simple and cheap. All the mechanics will be in a stainless steel box, and only a special tap will come out, which will dispense the right amount of juice until the cup presses the tap lever. Sol's eyes lit up with pleasure, although I noticed that the essence of the mechanic was not completely clear to him. He suggested that I make a life-size model so that he could imagine what it looked like before investing money in a real sample. At first, I did not understand what he meant by a full-size model.

When he said he wanted to make a wooden layout, I laughed heartily. Then, on reflection, he agreed to make a box of wood and a juice container of plywood. Naturally, there could be no question of any metal details.

By Sunday, all the materials were prepared and my hands, missing the tools, set to work. Having made the boxes, I showed how a box made of plywood, imitating the container with juice, will swing and shake the juice with pulp. But this did not convince him.

He thought a little, then went into the house and returned with a plastic bottle of orange juice, at the bottom of which lay the sediment. He put the bottle on the bottom of the plywood box and watched as the thick pulp on the bottom of the bottle gradually dissolves during shaking of the container. Solly, suddenly, became very serious and businesslike. We went home, and he said that for him, this product means a lot, because it opens the opportunity to start a business. After thanking me, he said that he would do everything possible to help me in the future, using his contacts if I had such a need. I said that I already need help, and told him about my grill, part of which I had already made. He listened very carefully to my story about how I came to create my grill and said that he was also interested in this business, but now he urgently needs to start making his product, and he asked me to order all the necessary parts. I found a small company, where they agreed to produce a single sample from a sheet metal with subsequent painting.

In the meantime, I continued to invest my money and make parts for the grill. When all the pieces were ready, I assembled the prototype for one week and looked with admiration at my brainchild, on which I spent more than a year.

When the prototype of dispenser was manufactured, Sol showed it to his relatives. They liked it, and we set up for making an industrial design. I ordered stainless steel parts in the same factory where the parts for my grill were made.

The finished in stainless steel juice dispenser worked perfectly. After that, we ordered ten more units, and Sol started selling them. Buyers were satisfied. Reminding Sol of his promise to help me after his product is on the market, I asked him to buy me tickets to America. I wanted to visit the international exhibition of products and equipment for the food industry. He agreed. Just a day before the scheduled departure, and after many reminders, Sol brought a ticket and gave the address of one of his friends in Chicago, where I would have an overnight stay. He mentioned to me that at the exibision I have to check and bring information about American's designs of the juice dipensers too.

I remembered his friend, because I saw him recently at Sol's house. I scraped everything I had on the bank account and went to the airport. The plane flew me to New York and during the transfer, I learned that Sol did not buy a ticket to Chicago. I had to give more than half of my own money for the flight to Chicago. Otherwise the whole trip would have been useless.

At the address given to me, I came to the district with the strange name – Divan. The door was opened by a man who did not recognize me. When I said that Sol Katz recommended me to him, he was a little embarrassed and asked me to come in.

Reuven, the owner of the house, asked about the purpose of my arrival to America and, having learned that I have no relatives or friends here, took me to the basement. There, next to the buzzing heating installation was a folding bed. I was lucky. His son, who owned this bed, was absent.

I knew Reuven was a handyman and had his own business. He had permission to repair all kinds of home appliances, as well as water pipe repair works. He had a mobile workshop with all the necessary tools and spare parts and was called at any time of the day or night in case of urgent work. Also, the work, most often, required a great physical efforts. But the job brought in an income that covered the expenses of his large family. His modest clothes and traces that left tools and work on his strong hands, instilled respect.

Having more than half a day left, I decided to walk in the city. I left the house and went along the way built up with two-story brick houses. Reaching the main street, I passed through a small bridge and paid attention to pedestrians, among which I saw many Orthodox Jews. Noticed a small synagogue building.

It seemed abandoned. Peeped in. A young man in a worn out black frock-coat met me and spoke to me in Yiddish. I answered him in Hebrew and asked how many people visit the synagogue. He shook his head. No, they almost don't come, and it will be soon closed because there are no people, even for a minyan. I continued my walk along the street, which became crowded and noticed that there were many Indians among pedestrians and also heard Arabic. Only at the end of the street, I saw a large synagogue. It was late to visit, and I went back home.

The whole family was home. Reuven's wife met me affably and introduced her children, two boys of ten years and an older girl. I was invited to dinner and, after the blessing of the meal, sitting at the table, I felt some restraint. Realizing that this was due to my presence, I thanked for the meal and went to the basement. Under the pleasant buzz of the stove, I fell asleep and woke up early.

The exhibition was far away and I had to travel with transfers to different buses. I spent at the show all three days from the morning until late evening. I went through all stands, kiosks, and pavilions, where various companies show their equipment. There were the pavilions where all kinds of food products were displayed and the visitors were offered to test whatever they liked. I had to snack from time to time and was not hungry.

American grills conquered me with quality of performance and exciting ideas, but I did not find anything like my design. That was enough to justify the purpose of my trip.

There were also a lot of trade exhibits for the sale of juices. They were high-quality workmanship, looked very attractive, and had a cooling system. But still, none of the dispensers looked like my design. I gave the preference to American design.

On the third day, at the request of the host, who invited me to the synagogue for the coming Sabbath, I came from the exhibition earlier. Respecting his hospitality, I could not refuse him.

With pride, he showed me a local synagogue, where, as I noticed, he was respected and welcomed warmly. As a guest, I was called to read one of the chapters of the Torah, and I coped with this, thanks to the knowledge of Hebrew, which I still have. Ruwen was pleased with me. On Saturday, I rested and, sitting in one of the rooms, decided to take a couple of notes about the exhibition. One of the owner's son's who looked into the room and saw what I was doing, ran out and brought his father. Reuven explained to me that on Saturday is forbidden to write, only to read. I apologized and put my notes away. I was convinced that I was right, believing that their family was warry that a non-religious person came to their family and they foresaw possible violations of their lifestyle.

When Saturday was over, Reuven said that due to my departure, he and his wife wanted to show me Chicago at night. I was happy about their proposal, since, apart from walking around the Divan area on the first day of arrival, I did not see the city.

On this occasion, Reuven and his wife were smartly dressed. He drove directly to the city center. The elevator of the tall tower lifted us to the entrance of rotating restaurant. Reuven said that the treatment would be at his expense and ordered several dishes and cocktails. Probably, he understood what a "rich" American I am if he had to arrange me in the basement of his house. Therefore, he made an indication that I do not need to participate in the payment for the dinner.

We spent the whole evening, admiring the city from a height of the tower. Cars like children's toys silently crawled along the arteries of Highways. The rotation of the restaurant opened up the changing panorama of the city, and we viewed with excitement the nightly Chicago flooded with myriad lights.

I saw my hospitable hosts are happy to have the opportunity to break away from the daily routine of life and enjoyed no less than me.

We returned home silently, as if, tried to keep the sense of the extraordinary beauty of the night city.

The next morning, thanking the hosts for their hospitality and a wonderful evening in Chicago, I went to the airport.

I have not forgotten the situation in New York where Sol left me without the ticket to Chicago, and when I meet Sol at work, expressed my outrage about this. Not at all embarrassed, he said that he had bought me a ticket to America, as he had promised. I had to take on all the other expenses, but he simply forgot to warn me about it.

A week passed, and he showed up at my home with an apology, that he did not understand me. He tried to convince me that it was impossible for us to terminate the relationship because of a minor, as he expressed, confusion, and assured that he was going to become my partner in business as soon as I finish all the official part of preparing patent documents for the juice dispenser.

I thought that having a patent for my design would give me the right to an individual share in the income from the sale. Also, if Sol, with his money and the support of wealthy relatives, become, as he assured me, my partner in the grill business, I need to continue to cooperate.

He took from the briefcase the document that he brought with him, as proof that an agreement with relatives was signed and acquainted me with its content.

Under this agreement, he had 51 percent in the business, his relatives 49 percent and 5 percent of each partner would go to the synagogue's charitable expenses.

I listened to him and thought about how he actually turned out to be ungrateful. He gives five percent to the synagogue, and to me, for all my work and time spent on the business which would provide him with income for life, he refused to give me even half of what he gave to the synagogue.

Satisfied that he had achieved profitable results for him with partners, he said that I needed to prepare the drawings and description of the invention for the patent.

"You will have no difficulty in preparing all the necessary documents and drawings because you have already done this work for your grill," he said.

I took up the job, believing that I would now have another patent for which Sol should pay me. I don't even mind if he adds his last name too.

A week later, I visited him at home with documents ready for filing for a patent. He met me, as always, affably. All the rooms were lined with wooden boxes in which household items were laid. The black piano was painted white, the paintings were gone from the walls, all the crystal vases, glasses already disappeared from the sideboard, and there were no carpets on the wooden floor. I stood and looked, not understanding what was happening, until Sol explained that they were preparing to immigrate to Israel.

Understanding that I was not only interested in this, he said that he would be developing business in Israel. Then he invited me to his home office, where everything was unchanged, and putting in front of me the papers, said that I should read and sign. The essence of the document was that I had to confirm that all my drawings were made according to the sketches that he, Sol Katz, gave me during the development; that I do not claim any rights to a patent and I undertake not to transmit any information to anyone about the invention.

"What it is?" I asked in perplexity.

"You must sign this document; otherwise, I will sue you and, you will have to return the amount of money I spent on your trip to America, as well as for legal fees."

I could not believe my eyes; I could not believe that he can so impudently lie. He, who could not even hold a pencil in his hand, states that I worked according to his sketches. He, to whom I had to explain what the essence of my idea was and how it would work. He sat in front of me and wrote down my every word when I told how to justify the profitability of the appliance. He had no idea how to start making parts and who to turn to if it wasn't for my personal contacts. Now he sat in front of me and waited for my signature, a complete lie of a humiliating document.

I felt an aversion to this man who prayed to God every day and knew by heart all Ten Commandments.

"You want to be an inventor, please, but in my eyes you are a nothingness and a scoundrel," I told him, and put my signature.

Many years later, I learned that already in Israel, his wife divorced him and, taking the children, left him.

Shortly before graduating from school, Orit warned me that she would not get a certificate because of her insufficiency in the English language. I remember, sometimes she was telling me about the difficulties in studying subjects, and I thought that she, just like all her Russian-speaking friends, would be able to finish school. I have never been called to the school, and I did not know she had problems.

In the constant care and support of the two families, the search for work and the desire to succeed with my inventions, I was distracted from her studies at school. And here is the result.

Now it was necessary to think about acquiring for her of any required profession. Given her immigrant status, I managed to get her into college for the economics course.

Fight for survival

Uranium mine in Namibia.
Daughter's wedding in Israel.
New job.
Unexpected dating.
Daughter's arrival in Africa.
Philippine Healer.
A grandfather at 46.

I lost my job at the Maurice's Siff factory. Despite the unfavorable times for the country's economy, I left work at the Siff plant without regret. I lost interest in my work, where I could not be useful, and he was tired of my constant reminders of the existing production problems that did not bother him.

The country continued to experience difficulties in all fields of industry. Unemployment has affected both specialists and unskilled labor.

Searches for work did not bring results. Finally, through the employment agency, I managed to find a temporary job with high pay at a uranium mine in Namibia. They needed an engineer to carry out ongoing projects.

I did not want to leave my daughter alone, but I did not have a way out. It was hard to find a job, and I ran out of savings after the financing the grill manufacture.

Before leaving to Namibia, I arranged the daughter's secure stay in Hillel boarding school. This Orthodox religious institution where girls and young men live in separate rooms and get three meals a day.

When I tried to see how Orit's room look like, the director of this school pushed me out the door, saying that in the rooms where the girls are living, men are not allowed to enter. After that, I even more believed in the reliability of my decision. With such Cerberus, I have nothing to worry about my daughter. I paid for her stay and was pleased that she got a roof and provided with food. The college that she started attending was not far. School friends lived nearby.

The ticket was bought by the company and I flew to the Namibia capital - Windhoek. From there, a small twin-engine aircraft with several passengers on board, after exhausting flight over the blazing heat of the Kalahari Desert landed in Swakopmund.

I knew very little about this country. Former German colony until 1920, it was called West Africa and was part of South Africa. The official languages were German and Afrikaans. The population is about two million, of which whites were only a few hundred thousand. Namibia is one of the world known exporters of uranium, diamonds, gold, and silver.

I was met at the airport, brought to the hotel on the ocean shore, and given 500 rands for pocket money. After having dinner in hotel, I went out for a walk to know the city.

Swakopmund is a small city by the ocean. Clean houses, well-groomed streets, small shops, cozy bars. I started with a walk along the deserted sandy beach. The wind threw cold spray of foaming waves in the face. It got dark, and I returned to the city.

Walked into the first on my way bar, ordered a beer mug. Behind tables, filled with bottles, with cigars in their hands set and calmly talked the visitors. I heard the German language. Perhaps, they were the inhabitants of the former German colony. Then I heard English with a strong European accent, and I thought that there are also many immigrants, like me. I did not hear loud and drunken voices, like in the bars of South Africa.

The next morning, the special bus delivered people to work. The sky was foggy. Uranium mining was 75 kilometers away. On an asphalt road, we drove through a flat desert dotted with stones and boulders among the rare bushes of cactus and thorns. When we approached the enterprise, the fog cleared and brightly glared the sun.

I met with the head of production. I learned that I was hired to replace the engineer who took a long vacation. If I like it here, we can talk about permanent employment.

Then he showd the projects that need urgent work and led me to the room that was occupied by a previous engineer. Now it became my place of work. I received a uniform - shoes, a special form of clothing - and a special identification document, without which nobody has the right to be at the production site. I was presented to the head of the design office, and then began to acquaint myself with the enterprise.

The extraction of uranium ore itself was located several kilometers away from the place of processing. We drove to a vast excavation pit in the ground where the trucks appeared on its bottom like toys. They were loaded with ore and climbed up on the serpentine road to the top. When they were at the exit of the pit, from where we observed them, they were the size of a two-story house, and their wheels were the size of the two human heights.

We returned to the plant, where I was introduced to the stages of processing the delivered by trucks ore. In the office, I began acquainting with the list of projects to be implemented, and chose one of them – with under the heading "urgent."

Then I left the office and went to the place of processing stage which was associated with my task. I walked along the wooden track with a handrail. Down, below my feet were enormous cylindrical tanks with an open top, where the ore passed through one of the processing phases. I was wearing a short-sleeved uniform shirt and short trousers. Soon I found the place that required my attention. Making notes and taking measures during the half an hour of studying the problem, I returned to his office. In this case no knowledge about the recycling process was required. The decision was purely technical, and I made a few sketches.

The next morning, waking up, I saw that my legs and hands were covered with red spots that were tingling. Sitting on the bus next to one of the draftsmen, the guy from Romania, told me that these spots are the result of a burn from the radioactive radiation. It is not dangerous, and soon they will disappear, he explained to me. That evening, he introduced me at the bar to his friends. The woman worked in our factory in the ordering department, and her husband was a collector of all sorts of gems and crystals. They invited us to visit their home.

I watched in amazement at the stones and crystals laid out

on the shelves that sparkled under the light of electrical globes in different colors. I did not see such diversity even in jewelry shops.

It turns out he found these amazing stones in the desert. Showing me a big dark brown stone, he said, that if you cut it, then there will be crystals inside.

From his explanation, it was clear that he knows and understands the origin of gems, he knows where to find them and how to discern an ordinary stone in the desert from the precious one. Then he showed me his workshop and tools for sawing and polishing them. In parting, he gave me a few crystals in different colors and polished cut of one of his stones.

Impressed by the collection I saw, I wanted to wander around the desert that I saw out of the bus window every morning in the haze of fog before sunrise.

One Sunday, I went to the outskirts of the city, behind which lay a gray and silent desert, wandered among the stones scattered around and tried to guess which one of them might be useful. Realizing that my attempt was useless, I returned to the city and decided to get acquainted with the shops. Small in size, they impressed me with a careful selection of quality products and low prices.

I got the idea to send my parents a package. My parents did not receive my letters, but the parcel from Namibia, a country hardly heard of in Minsk, I hoped, would pass through the custom-house.

I bought my mother beautiful shoes and a shawl made of Kashmir wool, and for my father, I bought a Scottish wool cardigan and summer shoes. I wrote a letter, put it in the bag and sent it from the local post office.

I learned, that they received the parcel, when I managed to come to Minsk nine years later, in 1989. I did not find my mother alive, she died three years before my arrival.

Dad sometimes wore a cardigan. The shoes were untouched - my sister said that he kept them as a gift from a son who did not forget him.

I keep his cardigan, which my sister gave me after her arrival in America, as the memory of our father.

The days passed monotonously and imperceptibly passed three months.
I was sitting in my office, busy with the next project. Suddenly Orit called me. I often spoke with her from my office.She said that she was going to get married and leaving for Israel. In a panic, not understanding what had happened, I asked her not to do anything without my permission and wait for my arrival.

I had to explain to the production manager what happened in my family, and he gave me a permit for a short leave. I booked a ticket, and that day, sitting next to the pilot, I was already flying through the desert to the capital of Namibia. From there immediately to Johannesburg.

My daughter met me with joy and told me the story of her acquaintance. There was a guy in the hostel whose mother died in Israel, and according to the Jewish trudition he had to sit on the floor for seven days, praying and never go out. This tradition is called Shiva. Zion, the name of this Israeli, was allocated a place on the first floor, next to the director's office. Orit every day brought him water and food from the dining room, and when the days of Shiva were over, they began to meet.

By profession, he is a diamond polisher and worked in South Africa under a contract that expired. In Israel, he has a family: a father, six brothers, and a sister. The whole family is religious. Zion at the age of two, was brought to Israel from Marocco, where his father was a rich man, carrying out orders for making the furniture for the royal palace.

Having decided to immigrate to Israel, he sent many boxes with carpets, furniture and everything necessary for living in a new country. When the boxes were open in Israel, all of them were empty. The big family of ten people found themselves in poverty.

After the influx of numerous immigrants, the life in the country was very difficult. Like many others, they were living in a tent, where wooden boxes of food products served as furniture. Years have passed. Father has aged. All the brothers had professions, work, and supported their old and disabled father.

The four elder brothers were married. Zion offered Orit to go with him to Israel, and when she turned 18, they could become husband and wife.

Having finished the story of her boyfriend, my daughter looked at me confidently, calmly awaiting my approval.

I was confused and did not know how to start such an unexpected conversation. I began by saying that she is only 17 years old, and it is still too early to think about the marriage. Zion is eight years older and has a relible occupation, but I don't know anything about him, and I'm not sure about his intentions.

Terrible thought came into my head. "What will happen to her if Zion, upon arrival in Israel, give up his words, and she will be alone without my support?"

But Orit did not agree with my fears and said that she believes him. In her voice, I felt a conviction in her decision. Then I decided to meet him.

With the cap on the back of his head, regular features, gray-blue eyes, sturdy build, just slightly below my daughter's height, he made a pleasant impression.

I immediately laid out to him all my doubts about their mutual solution after such a short acquaintance. I was also concerned that, in the event of a break in their relationship, Orit could be left alone in Israel. Zion assured that his intentions were the most genuine, and he thought about this at the boarding school when she first brought him food and expressed her condolences over the loss of his mother. When he learned about her life without a mother and insult by her stepmother, he firmly decided to become her husband and support her forever.

His words brought me back to the distant past. I remembered how Ida came to visit me at the hospital. Looking at the food she prepared for me and a radiant smile, I wanted her to be my wife. I was only twenty then.

A conversation with Zion calmed me down. I thought maybe this was her fate and I should not interfere. After all, now she will have a person who will take care of her and their future together. I bought a ticket for my daughter and took them to the airport. She often wrote letters to me and described her life in the family of the married sister of Zion. She was surrounded by care, taught to cook Moroccan food and considered as a part of their family. Zion came to visit her, but he lived in his father's apartment with his younger brother.

A year later, when Orit turned eighteen, I received an official invitation to the wedding and flew to Israel. Stopped at the hotel. The days preceding the wedding, I became acquainted with the large and warm Zion's family. They took over all the wedding expenses on themselves.

I was impressed seeing how the children treated their half-blind father. Every Friday, on the eve of the coming Saturday, the brothers, after work, even before coming to their family, came to see their father. Sitting over a cup of coffee, they kept his company and talked for about an hour. Then they went home. It really touched me. I never saw such respect to the parent like in this family.

The friendly relationship between the brothers was a sign that my daughter had a family of good people. The wedding was in a large hall.

Not surprisingly, in addition to a large family of brothers, sisters, and relatives of Zion, also many guests were invited to his wedding.

My daughter's uncle, Matvey, and his wife were also present at the wedding and we sat at the same table. Strangely enough, we sat side by side, but the conversation did not work out, as if there was never a past that united us.

After the wedding, as a customary, I took the newlyweds to the hotel, where I ordered a room specially designed for such events, and gave them a cash gift. The next day, after parting with my new relatives, I flew to Africa.

I never returned to Namibia. I had the money. The salary on the mine was four fold compare to my previous one. I decided to pay attention to my grill patent and find those who want to invest in its production.

First of all, I rented a large one bedroom apartment in an expensive area. The building was located opposite the shopping complex of various shops, cafes, and restaurants. From the window of my apartment, I saw the shopping mall. Now I could cross the square in a few minutes and make the necessary purchases in a store, without using a car in the garage for this purpose.

With employmnt I was lucky. I found the advertisement in the newspaper and phoned the chief designer of the plant, Michael Cohen, who needed a manager of the design office.

After a long conversation, he employed me. Then he began to show me the plant which produced standard furniture modules for offices and partitions made of rolled aluminum for enterprises and project organizations. Everything was simple and primitive, compared with what I had to do before, but the position, salary, and company car tempted me.

The design office consisted of four people. From a short conversation with them, I found out that three of them are working on a contract base. Seeing their drawings, I realized that these are just idlers who are doing useless and technically illiterate work. I fired them. Found two knowledgeable guys. The third was a man of about 65. He said that he worked as a designer many years ago, but now he was left without income and asked to allow him to return to his former profession. I promised to think, knowing that I would not take him to work. I was very sorry for him, but I was ashamed to say this to his face, and I sent him a letter of apology.

I remembered this incident many years later, when I had to look for work in America. I was already 60 years old and, even though that I knew and could do the job for which I was applying, was refused. The owner of the factory told me directly that he was looking for a young man, preferably a recent graduate, and therefore, due to my high qualifications, he cannot pay me less than I deserve. It was the standard phrase of refusal, which is often used in the country of equal opportunities. I replied that I sympathize with him very much and understand his problem - to find a young engineer at the age of twenty-five with my thirty-five years of experience in design.

After a while, the director called me and asked why I dismissed the designers. I had to explain that they were not qualified to do the work that was required of them, and it is not clear who could hire them. The next day I found out that it was director himself. From this, I concluded that the director is not an engineer, but only an administrative worker.

I saw his attractive secretary and other women in different departments, no less beautiful, and I understood in what really he got knowledge. The truth is the director was young, handsome, and single. He often held meetings and conferences of his managerial staff and chose hotels and clubs outside the city for this purpose. After director's brief report about financial success of our company, we spent the day enjoying the sun, drinks, food and swimming in the pool. I noticed that young women did not leave him alone for a minute.

I had a mutual understanding with the chief designer of the plant from the first days of work. I drew his attention to the poor quality of some products, and he agreed to my proposal to change the technology and design.

A few days later, he called me in and said that the director appoints me as the head of the product quality control department, without dismissing me as the head of the design department. I agreed. After reviewing the documentation of the new department, I paid attention to the complaints from the customers dissatisfied with the quality of the furniture. After visiting the customer and making sure that the claim was valid, I agreed to replace the entire batch of furniture with a new one.

The chief economist of the plant called me into his office for an explanation. I showed the protocol signed by the customer and me, where it is noted that everything supplied by the plant furniture was in the use of the customer for less than one year and was out of order. He became enraged when I read out to him the existing five-year factory guarantee on the quality of the furniture.

His point of view was that the customer had to take care of his property and repair it himself if it breaks. To my argument, why to give a five-year warranty to customers, he did not want to answer. We parted without reaching an agreement. But I saw that from this day I have an enemy.

The design office did not bring me any trouble, the work there was getting better, but the quality of the products still worried me, and I decided to pay more attention to this problem.

It is necessary to mention one more case with rejected furniture, which I found in the warehouse, and unpleasant meeting with the Chief economist again.

One of my old friends, Judy, was in charge of a school for children with Autism. She was one of the leading authorities in the country, with whom doctors consulted and parents came to talk about their children needed to be checked. The school existed on the donations from peole and enterprises. Once, Judy invited me to see her the school, which received a new, expanded facility. We have not met for a long time and, having learned where I work, she asked me to find an opportunity to help with the furniture. I was surprised seeing rooms in which there were no tables and chairs for teachers. In the dining room, where the children had nothing to sit on, and classes, where there were no bookshelves.

Making a list of necessary furniture, I promised to find out if I could help her with anything. She wrote a letter addressed to the director with a request to allocate for her school the furniture that is rejected or not needed by the plant. With this letter I had to turn to the Chief economist because this furniture had to be arranged as defected waste and written off. Knowing that I would receive a refusal, I went straight to the director. He read the letter and immediately signed it. I went to the warehouse of rejected furniture, found everything that was on my list, and issued a document for delivery. This was my gift to the woman who devoted her life to sick children.

Then followed the battle with the Cnief economist, who accused me of violating the financial discipline.

My proposals for improving product quality required the investment in the process of manufacturing and assembling products. I was waiting for a decision and found out that my foe had challenged the "unnecessary," as he said, costs.

Unfortunately, my immediate superior, for some reason, did not want to support me. Later, I learned that the chief economist prevented him from doing necessary improvements, as he did to me. I didn't want to go to the director, bypassing my boss.

I lost interest in production and took up my patent again. Completely reworked the design, making it easy and safe to work. I began to look for the possibility of manufacturing a prototype.

Several enterprises which manufactured parts for my grill did not want to make it as a part of their production.

After a short break, I appeared at Rola's house, where one member of the yoga group, returning from France, would show the film and talk about his trip. Not the first time I had to attend Etienne's shows. An immigrant from France, he attended yoga classes regularly. Good-natured, with a pleasant smile on the face, he played the guitar perfectly and sang all the famous and favorite tunes of French songs, and we all sang together with him. One day, he invited me to his apartment to show the devices he talked about at yoga. With astonishment, I looked at the walls of the rooms painted in different colors, illuminated by multi-colored lights. He showed me the electronic control devices made by him, and then demonstrated how his room interior changes under the switching on of different colors of light bulbs.

He was absorbed in studying the effect of color on the state of the human body for many years. He possessed also ability to see an aureole of different colors around the human body. Sometimes he did it as a favor to those who were at the yoga class.

He studied the unusual properties of the Egyptian pyramids and once he showed me how he sharpens the razor blades, placing them at a certain height in the pyramid he had built.

I decided to do the same, and built the pyramid with high precision, using a device made for me at the Siff's factory, and I tried to sharpen the razor blades too, but I could not see any changes.

Remaining in the room after Etien's lecture about trip to France, I stood and talked with Rola, who was interested in the fate of my patent.

Seeing the woman coming to us closer, Rola introduced us. Maria Pappas, as she introduced herself, said that she had heard our conversation and asked if I would like to share with her about my invention. After listening to my story with the grill, she wanted to see it in order to imagine how it looks like. We drove to my home, where the grill stood on the balcony.

I switched the power.

In a square case with glass walls, the lights were lit and metal pendants with fixtures started rotating around their own axis, following by the rotation around the center where the heating element was installed. The grill housing, made of polished stainless steel, which was heated to a high temperature and sparkled under the rays of light bulbs, made an impression. When I turned off the carousel, Maria asked if she could see my patent. After reading only the first page, she said that she would like to meet with me at home and discuss how she can help me. Judging by the Mercedes she drove, she was a wealthy woman.

We met the next day. Already not a young woman, she, the owner of the transport business, was looking for an opportunity to invest money in something that does not require large expenditures, but which has a reliable future. I offered to cooperate with her and be equal partners. Having asked how much money I needed to make a new improved prototype, she went into her office and returned with a pack of money in her hands. Having handed me the package, without requiring a receipt, she asked me to keep her in the matter of production and show her the documents with the all expenses. From that day I was again inspired by the hope that never left me.

Once, after buying food in one of the stores in the shopping center, which was located opposite the house where I rented the apartment, I was heading for the exit. Passing by one of the windows, I stopped at the sign - Antique and Jewelry.

A gray-haired man in horn-eyed glasses sat behind the counter, behind the thick glass of which the big blue eyes watched me curiously.

In the broken English, he asked what I was interested in his store. I answered him in Russian. He revived and introduced himself - Arcady Temkin. Realizing that I was not a purchaser of jewels, he decided to talk with me. Judging by the open book lying in front of him on the table, he rarely had buyers.

He was not the owner of the entire store, but only rented part of the store for his business, pointing to the second room, where the original owner's jewelry department was located. Naturally, he began to ask me about where I lived in Russia and how I got to South Africa, about my family, about my work and people I know. After receiving the answers to his questions, he offered to visit him at home, saying that he had no contacts among local immigrants. I accepted his invitation and came to see him with a bottle of wine. The wife was not at home. He brought a snack from the kitchen and we sat down at the table. Now he began to tell me about hismself.

All his life he lived in Moscow. He graduated from the law school and, working as a lawyer, he made a career and a lot of money. He made great connections with prosecutors and judges, and using his connections, saved people from harsh punishments and executions. He was paid with a lot of money, with which he bought jewelry. He managed to forward all of it to Israel. Being in ulpan, he met a young and beautiful woman. They were married and returned to her home in South Africa. His wife had a home in elite part of the city and the wealthy woman returned to her former life, which was interrupted for several months in an attempt to emigrate.

Arkady, did not need money, nevertheless, he decided to start trade in jewels - close to his soul affair. He had no shortage of valuables and jewellary. His wife introduced him to a friend, Rona, who was the daughter of the bank President, and her husband was a millionaire. After a divorce from her husband, who started an affair on the side, Rona remained in the two-story house with a servants and three children. Her ex-husband had his own property, where he was comforted by women bought for one night. Another interest of her ex-husband - collecting jewels and antique things - led him to the store that Temkin opened.

He was buying from Temkin the Faberge eggs, of which there were only a handful of pieces of art all over the world; some pieces of art packed in boxes, the appearance of which said that they were many hundreds of year's old, antique watches, Chinese vases that also were many thousands of years old. Large sums of money flowed from the collector's pocket into the pocket of a connoisseur of antique and antiquarian values.

Rona was a frequent visitor to the Temkin family, but I met her in the Temkin's shop, which I often visited after shopping at the grocery store next to him.

Her house was also nearby and, after a manicure, she came in to talk with him. One day, Temkin called and said that Rona wanted to talk to me and gave me her phone number. She asked me to come to her house. I rung the bell, the patterned metal doors of the fence opened and along a semicircular road I drove up to the entrance. The servant show me to a spacious room next to the hallway. Rona was waiting for me and asked if I wanted tea or coffee. I asked for tea. Sitting opposite me in the chair, she said that sometimes she had to attend charity evenings, and one of such evenings she needs to attend tomorrow. She wanted to know if I would agree to accompany her. Naturally, I agreed. The next day, I arrived wearing my best suit, the sleeves of a white shirt with silver cufflinks were slightly below the sleeves of the jacket and the gray triangle of the scarf in the left upper pocket.

Looking at my clothes, she nodded her head approvingly. She herself was wearing a black velvet tight dress and a modest white pearl necklace; on the right hand a sparkling gold-colored diamond in a wide frame, and in the left hand she held a small handbag, iridescent with stones. We got into the car and her chauffeur drove us to the destination. She took my arm and we entered the hall full of tobacco smoke, the smell of perfume, and noisy conversations. There were people who, as I understood, knew each other for a long time and met more than once. I paid attention to how everyone turned the head in our direction and exchanged views. We approached a small group of men. Rona asked me for the envelope, which she gave me before leaving, and handed it to one of them. He bowed and thanked her. We continued our way to the buffet, where, ordering drinks, we went aside with glasses in hand. One pair came up to us. The woman, taking Rona's arm, and apologizing, took her aside. Her husband said that he had not met with me yet and was interested in what business I was in. When he learned that I was just an engineer, and my accent indicated that I was in the country not so long, his face stopped expressing interest and he began to puff out his cigar. Probably, Rona understood my position and, taking me by the arm, led off, stopping and briefly exchanging greetings with those present. The latter looked at me with surprised eyes. Having made the appropriate effect, she said she was tired and it was time for us to return. The driver was waiting and in no time we were back to her residence. She thanked me for keeping company with her, and I left the hospitable home. Temkin, finding out that Rona invited me, was pleased. He came to the conclusion that she likes me. To my remark that I simply did her a favor, and that this does not mean anything, he smiled, saying that I do not understand women. Then he told me that Rona, after a divorce from her first husband, was remarried. The husband turned out to be an idler and a drunkard, and she, a year later, divorced him too, paying him a huge amount of money. The stress led to the illness, and when she recovered, she did not want to meet with anyone.

To make sure that he was not mistaken, Arkady invited Rona to his home for dinner and me too. We met again. She greeted me affably. We sat next to the table, exchanging banal phrases. I left first, thanking for the reception and referring to the early rise to work.

Temkin began to work hard on the fate of our acquaintance, saying that Rona spoke positively about me in a conversation with his wife. I saw that he does it wholeheartedly.

Indeed, Rona called and invited me to her place for dinner. Her two daughters and a son were sitting at the table. Only the eldest daughter answered to my greeting. The younger daughter and son ignored my presence and continued to talk among themselves, not paying attention to me. I noticed that Rona ate only salad and soup, and when the fried meat was on the table, her plate remained empty. Seeing my inquiring look, Rona said that she had been a vegetarian all her life and could not touch meat. The children behaved ugly at the table. For no reason, the younger daughter and son looked at each other and laughed.

The son responded to the comments of the mother with curses that shocked me. Then he began to tell his mom what dad promised him to buy.

After dinner, Rona felt uncomfortable, realizing that the children's behavior had spoiled the evening, but saying goodbye, I did not make any comments.

The eldest Rona's daughter, lived in Israel. From Temkin I knew that her mother provided her with an apartment and everything necessary. Having seen a fat and unattractive girl at the table, I understood the reason for her search for happiness in Israel.

Temkin also told me that the eldest daughter, trying to attract attention to herself, arranged an open house to everyone, where there was always food, drinks and even drugs. Upon learning that the daughter is in such company, Rona urgently left for Israel and forced her daughter to stop the behavior discrediting their family.

At about the same time period when I already acquainted with Temkin, a man, I did not know, called me. His name Mark Gizis and he wanted to meet with me, saying that a person who knows me in Israel gave him my phone number. I did not remember the person, but nevertheless, I invited him to my home. Mark, a little above average height, with a beautiful short-haired little beard and short neat mustaches, began to tell me the story of his family life, which was the reason for his arrival in South Africa.

He told me about his wife, who was dating a neighbor. A girl was born, and he does not believe that it is his daughter. Unable to bear the torture of doubt, he decided to leave his family and start a new life in Africa. His expressive, almost blue eyes spoke convincingly of his family tragedy. He arrived in Johannesburg a week ago, got in a cheap hotel, and he has no one in this country. According to him, he can do any work that requires skilled hands. In the past, he graduated from a technical college, a jazz lover, playing the saxophone, and also doing massages.

From the English language uses two expressions: "I can" and "don't worry." Everything else he tried to explain with hands, and facial expressions. I was thinking about how to help him and recalled my friend Sasha Goldman. A builder by speciality, he came from Israel a few years ago. He was looking for a job for a long time, and now he is responsible for a large object that is being built somewhere in the province. His family lives in the city and through his wife I learned when Sasha comes to see them. In one of his visits to the family, we met. I told him that my new acquaintance came from Israel. By specialty builder. Looking for job. English he does not know. I asked if Sasha could give him a job at his building site. He did not refuse.

About a month has passed. Sasha calls me and says that Mark has no idea about the construction business and he dismissed him. Mark appeared again at my home. Joyful and smiling, with a little lamb carcass in his hands, he immediately began to carve it in my kitchen for frying in the oven. From that day on, Mark became my shadow, and walked with me, wherever I went. When I appeared with Mark at Temkin's house, he felt there more comfortable, than I was. When Temkin's wife was cooking in the kitchen, he tried to show her culinary skills, and when she cleared the table, he helped her carry the dishes to the kitchen. At the table he was a master of ceremonies and uttered pretentious toasts, and after dinner he entertained us with anecdotes and stories from his life.

Upon learning that Mark is a builder by specialty, Temkin said that he needed to build a large safe at home and he is looking for a person he could trust this work. Since Mark is my friend, he would like to entrust this work to him. I sat and was silent. Mark happily exclaimed that this is the simplest of the works that he had to do, and he is ready to do it immediately. Temkin said that he needs a solid concrete walls in the room where he can store his jewelry. He has a large number of icons that are in demand and expensive paintings, which are masterpieces of famous artists. He also has gold, silver and crystal products, which he does not wish to keep in his shop due to their high cost and value.

Without losing time, he took Mark to a room adjacent to the back of the house, which he wanted to convert to a safe, and asked Mark to provide a budget for building materials to know how much money he needed to allocate. Then he said that Mark does not have to worry about pay.

On the way home, I asked Mark if he was familiar with the construction of safes and what kind of the standard requirements were imposed on them. He waved his hand, saying that it is just a reinforced concrete box, and the most complicated thing is the safe itself which will be purchased. After this visit, I did not see Mark or Temkin for a long time.

I met regularely with Maria, discussing issues of our cooperation and showing the documents on the costs of materials. We became friends. She shared with me her family issues, her brother's illness, and the discord among the siblings because of a legacy inheritance, in which she did not want to participate. She told me about her personal life. For many years she has a man, also a Greek, but he is much older than she is, and very rich. He has already made proposals to her several times, but she cannot yet to make a decision. Once, they went to the restaurant together, and during the dance she fell on a slippery parquet, breaking a hand. He hired a lawyer who helped her win the case. Having received a large amount of money, Maria started her transport business, which she conducted from home.

During one of my visits, I found a man with a strong Afrikaans accent. He sat with us at the table and listened attentively about my next report. Upon learning that one sample was almost assembled by me, and I have the details for the other two, Maria was delighted. We agreed on a time when I can show it to them.

During previous years, my hopes were often replaced by grief. I believed people in their willingness to help and cooperate, and then they retract from their words and promises. They did not leave my memory, but my constant belief that there are decent and honest people did not disappear. I believed, a ray of hope had finally appeared in my life.

It was the end of February, and I decided to celebrate my birthday. I ordered a room in the Chinese restaurant of the most famous hotel in Johannesburg, and invited my new acquaintances. Naturally, Mark was present too. The evening was a success, everyone liked the dishes, vodka and delicious dessert with French champagne. Temkin gave me a gift – a golden teaspoon, Rona gave me an amazing set of chess, and Maria, who came with her partner, gave me a very beautiful Greek vase.

Despite the fact that I had to pay for this evening more than half of my monthly salary, I was pleased that I was able to treat people with whom I had a friendly and useful relationship.

The call of Temkin after a couple of days made me terrified. He said that Mark caused him tremendous damage and wanted me to see it. It turned out that all the precious things in the safe, which he did not have a chance to open for almost a week, were covered with drops of water. The air in the room with cement walls was humid, like the smell of air in a cellar that was not ventilated. He was especially worried about icons and paintings saturated with moisture.

I found Mark, who celebrated his good fortune in cafes and clubs, and ordered him to immediately come to Temkin. The "builder" had to hammer the concrete wall of the safe in order to make access to fresh air and put a grill. I felt guilty that the person, who accepted us at home as friends, suffered a tremendous damage. Fortunately, after a few days all things were dried and cleaned. With the exception of fear and worries, Temkin did not suffer any big loss. He paid Mark for the work, but less than Mark expected, and I was embroiled in an unpleasant for me debate that ended in a spoiled relationship with Temkin.

Mark's next victim was Rona. I came to visit her, but this time I was with Mark, who co-accompanied me everywhere. Rona, having learned that he was an unemployed "builder," asked if he could paint her house.

Mark, with the help of my translation, assured again that this is the simplest work that he had to do in his building practice. Naturally, she wanted to give him the opportunity to earn some money. She did not need to do it to save money. For her it was a charity. After discussing the matters of work, Mark went out to inspect the building. Rona, staying with me, said that in her personal life these last years were so many problems, she did not think about painting the house.

I realized that Temkin, perhaps ashamed of his slip, did not tell her anything about Mark's "work" with the safe. When I went out to see the building outside, I noticed that the old paint was peeling off in many places, and most of all, on the second floor of the building. I drew Mark's attention to the fact that he has to remove the paint before painting in the places where it was damaged and wash the entire surface from dust. He also have to build a structure to work at the height of the second floor. When I was asked where he was going to find a workers, he replied that he would do all the work himself, and there would be no structure around the building. I haven't seen him for more than a month, and Rona too.

Once, she called me and invited me to dinner, Mark was already there. During the lunch dedicated to the end of the house painting, Rona noticed that she would like to replace the fountain with a more modern look. "The Builder," he immediately declared that he could make a work of art out of the fountain.

The fountain in question, was very attractive and I did not see anything like this in the houses I had to visit. It was inside the house and greeted the visitors with a pleasant and gentle murmur of water from a huge vase with edges in the form of petals. It was located in the center of a round pool where goldfish and lilies bloomed. Thin trickles of water from the fountain of the center of the vase rose high and sparkled under the rays of lamps of different colors. The location of the fountain by the architect was also chosen correctly. It was also visible from the dining room. I liked the fountain, and I did not understand why it had to be redone. But I did not want to express my opinion, and was annoyed that Mark takes up the work he clearly does not understand.

The next day, Rona called me and said that she was going to visit her mom, and since she lives on the same street where I live, would I mind to join her there for a cup of tea.

I appeared without delay. The door was opened by the maid and she led me into a very spacious room with high ceilings. There are plush curtains on the windows, pictures in gilded frames on the walls, a large old clock in the corner of the room, a carpet on the floor, in the middle of which stood a small table and armchairs of old work.

Rona was sitting in one of the chairs, and her mother was in the second. She was small, with white hair and a deeply wrinkled face with brightly painted lips; in a dress that indicated more about the time of her youth than about her age, this woman caused sympathy and respect. Her aristocratic manner of greeting pleasantly surprised me. I realized that Rona, to some extent, inherited her mother's manner of conversion. Remembering a meeting with her children, spoiled by the power of money, I saw a sharp contrast between their upbringing and the upbringing that Rona received in her mother's family.

The old woman's hand shaked a little when she brought the cup to her lips, but nothing spilled. She was interested in my accent and I satisfied her curiosity, waiting for the following questions. They followed after a short pause. Then the old woman apologized for having to leave us.

It became clear to me that people will always see an immigrant in me, and my accent will be the first thing that will interest them. Perhaps this meeting was decisive for our future relationship, and Rona wanted to know her mother opinion.

The next call surprised me. It was a call from a woman who said that Mark Gizis is her husband, and begged me to meet with her. I did not mind, and we went to the café.

Not tall, with a beautiful figure, a lovely woman sat in front of me, and with tears in her eyes, was telling how she tried to find me because somebody said to her that I knew her husband.

Mark left the family entirely unexpectedly, accusing her of having an affair with a neighbor to justify his departure from Israel. She showed me a photo of a daughter. A girl with blue eyes, like Mark's, with his features and mother's hair, was looking at me. Looking at me imploringly, she asked only one thing - to help her meet her husband. I promised.

I told Mark about the meeting with his wife, and her request to meet with him. He flatly refused. I told him that if he does not do what I said, I don't want to see him anymore. He realized that it was serious and immediately agreed.

I have not seen him all week, during which he spent all his days with the wife. Before leaving, she called to thank for what I did for her and said that they are now again one family. She was leaving happy, but I could not imagine how he could leave his family and children. Taking into consideration my family broken life, I wanted to help the man who came to me with a similar story. It turns out he just lied to me.

The money that he had after the work he had done was more than enough to pay for everything needed, and he moved to the hotel.

Soon I got another call - emigrant from Israel. I had no idea that I had become so famous in Israel lately, among those who are looking to come to South Africa. I went to the hotel where he was waiting for me. I saw a person with an accent from a rural dweller, which was often among the emigrants who came to Israel from small towns of Belarus. He told me that he is looking for a job and wants to stay in Africa because he has problems with his family. In Israel, he lost his job. No money left. He paid for the hotel only for two days. Again, family history.

A few more of these fugitives and I could open a club for people experiencing problems in the family life. An unattractive, dark and unshaven face, of short stature, sloppily dressed, he gave the impression of a beggar, but his profession was excellent - a welder. When I learned that he could weld stainless steel parts, I contacted the company, where I had ordered parts for my projects for the last four years, explained the situation and asked whether they had a job opportunity for the welder. They agreed to see him, and the next day, we arrived at the plant.

The test was successful, and they hired him. He lived in my apartment until the first payday, then he settled in a cheap hotel, and I have not seen him for more than a month. His appearance in my apartment with a woman of his age, whom he called his girlfriend, was unexpected for me. He was well dressed, shaved, and even looked a little plump. I asked him how he managed to converse with her, (because Ellochka from "The Twelve Chairs," in comparison with him, could be considered a polyglot), to which he smiled smugly and replied that they did not need the language, they both know what they need. The woman had a European face with slightly dark skin, she was not white, so there were many in Africa. She sat modestly, not knowing what we were talking about among ourselves. From a conversation with her, I learned that she was washing and ironing his clothes, preparing him food and that he lives in her apartment. Osip, so she called her man in life, promised to marry her. I said that I am very happy for them.

I saw him six months later when he appeared in my apartment with his wife, who came from Israel. They left at my place a carpet, several suitcases, and several packed boxes, asking me to hold them before they going to fly back home, to Israel. Now they were leaving for a week on a vacation tour and did not want to leave their purchases at the hotel. Returning from the trip, they loaded their "wealth" into the taxi and, forgetting to say goodbye, hurriedly left.

I returned to my business with Maria. The grill with the improved design was ready for testing. I suggested to do it in my apartment.

Maria bought chickens, meat, vegetables, and wine. I wanted to show what I have been working on for many years and to find out what my acquaintances and friends think about my invention. I invited Rona first. Maria came with her friend, whom I had already seen at her house, Rola came with two women from her class, and Sasha Goldman came alone. We have not met for a long time, and I was glad that he found time for me. Even so I let him down with Mark, "the builder," our relationship did not suffer. I told him about my invention and said that he could see it in my home. When I learned that he was already the director of a large construction company, I was genuinely pleased with his success. I was also happy with the news that Sasha employed Izya Gilis.

Sasha worked at a large construction site located in Botswana – not far from the border with South Africa. They needed a cook to prepare meals for administration, and Sasha remembered how Izya always entertained all of us at his home. As a cook, he was given money for the purchase of necessary food products, which he delivered in his car to the kitchen and the dining room of the company.

I recalled my regular visits to Izya during his work in Botswana, and some food supplies that he kept in the house. He could not make money in Africa, as it was possible in Lithuania, but his business qualities manifested in the form of not forgetting himself too.

The guests with glasses in their hands conversed while watching the carousel of chickens, which began to acquire a brown color. Serving portions, I saw that everyone, except for Rona, was interested in testing the juicy meat, and wondered how quickly this grill fried the chiken. The opinion of women was outstanding - everyone concluded that the chicken meat was delicious.

Maria, pleased with a successful demonstration, offered to meet me next week. On the appointed day, I came to her house, where, besides us, her friend was present too.

She put in front of me a document stating that the name of Maria Pappas I must include in the patent, and also that she becomes the owner of the license and director of the company, in which I will have 49 percent of the shares.

I was immensely surprised and explained that the patent is already five years old, and it is impossible to change the name of the owner of the patent. Also, I do not agree that the patent will belong to her. I reminded her of ourinitrial agreement, where nothing that she requires now we discussed. She replied that, on the advice of a lawyer, she wanted to protect her future, and she was ready to invest her money only if I agreed to her terms.

I refused, and Maria never called me again. No doubt, our cooperation would be successful. Her financial support and connections could be the basis for a small but stable business if she had not offer humiliating conditions. Despite the termination of our business relationship, she left a very favorable opinion of herself. I could not blame her for anything. The terms were dictated to her by a man who did not know me. Perhaps, being in her place, I would suggest the same. We both lost.

My immediate boss, the Chief designer Michael Cohen, unexpectedly immigrated to Canada. Now I understood his indifferent attitude to the technical problems he had no authority to solve. His and my attempts to introduce qualitative changes in the production met resistance from the head of the finance department.

The Chief designer was my only defense against the factory economist, who now had the opportunities to settle accounts with me. I was not surprised when the director called me and said that the company no longer needed my services. But he allowed me to use the company's car for another week allowing me to buy my own.

Keeping in mind the possibility of the orders for my grill, I registered my company, ordered a stamp with a seal and several forms with the name of the company in case of the business correspondence.

Knowing that I had a lot of free time, Rona suggested that I go with her to Lesotho, where she has business to do on the farm, which she inherited from her father.

There is amassive residence for visiting owners on the farm, and it is always ready for them at any time. The farm management had already been notified about the visit and we had rooms prepared. Lesotho is a small independent state in South Africa.

We drove in my car. The third in our company was a young guy, the groom of the eldest fat daughter.

The road was long. On such trips, I liked always listen to music. I set a cassette with the Beethoven's Ninth Symphony, which the daughter's fiancé did not know, and was surprised that I might like it.

After many hours spent on the road, we crossed the border post and were on the territory Lesotho. An hour later, we arrived on the farm. The house was impressive in size and the quality of the interior decoration. The dining room was not worse than the halls of the best restaurants in Johannesburg. In this establishment, which is far from the civilized life, the waiters in uniform and white gloves served dishes.

After dinner, Rona immediately went to her room, and the guy offered to sit over a glass of wine in the next cozy hall. After drinking almost half of the bottle in silence, he suddenly turned to me with a smile and in malicious voice said that, as far as he understood, I was interested in Rona just because she was a wealthy woman.

I was surprised at therudeness of this offspring from a rich family and said that his remark was an insult not only for me but also disrespect for the woman whose daughter he is going to marry.

The next morning, at breakfast, I did not talk with either Rona or this young scoundrel who grew up in a family where everything was determined only by money. Rona looked at me and, unable to bear it, asked if I slept well. Indeed, I could not fall asleep for a long time, thinking of people who did not know and never will know what it means to ensure that a family has a roof over their heads, that the family has enough for the children not be hungry and dressed, and they could study and get an education.

These people are born and live in a world where they have no problems, where everything is available to them.

Rona finished her business, and farm workers began to acquaint us with their farm. We saw a sugar cane processing plant, the endless fields of which stretched for many kilometers. Then follow our guide we saw the livestock, vegetable farms, and machinery, equipment and repair shops. Everything looked impressive and in good condition.

After leaving the farm, on the way back to Johannesburg, I listened to Mozart and Chopin. I didn't want to talk, although I saw that the bridegroom could hardly endure my pleasure from music. I sighed with relief when I brought them home.

It took a long time before Rona called me again. All in tears, she pointed to the fountain. Mark destroyed beautiful work done by a real master. He spoiled everything, not to mention flooded parquet floor. I could not imagine such an ugly not only design but also quality.

I wanted to call Mark and ask him to come immediately, but she indignantly said that it would be better to hire employees of any company and pay any amount to remove and rebuild everything, but she does not want to see Mark. Then she led me outside and showed up on the peeling paint of the building, which she had again needed to take care of.

Since then, Rona has never invited me. I was ashamed that I did not save her from this crook. Because of Mark, I lost the friendship of two good people. They may have seen Mark as a close friend of mine, which he never was to me.

The unexpected letter from my daughter from Israel, saying that she and Zion were soon coming to Johannesburg, excited me. I began searching for a larger apartment so that they had their private room and bath. I was lucky. Rola introduced me to a woman who came to visit her. Anna, with sparkling brown eyes and a beautiful figure, was already not young, but she looked attractive. Having learned that my daughter comes from Israel, and I urgently need an apartment with two baths, she said that in the house where she had recently settled, there is such an apartment for rent. Adjacent to Anna's apartment, it had everything necessary - two large bedrooms, two bathrooms, a spacious living room, and a well-equipped kitchen.

It was cheaper than the one I had in a prestigious area of the city. Located in a quiet area of private houses, the apartment was near the main road connecting the airport with the city - just a few kilometers from the area where Isya Gillis lived.

The white population there, like Anna herself, spoke Afrikaans, although she had excellent English without any accent. The apartment was located far from the city center, near the main road connecting Airport with the city. Just a few kilometers from the area where Isya Gilis lived.

Returning to Rola, to thank her for the help in resolving the issue with the apartment, I found out that Rola and Anna are old friends. Anna recently returned from Cape Town, where she lived for many years and broke up with a man who was her life partner. He was rich, and part of his wealth was on her fingers in the form of diamond rings.

"This is her weakness," Rola added, smiling, "she likes to collect diamonds."

"Well, now we have something in common - the husband of my daughter is a diamond polishing specialist," I said. Drawing attention to the fact that I am often coughing, Rola looked at me carefully and asked if I were to see a doctor.

"It doesn't bother me," I replied, "and I did not think about the visit to the doctor."

Mark, whom I noticed at Rola house, was sitting next to a very nice and calm woman.

Once he came with me to Rola and found what attracted him most. Not yoga classes - he was interested in women. But since his English language remained in the embryonic state, he tried not to use it. His silence and mystery attracted women, and his piercing eyes and a charming smile replaced his words, and women adored him.

I knew this woman was married. Once she invited a few people from the yoga class to visit her house. Mark and I were among invited. Her husband is an intelligent person, an engineer, and they have two adult children.

We all knew each other and a little about the families, because Rola could skillfully ask the details of the personal life of her yoga class members during the general conversation around the table with tea, and fresh rolls, and this made everyone present feel part of the team.

Seeing me, Mark left his victim and approached me. Looking at me with his laughing eyes, which helped him so well and now radiated the joy of the meeting, he told me that his massage practice is appreciated by many in our group. The only thing that reassured me was that doing massage he could not bring any harm to his clients because his "building" knowledge was not required here. In any case, no one will complain to me.

With the arrival of my daughter and Zion, I paid them all my attention. Orit was already six months pregnant. Now the house had a real housewife, and the house became kosher. Zion did not have the right to work, and he agreed to work at the cattle's slaughterhouse, where he monitored the observance of kashrut. The work was dirty, with meager pay, but he decided on the condition that the religious organization would apply for his permanent residence permit. I managed to sell one of my grills to make it easier to support an increased family.

Rola, noticing that I was still coughing, suggested that I join the group that she organized for a trip to Maurishius, a resort place near the island of Madagascar, for the treatment by a healer from the Philippines. I could not afford such an expensive trip. Having learned the reason, Rola offered to lend me the necessary amount, and I agreed. My daughter said that I should not worry; she will give birth after my arrival.

Maurishius greeted us with a turquoise-blue ocean sparkling under the rays of the sun. In my bungalow, like everyone else, I had my room with a view of the water.

In the resort, there were outdoor tables with fruits and juices, meals with cold snacks, various kinds of hot meat dishes, pancakes, and salads. The staff was unusually friendly.

The same day I was on the shore. The clean sandy beach with palm trees, the blue sky, and the transparent water fascinated me, and I remained on the coast in complete silence, with only a slight splash of the waves. When the sun started to burn the skin, I had to leave the beautiful environment and return to the bungalow.

The Philippine healer arrived the next day. He looked like an ordinary man. Below average height, no longer young, in a jacket, trousers, and cowboy boots, he did not have an impression of a healer.

In the restaurant, at the long table of our group, he sat next to Rola, and I noticed that he enjoyed eating everything that served on the table, and drank wine as everyone else.

In the evening, invited to a small hall, we listened to what he told us about himself. We heard how, accidentally, while still a little boy, he found in himself the qualities of foresight, which he did not know about before. These qualities allowed him to be accepted by the Grand Master to learn the art of healing. It took him more than twenty years to study. Many years later, after graduation, only with the permission of his teacher, he was able to start to treat people independently.

He explained, and everyone must realize that he cannot cure all diseases. He does what he has learned and tries to do everything possible to help people who need his help. He heard that among our group, there is a man who was taken directly from the hospital, where he was dying of cancer. Concerning him him, as a healer, this is unjust, because he is not a God and does not perform miracles.

Speaking about the procedure of the treatment itself, he asked to observe the absolute silence to allow him to focus on treatment. He assured he would do everything so that we would go home in a better condition than the one in which we came to the island for treatment.

Everyone was assigned the day and time of admission. Except for those who were supposed to undergo treatment, everyone else was free to spend time on the beach.

Food lovers came to the club hall, where it was not hot like the ouside and continuous supply of food and drinks. Suddenly, a beautiful woman asked me to accompany her on a walk around the island.

I noticed her at the airport when she was saying goodbye to her husband, who was holding a little boy in his arms. On the plane, our seats were next to each other. Tall, with a face on which black eyes, lush black hair, and beautiful brightly painted lips drew my attention, she was attractive. Jenny, it was the name of my stranger, ordered a taxi, wanting to see the neighborhood and at the same time to visit the neighboring village, where she did not dare to go alone. The locals in the village greeted us warmly and we spent all day together.

All the next day was on the sandy beach. For many years in Israel and Africa, I did not have a real vacation. This one was my first real holiday, which I did not consider for myself to be a needed treatment, although my cough did not stop. In the evening, in the restaurant, Jenny came to the table and set next to me. Since then, we have spent a lot of time together, but only in the company of others. She did not want gossip, because so many people knew her. She was in the family business of ready-made clothes and often traveled to Europe, ordering what she thought was necessary for several stores owned by her family in the city. Her husband, a lawyer, much older than her, had his own law office. Their only son is three years old. I noticed that she did not drink any juice and coffee, but only red wine and mineral water. She said that she had one kidney removed.

One week after returning from Mauritius, she gave a big reception at her home with refreshments and asked Rola that she wanted me to see me too.

I had my treatment on the third day. Alex, the healer, asked me a bout my complaint and I told him about the frequent dry cough. He asked me to lie down and relax.

I saw his hands and the white powder with which he sprinkled the spot on the recess on my throat. Then I felt his finger touch the notch in my throat, and he began to press harder and harder on the skin. My eyes closed involuntarily. There was no pain. I lost the feeling of the environment and did not know how long the procedure lasted. Awakened by the sound of his voice. I heard him say to me that everything is over and I can get up. I sat and saw that people in the room silently looked at me. It is difficult for me to describe my feelings at this moment. Alex told me to go back to my room and lay in the bed for two hours. In the sun, until the end of the day, he did not recommend to appear categorically.

The tickling sensation in the throat that caused the cough disappeared, and since then, it has never returned.

Two days later, Anna called me and congratulated with the birth of the granddaughter. It turns out that Orit was alone at home. Zion was at work. Anna went to check in and, seeing that she was giving birth, immediately took her to the hospital.

Two days later I was holding my granddaughter in my arms. Her given name was Simha, meaning in Hebrew, Joy. At the age of 46, I became a grandfather. The second joyful event was that Zion received a residence and work permit. He immediately began working in his specialty as a diamond polisher. And soon they moved to a two-bedroom apartment in the area near the synagogue. I moved to the same house, where I also rented a two-bedroom apartment. We were together again.

But my loneliness in the apartment did not last long. Mark appeared on the threshold and said that if I didn't take him to my apartment, he would be on the street, as he had nothing to pay for the hotel. I could not refuse. He again had a roof and food, but I did not help him with the work. He understood that.

The participation, I showed towards him when we first met, disappeared. I saw in him a person who had caused me a lot of trouble, ruining my relationship with people I valued friendship.

Naomi

A call from a stranger.
Sasha Goldman.
Naomi. We became friends.
Zion luck in business.
My son Bar Mitzvah.
The last business attempt.

As always, calls from people unknown to me usually began by asking to help. This call was from a woman who came from Israel, and she did not need any help. I calmed down when I learned that she brought me a letter from Matvei, brother of Ida.

I remember, I came straight from work, sweating, in my silk suit, before I could go home and change clothes. The cafe had several visitors. The stranger was sitting at a table at the entrance. Our eyes met, and we both smiled, realizing that we were not mistaken. There was a cup of coffee in front of her and a cigarette in her hand: big blue eyes, short hair cut of black hair, elongated face, and plump lips. I sat at the table opposite and extended my hand to her. She already knew my name, and when she introduced herself as Naomi Muscatel, I involuntarily exclaimed. "This last name reminds me of a person I met at the Hotel Alon many years ago when I came to Africa for the first time. He was an Israeli businessman with whom I had friendly relations." "This is my ex-husband," without much interest in what she heard, said Naomi calmly and handed me the letter.

I apologized and eagerly opened the letter. Matvey wrote that he was sending me a letter through a woman when he learned that she was leaving for South Africa. In the letter, he wrote that the younger son of his elder brother had arrived in Israel. He mentioned the events in his family, a little about our mutual acquaintances, and finished the letter with the message that my mother was very ill.

I was thinking about this line, which reminded me that I hadn't received letters from my parents for eleven years, and the KGB don't let them get my letters too.

I remembered that in a few days my mother's birthday. Seeing that I was no longer reading and disconnected with my thoughts, Naomi got up. I thanked for the letter, and we parted.

Then, during a meeting in a cafe, I could not imagine that this meeting would be the beginning of our relationship, and that this would be my first attachment to a woman since I lost my wife. I did not know then that this woman of hard fate, intellect, and erudition, would become a woman in whom I would see something that I did not find in anyone with whom I had met in Israel and Africa.

Over time, she told me about her marriage and family life, about herself what other women would never have said, but with all her sincerity, I felt that she kept in herself what I would never find out. She knew and loved music, had an excellent memory, and could talk with people on any topic. I felt in her a woman, behind the calm face of which there was lurking uncertainty, and whom I, not without reason, was jealous. She was a woman of contradictions and mistrust, who many times left me and returned. And I left her only once and forever. Receiving her tearful letters asking me to come back, did not change my mind. I am keeping them to this day.

Despite frequent and long breaks over ten years of our intimacy, I never tried to be with other women. It was not only loyalty. It was a feeling that no one, except Naomi, could give me intellectual and physical satisfaction, despite the pain of separation and uncertainty in our interrelationship.

On my mom birthday, I went to the central telegraph office and ordered a telephone conversation with Minsk. I was there from morning to evening. The employees of the international telegraph station sincerely tried to help me and did not understand why my call not accepted in Minsk. When, already in the morning, they gave me a direct connection, so that I could make sure that it was not their fault, I heard the answer from a telephone operator in Minsk that my parents' phone was not answering. When I asked what time it was in Minsk, she replied - two in the morning. When I told her that my old parents could not be not at home at that time, she hung up.

Six months later, Matvey wrote me a letter with a message that my mother passed away after a long battle with cancer.

All the failures during my immigration against the background of this message seemed to be insignificant.

I sat and recalled the past in which mother was everything in my life. The time of my childhood passed before me: an idyllic childhood in the circle of my parents and brother, to all of whom I caused a lot of trouble and grief with never stopped adventures. My happy childhood, in which, surrounded by care and in love, I learned the world. Then the horror of the outbreak of war and a sad parting with the father drafted into the army on the first day of the the German invasion.

A terrible time in the ghetto, where mom was all in my life after German soldiers killed my brother during the pogrom. Hunger, disease, and a constant sense of danger and uncertainty behind the barbed wire of the ghetto. Escape from the ghetto and long days and weeks of wandering in search for partisans. Rescue in the partisan detachment - life in the forest.

The liberation of Minsk. The end of the war and the father's return from the front. Severe conditions of post-war life. Birth of a sister. Dangerous post-war years and the prosecution of the Jews. And long months of being in constant anticipation of the arrest of our parents.

In spite of the poverty in the post-war life, the unforgettable years in the school and the graduation. Beginning of student life and getting the diploma. My family life. The loss of my wife and departure to Israel with a small daughter.

In all these events there was not a single day and minute without my mother's constant care; there was not a single day without her worry for everything and each of us. She lived till her last minute for all of us. It hurts me that I could not be near her at her last days and say how much I love her; touch her hands, which never knew tiredness, creating an atmosphere of home comfort and reliability of family life. There remained only a memory and gratitude, which, unfortunately, I could not express enouth to her personally during her life.

Being close to the hotel where Naomi stay, I decided to visit her. She eagerly invited me to her place and put a full plate of the salad made by her recipe on the table and, sitting opposite with a cigarette in her hand, watched how I with an appetite swallow up an unusual tasty dish. She spoke very little about herself but asked more about me. It was understandable - we did not know each other.

Winter was over. It was getting warmer, and I suggested we spend the day together in one of the parks. She did not refuse. I took a camera and made some pictures. Looking through the photos later, I saw that she was very photogenic. She remained a mystery to me, but I did not want to force her to talk about what she was not ready.

At the next meeting, Naomi told me that her older sister lives in Johannesburg. She has four children. Three adults and one - a schoolboy. Husband architect. The second sister is in Cape Town with her husband and three daughters.

Her father and mother live in a kibbutz. Former husband with children lives in Israel. All children are adults, the eldest is in the institute, and the rest are still in school.

A close friend of Naomi recently moved with her husband from Rhodesia, and they live in a prestigious area of the city.

That's all that I learned from her. She didn't have a car and got to work by bus. Her clothing was modest, but I liked her style. I never saw her in a dress, she wore only pants and beautiful sweaters, or shirts.

Once, having come to her in the evening, I found a strong-built man in her apartment. A short, wide-shouldered Israeli with mighty shovels-hands greeted me affably. I left late at night, but the Israeli stayed. The next day I asked her about the late visitor. She, seeing nothing special in my question, calmly said that she had accidentally met him. Chatting with him and seeing that he is a fascinating person, she invited him to visit. I did not come for a long time and did not call.

Accidentally meeting her on the street, I learned that she had recently met a musician who invited her to his organ concert in the church. When I offered to keep her company, she replied that it would be of no interest to me.

The next visit to her surprised me even more. When she opened the door, I saw a man in a bathrobe wiping his wet head. On the table, I saw a magazine with a pornographic picture. It turns out that her new acquaintance came to visit her from Pretoria. The magazine belonged to him. I did not understand why she likes to show me her relationships with men, without being embarrassed and not thinking about how I can react to this. I replied to myself: she is a free woman who has not given anyone any obligations, and her personal life is her own business. I stopped visiting her.

A meeting with Sasha Goldman diverted me from all other cases. Sasha came to me with a personal request. I have to give much more details to this story because from that day I was connected with Sasha and his affairs for asubstential time.

Together with Michael Sperling, who was the President of the construction company, Sasha was the Director responsible for the construction of more than a thousand units of residential buildings. The whole project was much significant. It also included a Zoo, a sports complex with a stadium and a swimming pool, administrative buildings, and buildings for service personnel.

The state of Botswana funded the whole project wich Shabtai Kalmanovich, who was the representative of Israel in Botswana, received from the President of the Botswana Republic. Shabtai called the president of Botswana as his friend.

Now about the Kalmanovich. He came to Israel from Lithuanian city of Kaunas in 1971. It was the year of the first legal emigration of Jews from the Soviet Union. He had a degree in chemical engineering. Being in the Soviet Union also a Komsomol worker in the past, for some reason he was attracted to social activities more than the work of an engineer, although in those years engineers could find a job in Israel.

A year after his arrival, his past activities and oratorical skills began to manifest themselves in the field of politics. He began campaigning among Russian émigrés and helped a Jewish magnate who had fled from France to become elected to the

Israeli Knesset. A multimillionaire who did not know Hebrew made Kalmanovich his assistant. In this duty, Shabtai was present at his boss's business meetings, where he had to meet with members of the Knesset, prominent peole in business, and representatives of various organizations who were seeking financial assistance from the oil magnate. Many of them asked Kalmanovich for a personal meeting with his boss. Using contacts for the own purposes, and help from his boss, Kalmanovich eventually managed to become a wealthy person, open his company and start investing money in profitable activities. As a representative of Israel in Botswana and establishing friendly relations with the president himself, he received an order for a massive construction project. He created a group of civil engineers from Israel, headed by an engineer, an immigrant from the Soviet Union, Sperling, and began successfully implement this project.

By this time, Kalmanovich was already a millionaire. He buys a plane, buys expensive mansions abroad, conducts extensive trading activities, and travels around the world.

When I met Sasha, I had no idea who Shabtai Kalmanovich was. Sasha told me only that this is his biggest boss, who pays engineers big salaries and fees. Therefore, everyone diligently fulfilled his demands and never let him down.

Now about Sasha's request. Kalmanovich, before leaving for China, personally asked Sasha to establish contact with the President of the De Beers Company and to meet with him on the day when Kalmanovich arrives from China. The theme of the meeting: the development of gold mines in Sierra Leone.

De Beers Company is the largest privately owned diamond mine development and sales company in the world that has a diamond business in three countries in Africa: Namibia, Botswana, and South Africa. The headquarters of all operations in Africa was in Johannesburg.

Why Kalmanovich wanted De Beers to have interest in the development of gold mines, I could not imagine. I do not think that he confused gold with diamonds.

It would never occur to me that someone of my acquaintances, in this case I mean Sasha, might be interested in this huge, monolithic and granite-covered, high De Beers building in the center of the city.

Sasha explained that he should, and he repeated, should do it, whatever it cost him. It is crusial for him, and he came to the conclusion that of all those whom he knows, no one can do this better than me and agrees to fulfill any of my requests and help me if I need anything. As a company director, he can return the favor. There was little time left - Kalmanovich gave him one week to complete this task.

I listened with interest to the story of his project and his boss, but the request for help of this magnitude surprised me. With all due respect to Sasha, I could not fulfill such a request.

To meet with the man who runs the most significant international corporation, for me, a man from the street is merely impossible. But Sasha categorically objected, saying that he believed in my abilities and gave an example of my acquaintance with Rona, daughter of the president of the Barclays bank.
The mention of Rona made me think that maybe she knew the names of the people her father was dealing with. She probably also knows the name of President De Beers.
"Well, I will try," I said to Sasha without confidence in my voice.

I did not think at all about gratitude from Sasha, because I was sure that I would not be able to fulfill his request. But it was also a reason to meet Rona.
She accepted me affably, but without the former smile. When I laid out the matter of my visit, she looked at me with surprise and even suspicion. In her eyes, I read without doubt - my friendship with Mark left its mark here. Moreover, now she saw in me another, Mark, a man she better stay away. I was not surprised when she let me know that she did not know anyone who could help me. She does not know the name of the head of this company, and she doubts that he will accept someone without the recommendation of a person known to him. Coldly saying goodbye, she stood up. I left her house with a shattered hope.

I had nowhere else to go and wanted to call Sasha, but decided to wait. I did not want to upset him immediately. In his voice, I felt such a belief in me that I decided to think about how I can help him.

The next morning, quite unexpectedly for myself, I shaved, put on my best suit, in which I was traveling with Rona to a charity evening, and went to De Beers. Even if they don't let me come in, I thought, it will be interesting to see what this institution looks like, which holds in its hands the diamond trade on many continents.

The massive and high door from pressing on the handle opened unexpectedly easy. Opposite the entrance in the depths of the hall behind the also massive table was an elderly man in a formal suit. I approached and said that I needed to see the President of the company about essential matter. He opened a book of visitors on a table and asked to fill in the required information. After reading, he picked up the phone and said that the visitor needs to see the President. A few minutes later, a slender middle-aged woman came out of the elevator with a beautiful short gray hair and in a strict suit. After reading my entry in the visitors' book, she asked for my last name, and I followed her to the elevator. Coming out of the elevator, we were in a reception room with large windows and an impressive polished table with several telephones and a stack of neatly folded documents. After carefully listening to the reason for my visit, she went into the presidential office and closed the door behind her. I sat in the chair without breathing; I could not believe that it was real. I was ready to be politely escorted from the reception to the elevator.

At that moment the secretary opened the door, invited me to come in, and closed the door behind me. In the corner of a large and sunny room at the table, I saw a very handsome man: beautiful mane silver-gray hair, prominent forehead, glasses, square chin. The collar of the white shirt is open, and the tie knot lowered. Through the horn-rimmed glasses, big gray eyes were carefully watching me. In the ashtray on the table lay a cigar.

Taking off his glasses and putting them in front of him on the table, he pointed to a chair and asked me about the essence of the matter that led me to him. His noble manner of speech and accent reminded me of my first employer, Mr. Logan. It suddenly occurred to me to say that I am here as a representative of the famous businessman Shabtai Kalmanovich, who has many different businesses in Africa.

The thing he wants to discuss is that, as a friend of the President of Sierra Leone, he has a concession to develop an entirely new, yet unknown, Goldfield and he would like to discuss the idea of the cooperation. He arrives from China precisely one week from now and stops in Johannesburg only for one day.

Therefore, he would be very grateful to you if you could give him half an hour of your time.

I shut up, waiting for a response. The President thought for a moment and pulled on his cigar. I waited for a failure. Having made a few more cigar puffs, he firmly pressed the bell button. The secretary came in. He asked her to take the necessary data from me and find half an hour for him to meet with Shabtai Kalmanovich. Thanking the President for seeing me and the positive reply to the matter of my visit, I followed the secretary. After she made an entry in her book of the provided information, and before leaving the reception room, I asked for her phone number and thanked for the help. With a business card and a phone number in my pocket, I went down to the lobby.

I left the building and could not yet realize that I had succeeded in what seemed impossible. Calling Sasha I calmly, even somehow ordinary, said that I had met with the president De Beers and that he will receive Kalmanovich at his appointed day. He was silent. I realized that he did not believe what I told him. I could only hear his breath on the phone. Finally realizing that I was not making a fool of him him, he said that he was leaving for me to meet.

After hearing about my visit, Sasha happily and excitedly said that I had done for him an unimaginable favor.
"You see now, I was right that you would succeed," he said, shaking my hand.

The day before Kalmanovich's arrival, I called the secretary and made sure that the meeting was not canceled and held according to the schedule.

On the day of Kalmanovich's arrival, Sperling, Sasha and I arrived at the airport in advance and found out that the plane was twenty minutes late. We began to worry. To be late for such meeting is inexcusable.

When we saw Kalmanovich coming towards our car, we sighed with relief. I saw him for the first time.

Medium height, youthful, friendly face, very sympathetic, with familiar shaking of the hand, he was dressed in denim, in the hands a brown leather bag. Seated in the back seat, he opened it, took out a suit and a shirt and tie. The car rushed to the city, and Shabtai, without haste, quietly began to change clothes. We arrived on time. We had to wait a few minutes, and the secretary shows us all to the office. I introduced Kalmanovich and his two directors to the President. Shaking hands with everyone, he returned to the table and invited Kalmanovich to sit opposite. We sat behind at the wall. Kalmanovich took off his jacket, hung it on the back of a chair, unbuttoned his tie, and sat down in a chair, lounging and putting his legs one on another. I was shocked at his posture. I did not expect such disrespect for the president from a person who met with business and government officials from many countries. I was sure that he should have the concept of etiquette, and I did not understand his behavior now.

In limited English, he began with enthusiasm to talk about his friendship with the President of Sierra Leone and that he had permission to develop a gold mine. The purpose of his visit is to find out how much De Beers will be interested in his proposal for joint development. The president asked Kalmanovich if he had proof of the presence of gold at the proposed development site. The latter, as if expecting this question, took out a small bag of cloth from his pocket and, opening it, poured out its contents onto the table. The President unfolded the map and suggested to indicate the place where the sample obtained.

Kalmanovich, carefully looking at the map, pointed to a point. With a satisfied nod, the president confirmed that Kalmanovich was not mistaken. He knows this place. But before he can give a final answer to the proposal, which to some extent interested him, he needs time to discuss this proposal on the board of directors. We left his office with hope.

Sasha came to me the next day and asked what he could do for me. I have been out of work for five months. The Jewish organization decided to gave me a small amount of money, but I needed a guarantor who agreed to put the signature on a document obliging the guarantor or me to pay the debt. None of the émigrés with whom I was familiar wanted to sign a guarantee. Of those local Jews with whom I was familiar, no one wanted to sign. I was ashamed to ask some of them. I remembered the brother of Dorit, whom I had never met after returning, and decided to visit him. When he heard about my request, he immediately signed, without asking anything. The next day I got the money. It allowed me to hold out until the next opportunity when I got a loan from the bank. I paid off the Jewish organization with the money from the bank.

By the time I met Sasha, my debt in the bank had grown to thirty thousand rands. I did not imagine how to return it.

I hesitantly told him the money I owe, wondering if he could pay such amount. Sasha said that there were no problems with this and asked to bring documents from the bank. Two days later, he brought me proof of the payment by his company to the bank and regretted that he could not get me a job, where he needed only civil engineers.

My own company, existing only on paper, did not bring me any business. But the stamp of my company and the official letter signed by me, certifying that I am sending my employee abroad in connection with the interests of the company, was used only by the Zilberfarb family, my friends, emigrants from Kyiv. He and his wife have been in Africa for twenty years. Both of them were engineers and employed by state-owned enterprises. They combined their work in the profession with activities bringing them additional income. Under the guise of business travel, they managed to transport dollars to banks in Europe.

Many years later, I met them in America when I came to visit my childhood friend, Ilya Bass, who lived in the same city. Zilberfarbs received a pension from Africa and did not need to work.

My search for a job was a success. I signed a contract work as a draftsman with high hourly pay. My drawings differed in the quality of execution, and I performed the tasks much faster than all those working in a department. When I began to make comments on the problems in the design, the chief engineer Kevin McCain became interested in me and invited me to talk.

When he learned that I was an engineer with many years of experience in design work, he listened to my comments and ordered to bring all drawings to me for a checkup before the detailing.

In the meantime, many unexpected events have happened in my life. The first such event was unexpected arrival Mark's family from Israel straight to my house. I did not refuse his request to stay at my apartment until they found an apartment for themselves, and allowed them to stay with me for several days. I conceded my big bedroom to Mark with his wife and daughter, and for myself, I occupied a small bedroom. I had to buy for myself another bed. The arrived family turned out to be a big one. In addition to Mark's wife and daughter, his son with his wife also came. Mark's son is twenty years old, and his wife is even less. They got married before leaving for South Africa. The son with his wife had to spend the night in the living room on the couch.

What were the plans of the family, it was not clear to me, and I was not able and did not have a desire to be involved in solving their problems. I worked a lot, came home from work late, and tried to spend the weekend with my son. My guests were complete hosts in my apartment, where there were products in the refrigerator, and I only came to spend the night. Days passed, then weeks, and my guests were not going to move anywhere. I explained to them everything they wanted to know about getting a job, but could not help in any way - there was no time. Besides, I did not see any opportunity for them to find a job where no one in the family knew English.

I did not refuse to arrange their daughter Dolly in a kindergarten not far from home, which was also not easy due to their guest status in the country. Mark's wife was an excellent chemical engineer, but she couldn't find a job. The newlyweds had no specialty. It went on for several months. The refrigerator, which I regularly filled with food, was often found empty. The complete lack of a sense of my own home began to oppress me, and even though that the family of my daughter was near, I decided to leave the apartment to the Mark family and move out.

When I told Mark's wife that I was moving and leaving the entire apartment to them, she asked in surprise if it was really uncomfartable to live with them. "It turns out that it is I who live with them, and not they with me," I thought. At her request, I left her a rare edition of a book with technical terms in all areas of industry in English.

After six months, when they saw that they were unable to maintain themselves, they all returned to Israel.

After moving to the area where I used to live, I bought myself a new Danish living room furniture and a beautiful bamboo shell chair. Now I felt I have my own house. The furniture shined, the carpets cleaned, the laundry is done, the ironed shirts hung in the closet on hangers, socks stacked on the shelf, and the dishes in the kitchen were like new. I never saw my servant. She had her apartment key and came once a week, and her payment for work was always on the table.

The thoughts about Naomi did not leave me. We met. She asked me about my work, the family of my daughter, son and did not forget about my patent for the grill.

Her calm speech, an attentive gaze of blue eyes, in which I first saw something warm and trusting, made me see in her a different woman. I even wanted to touch her to make sure that this is the same Naomi, who felt complete indifference to me. Now I have a desire to learn more about her, besides what I already knew. This time, she did not mind, and after making two cups of coffee, she began to tell me about her life.

She was born in Zambia, where her mother's sister sheltered them. Sister's husband was engaged in the construction of roads and was already a wealthy man. He helped Naomi's father, a professional carpenter, to find work. A few years later, Naomi's family moved to Rhodesia, where her father was able to open his carpentry workshop. It was the beginning of the work that he successfully developed. Naomi grew up and educated in Rhodesia. Then the family lived in South Africa for several years. Later, the whole family immigrated to Israel, where the father once met a guy from the same village where he was born, and forced Naomi, against her will, to marry this man. Naomi did not love her husband but, bore him three sons and a daughter. Her husband's manners, his lack of intelligence, his complete indifference to her interests and desires, were hurting her. Never helping her with household chores and with children, he was often on business-related trips, and Naomi, constantly pregnant for the first ten years of their life together, bore the burden of caring for and raising four children.

"With one in her arms, and the rest close," she described to me her daily family life.

When the children became adults and independent, Naomi decided to divorce her husband. Her father, dissatisfied with Naomi decision, forbade her divorce. She, in spite of the prohibition, left her husband with children and began to live separately. Her father, in punishment, deprived her of financiall support.

Needing income, Naomi decided to acquire the profession of the hygienist and entered the University of Jerusalem. During this period of her life, she had friends with whom she could visit cafes and various entertainment activities, as well as be in their company.

Her friends, experienced single women, taught Naomi how to attract a man if there is a desire to meet. Tips based on their own experience always gave positive results. And Naomi had to make sure of that soon. One of these men was married and twenty years older. His unusual for his age experience and potency so fascinated her that she lost her head and they were in the heat of passion for more than a year.

This mutual fascination ended only when this "real man" declared that he could not return the debt to her, saying that her father would not be impoverished. Naomi was in a hopeless situation: she withdrew money from her father's account without his permission. Her father punished Naomi by selling the apartment in which she lived, and did not give her the money from the sale as remuneration for taken money from his account.

After graduating from university, she began to earn money and became independent. However, the spoiled relations with her father because of the divorce and hostility of her daughter, who did not want to live with her mother, as well as the study of her elder sons at the university, led her to leave Israel. She came to Africa, where she had citizenship.

I was amazed at how simply and frankly she spoke about her relationship with her lover, revealing the details that I omitted here, which women will never tell anyone. It was this openness that showed me the strength of her character and the recognition of her mistakes without excuses. She sat in front of me; her eyes looked at me eagerly, trying to grasp how I would react to what I heard from her.

I thought about her children, and as if reading my thoughts, she began to talk about their successes in school, about how she often met them when her husband was away, she cooked, cleaned the apartment, washed. But now they are all already adult and independent, and even shy when she takes care of them.

After this frank conversation, we began to meet and became close friends.

Each of us had something to tell about the past. We often recalled episodes in our life and, inconspicuously, found that we felt together well and free.

Melodies from operas or symphonies sounded softly in the room. Naomi asked if I knew from where and who the composer was. Often I answered correctly. "Do you know that Richard Wagner was Hitler's favorite composer?" I asked her. She did not.

Every time I came, she made her salads and watched my satisfaction with her culinary skills. During one of the visits, behind the door in the corridor, there were knocks at the neighbor's next door and shouts. Naomi said that recently, someone had knocked on her door several times. She was scared. The area where she lived was not the best. The walking at night in the area became dangerous.

Considering the hotel and the area around not safe, I timidly invited her to move in with me, letting her know that I was interested in a close relationship. She agreed.

The next day I helped her pack a few things that fit in my car, and we left the hotel.

My daughter's family moved into a three-room apartment. They needed an extra room because a son was born in their family, named Eitan. Zion was lucky with the job. One of the wealthiest families, that had its own diamond mine, needed a qualified specialist who could work on diamond processing. Miss Laub, the name of the owner of this mine, appealed to the Rabbi, who was present at her dinner. He offered her to speak with Zion Iloz and gave her a recommendation of a person whom she can trust.

Zion became the head of the laboratory, purchased the necessary equipment, hired specialists to work, and launched production. Payment terms were excellent. About a year has passed, and the owner of the business offered Zion to teach her grandson about everything related to the processing of diamonds. Half a year after this conversation, Zion lost his job. But the reward, in the form of an impressive amount of money, helped him start his own business.

I want to dwell on one of the embarrassing me events associated with meeting Miss Laub's assistant. It was a funny incident, long before Zion returned to Africa. Miss Kay, seeing my growing tummy, introduced me to a tennis coach, saying that I needed to play sports. I gained extra weight - the jacket I could not fasten on me. This happened during the period of my return to Africa after receiving citizenship. Working under the contract for one year, I was fond of sandwiches with fatty smoked meat.

At the first training session, it turned out that I was not able to play tennis. And my coach, a tall, athletic young woman, with a light down of hair on her face, said that I needed to train a lot before I saw positive results. After I had a hard time catching my breath, running and picking up tennis balls, my trainer asked if I would like to keep her company in the evening, since she should be present at the dinner and she needs a partner. I agreed.

There I saw Miss Kay too and introduced to the owner of the house - Miss Laub. A widow who lost her husband a long time ago, she looked like a patriarch. Next to her at the head of the table, sat the Chief Rabbi of the city. "He will not leave this house without a good reward," I thought. The dinner was beautiful and ceremonial. Amazing dishes, crystal glasses, gold-plated knives and forks and, if it were not for my neighbor coach, I would hardly have known when and what to use. After dinner my coach left with me, and when I asked if I could take her home, she replied that she did not need to go anywhere. She lives with Miss Laub, where she has her outhouse, for which she does not pay anything. Instead of paying, she renders petty services to the hostess of the house - accompanies her on trips on personal and other matters.

My trainer decided to have the next training session at her friend's place. We arrived at a large house with a swimming pool and a tennis court. She mocked my still fat body for a long time, after which we entered the house. The hostess, a gorgeous and slim woman, brought us glasses of juice and saying that she needed to do something, left. My trainer said that her friend is married and her husband is a very famous doctor. She often visits her, and they play tennis together. Then, asking me to rest, she said that she needed to discuss something with her friend and talk in person. I began to look around the room. A spacious room with windows up to the ceiling, a floor lined with granite slabs, modern furniture, many all sorts of vases and several copies of famous female sculptures. On the tables fashion magazines and architecture. Much time has passed, but my coach did not return. To look for her in a house that is unknown to me, I did not dare. I left the house and wandered around the garden among beautiful flower beds and fruit trees. But the sun and humid air led me back inside.

When I saw my coach, she looked slightly confused and her usually pale face was pink and sweaty, although the apartment had air conditioner. Her friend didn't come out to say goodbye to us.

A few days later, by chance meeting with one of the residents, I told about my visit to Miss Laub and about my partner at the dinner. He laughed for a long time and then explained. Everyone in the city knows that my coach is a lesbian, she lives with Miss Laub, for whom she works as a driver, and her father was a close friend of the Laub family. The reason why I was invited to Miss Laub's house is that in the presence of the Chief Rabbi Miss Laub wanted to show that her employee, who was considered a member of her family, is dating a man and rumors of her lesbianism are wrong. As far as I understood my participation in this story, Miss Kay fulfilled the request of Miss Laub.

My son grew up, and I talked to him as an adult. It seemed to me that quite recently I watched films with him, where I shuddered in horror, and my son, smiling, told me not to be afraid, because it's all not true. We went to the park, where he shot a pneumatic gun, visited my friend Izya, where he swam in the pool. We climbed to the observation deck of a high-rise building in the center of Johannesburg, from where there was a view of the whole city panorama. We made long trips to mineral springs, where we swem in a mineral water pool. Together with Naomi, we visited her older sister's Ruth family, where her youngest son, David, was the same age as Ami, and he had his room with numerous games.

At school, my son was one of the best students and remained so until his graduation.

And now he began, at his mother's initiative, to come to the synagogue for Bar Mitzvah preparation. I was puzzled. Most recently, she went to church with him, where he was given another name, Nikita as if emphasizing her displeasure with the name Amichai, which I gave him in Israel. I knew that my son went to a speech therapist to get rid of the inherent in all native Israelis pronunciation because Ami at the age of two years already fluent spoke Hebrew.

Rabbi Dov, a brilliant person and erudite, said that if my son goes to the synagogue to study Torah, then his father, at least because of his son, needs to visit the synagogue too. It was logical, and I agreed.

It was my first visit to the synagogue since we immigrated to South Africa. I liked the people, the service ceremony, the Rabbi's subsequent conversations with the attendees, during which he explained the events described in the Torah, and how they understood at present.

In short, I began to regularly attend synagogue and unofficial meetings with the rabbi at his home. Sitting behind a table, he talked with us on various topics, whether economic or political, family or social.

I was pleased to hear from Rabbi Dov that my son, the only one of all his students, who asked him questions that relate to the topic of the study.

On Bar Mitzvah's day, I came to the synagogue with Naomi. Ami was thirteen years old and, according to Jewish tradition, he was already considered an adult. I sat in the hall, listened to my son reading the Torah, and thought that all the difficulties that had fallen to me with the emigration were incomparable with the happiness that my son had given me that day.

Having no money, starting a business with the manufacture of grills had no prospects, so I left the idea of looking for investors.

Being in one of the shopping malls, I accidentally turned my attention to a modest table among the stalls, at which were sitting two people. I came closer and read the inscription on the poster in front of them, which said that they interested in new ideas and products. I began to talk with them and found out that they came from England and are trying to find projects that, in their novelty, could attract their interest. When they explained to me that they have contacts with companies that were looking for opportunities to invest in new developments, I could not immediately believe what I heard.

Continuing to elicit in what area of the industry these projects should be, I learned that they are interested in new ideas and inventions and that they decide which plan suits them. I said that I have a patent and a working grill prototype. They asked if they could seeit today, and I brought them to my house.

After seeing how my grill works, they got acquainted with the patent and then asked me to tdeliver it to their company for the demonstration. They made me understand that the opinion of the staff is crucial to confirm the correctness of their choice. The next day I brought a grill, loaded it with whole chickens and, when they were coocked, the all department was fed with juicy chicken, and had wine. Everyone liked the grill. The British shook hands with me and said that they would immediately start a project.

We agreed on the next meeting again in their department. The meeting was purely business. I received an explanation of how they procced with the chosen product. As a rule, the company enters into a contract for cooperation with the author of the patent.

The contract and the document details the financing of the project was drawn up by a lawyer of their firm. The size of the payment of remuneration for the patent and future income from the sale of the product are highlighted. Their company assumes all costs for the document preparation and the feasibility of the project, to justify the profitability of investments. The last document is essential, and its preparation will take at least two months. They asked if I agree to receive one million dollars for my patent. I agreed even before I realized what amount was in question. Returning home, I already felt like a millionaire. Suddenly for myself, I noticed that I had become calm and confident.

Exactly one month later, I was introduced to a document that described the work of the company during the first five years of the production. The company is going to demonstrate the grill in five countries in Europe and America. The document included the costs of the company to participate in international exhibitions. I had a duty to take part in all presentations and be responsible for the manufacture of products.

They explained that I would have to appear before the commission of investors, which would consider my project. On the day of the review of my project by the commission, I was calm, assured by the British that this was just a legal procedure since they already checked all the documentation.

In the hall I saw six people at the table. The one who sat in the center asked how much I want to get for my patent. Remembering the proposal of the British, I called the sum of one million. Then he asked, "Rands or dollars?"

"Dollars," I replied, remembering the previous proposition.

"We cannot pay more than two hundred and fifty thousand dollars," he replied. "I agree," I replied.

Confident that I would have additional income from the sale of products, this amount was acceptable.

The members of the commission exchanged amongst them some remarks and said that I was free.

The British explained that now, investors should submit my project to the State fiscal commission, which considers the financing of products and patents, which will be made abroad.

Two weeks later, I was informed that the State commission did not give permit to investors to go ahead with my project. The British said that only my project, of their three projects they worked on and previously approved, was refused. The reason – a week before the submission of the project to the State commission, the government issued a decree on stopping the outflow of funds from the country. Investors did not know about the change in the government policy. An unforeseen government decision stopped the guaranteed success of the project.

The star of luck shone me a few months. Documents and calculations were made by professionals. Forecasts for future business development have been carefully developed. All the circumstances and the desire of investors were real.

I was experiencing this failure alone. Naomi was in Israel. Of my friends and acquaintances, no one knew about my contacts with investors.

Chilean project

Kalmanovich arrested. New offer from Sasha.
Chilean project. A trip to Minsk.
Apartment purchase. Successful employment.
Inexplicable behavior of Naomi.
Meeting with sister in America.
Naomi and our farewell trips.
Cafe - my new hobby.
Departure to Israel.

The failure to sell the patent plunged me into depression for a long time. Work brought a good income, but knowing that this was a temporary contract, did not bring satisfaction.

Sasha's visit and his proposal to work on a new project revived me from a depressed state and made my head work.

But before talking about his proposal, I need to dwell on some of the details from the recent past. His work in Botswana on the project of Shabtai Kalmanovich was entirely and unexpectedly discontinued. The construction company was closed. Its owner, Shabtai Kalmanovich, was arrested in December 1987 by Israeli intelligence for spying for the Soviet Union and sentenced to nine years in prison.

Alexander Bovin, Ambassador of the Soviet Union to Israel, in his book "Five years among Jews and workers of the KGB," cites an article by the famous Israeli journalist Ze'ev Bar-Am, which I quote below.

"And he was the "star boy" of Aliya of the 70s, her symbol, the embodiment of a fulfilled dream, a source of particular pride: know our pier! The only one who managed to climb the shining peak of financial success and see the sky in diamonds.

His career dazzled and fascinated. For 17 years, this playboy has managed to create a financial empire with business connections on three continents. All the doors were wide open before him. Politicians and businessmen, military and scientists, writers and cultural figures have experienced his charm. Unlike James Bond, he did not possess the development of musculature, did not strike the imagination with his presence of mind and icy composure in extreme situations.

But he masterly played on nerves and psychology. He could be sober and prudent, boastful and cynical, prohibitively frank and deceitfully deceitful. And he knew how to be generous. He loved to say. "If I make a lot of money, then everyone who surrounds me wins." He was talkative, unbalanced, self-centered. Overly loved women and all the luxury that can be purchased for big money. "It smells of money from him," it was said of him. And he, like a boy, boasted about his wealth, villas, connections, and Rolls-Royce, bought from Ceausescu.

If there is such a definition as an antispy, then it entirely fits Kalmanovich. Too much, he attracted everyone's attention. And he was, apparently, not just a spy, but an ace of intelligence. Maybe even a "grand master of spying." Perhaps in this characteristic is a surplus of literature. But there is no other way - the story of the spy should not be boring. "

The government of the Soviet Union, at first unofficially, through Joseph Kobzon, who was then a deputy of the Supreme Soviet, made attempts to free their spy. Before the arrest, Kalmanovich and Kobzon were close friends and were on friendly terms with each others family. Kobzon flew to Israel, visited Kalmanovich in prison, who was sick and had a surgery. No one did more to liberate Kalmanovich than his friend Kobzon, at whose request the Israeli leadership was approached by Gorbachev personally, Minister of the Interior, Vice-President and Minister of Culture of Russia. Kobzon turned to Alexander Bovin, who was the ambassador to Israel at that time. Bovin visited Israeli Prime Minister Shamir, and then wrote a letter to the new Prime Minister Rabin. In March 1993, Kalmanovich was released early. He flew to Moscow, where Kobzon helped him with his connections and Kalmanovich was actively involved in business. In March 1995, Kalmanovich with his bride. came to Israel for a visit.

None of the company's executives in Botswana could imagine that Kalmanovich, the owner of the company, was a Soviet spy who had generously distributed cash bonuses to them for many years, thanks to which they all could have a secure future.

Sasha managed to provide not only himself. To a large extent, he also helped her sister. Tanya's husband worked in Sasha's company on construction in Botswana. He earned enough money that allowed him to buy a modern two-story house in one of the prestigious areas of Johannesburg, and after returning to Israel, he becomes the owner of the restaurant.

Sasha did not care about the loss of work. He was secure and calmly looked at the new opportunities that soon appeared. He met with two emigrants who earned a cosiderable amount of money from the sale of oil in the Soviet Union at that time, and quickly went abroad. They found in Sasha, a person with cash, contacts, knowledge, and experience in the business. Three businessmen set up a company and bought a fish factory in Chile, which had its own fishing fleet and a canned fish factory. Then they started with the opening in the factory a fish smoking shop. It was a successful idea the companions decided to start with drying the fish – an additional business.

Sasha came to me with a proposal to take up this project, and if I manage to do this, he will talk about paying for work later. I trusted Sasha. His word did not need a signature on paper.

I never had anything to do with fish, except that I ate stuffed fish made by my mom on holidays and tried to fish unsuccessfully on the lake. Dried fish I saw only in the store and loved to feast on it while drinking beer. But about the production of drying fish had no idea. Sasha insisted, and I gave up.

Since I left the Union, I have not parted with the technical literature, in which I found all the necessary information and calculations, which I used in my work. I also had a technical encyclopedia and decided to check if it contains the information I need. I was lucky. I found a description of the fish drying process, the description of the chambers in which the drying takes place, the basic parameters that must be observed and even the elementary calculations of the installation capacity, based on the required volume of the finished product.

The encyclopedia also compared the use of a different type of fuel for heating the drying chambers and a description of the product loading line. I studied the book and did calculations while studying the material. I did not manage to find specialists for consultation.

After that, I met Sasha and said that I understood a little and agree to take up this project. But to go on with the job, I need to know what kind of volume they expect. This figure was ready for me. Coming home from work, I started a project. When the calculations were done, and the electrical circuit was on paper, I asked my acquaintance, an electrical engineer, to check the calculations. It took him twenty minutes to verify and correct the electrical circuit. After that, I took up with the drawings. When the power unit was ready, I made a specification of the equipment and calculated the cost of the fish drying production line. I called Sasha showed him my calculations, drawings, and installation costs, based on the prices I found in the catalogs.

All my work took about a month. When I told Sasha that the whole line for drying fish would cost them 30 thousand dollars, he shook my hand and said that I won the competition. I did not understand what was going on, and he explained that their company ordered an assessment of this project in another organization, and their figure was four times more than what I gave them. He asked me for the drawings and said that we would talk about the payment later. He returned to me the next week and said that he had already sent the blueprints to Chile and I would have to fly to supervise the fabrication.

Speaking about payment, he asked about my requirements. My first condition was to pay for my trip to Minsk, to see my father and sister. Sasha did not mind but said that first, I must fly to Chile and finish the project for drying fish. In addition to the cost of tickets to Minsk, he promised to pay three thousand dollars for my work on the project.

A month later, the answer came from Chile that everything is ready and waiting for my arrival. I took a vacation at work and flew. The flight was long with landings in Rio de Janeiro, Montevideo and Santiago. From the capital of Chile, a small and very old-fashioned plane was flying to a small town on the ocean coast, called Caldera. The plane made a lot of landings, each time the passengers went out, and new ones appeared. It was very dark when the plane landed, and I noticed that all the passengers were leaving. After making sure that on the flight, except for me, there was no one left, I was the last to leave the plane and went to get my luggage. There was no luggage. I turned to one of the workers and showed him the baggage receipt. He pointed in the direction of the plane that was already in the air and said that my luggage had flown away and added that I also had to be on the flight because my final destination was the next one.

It was the last flight, and he advised to spend the night in a hotel. In the morning, there was a knock at the door. A young guy stood on the threshold and said that he had been sent to meet me at the airport. Having found out where I got off the plane, he got my luggage and came to pick me up. At the airport, he found out in what hotel I was staying.

What a right country, I thought, no bureaucracy and red tape. The driver explained at customs that the company sent him to meet an engineer from Africa, who, because of ignorance of the language, had mistakenly left the plane at the previous stop and they let him have my baggage without a receipt. I do not think I would receive such care and attention in another country.

We arrived in the city during the day. For me was prepared a place in the house of the owners of the factory and it was also the residence of the chief engineer-consultant of the plant. A native of South Africa, he worked in Chile under contract. A mechanical engineer by education, he was responsible for the work of all power and heat installations in the factory. His name was Patrick.

A little older than me, the wary look of gray eyes, after acquaintance, he led me through the steps of a narrow staircase up to my room. I left my luggage and went back down. Pat said the house serves as a stopover for business owners when they come for business for a few days. He has been here for a long time, working under a contract for more than twenty years.

He was already informed about my arrival, and he knew about the project of the fish drying, but he immediately said that he had nothing to do with this project. All my contacts related to the implementation of the project, only through the director of the plant. Personally, its functions include the delivery of me to the factory, care about nutrition and general familiarization with the production. Then he introduced me to the kitchen, wherein the refrigerator, I can take any food, but warned that after cooking, we will take turns washing dishes and doing the cleaning.

Being in the country for many years, he was fluent in Spanish and said he would take patronage over me if the need for a translation is needed. In the jeep that was put at his disposal, we arrived at the plant, and he introduced me to the director.

A middle-aged man, blond, tall, of large build, greeted me with a smile. He asked if I had settled well and regretted that I had landed badly.

It turns out, as I learned later, after returning to Johannesburg, that Sasha's business partner called the director and, having learned that I got off the plane ahead of time, immediately told Sasha. "I learned from the plant director that our "Kulibin" in Chile was lost.

When they were told that I had been already found, they started laughing and often recalled this funny story.

Then the director introduced me to the Chief Electrician, who was building a power unit for a drying line. He brought me to the site, where I saw a detached house with a flat roof, resembling a container for long-distance deliveries. Having opened the door, we entered a room where the entire wall was a dashboard covered with dozens of electronic relays and appliances, from which thick wiring harnesses were drawn to a massive electric motor mounted on a concrete base. On the motor shaft was a fan, whose blades with a diameter of one and a half meters were located behind the grating of a cylindrical housing with heating elements. The work was done so professionally that I was filled with respect for this person. He said that the assembly was completed a week ago and the test was successful.

Since, to my satisfaction, the most essential part of the project has already been made, I was not worried about the simple work on making the tunnel where the fish would be slowly moving through in the hot air in the process of drying. While the preparatory work was going on, I began to get acquainted with the plant and the process of preserving fish products. I started from the pier where fishing vessels came and unloaded fish. Then

I looked at how it was prepared for the cleaning and washing process, transporting to the workshop, where it was placed in jars and placed in airtight chambers in which they were exposed to high temperatures. In a word, I looked through the whole process right up to the packaging of the finished product.

I was particularly interested in the shop where the fish smoked. It was a new workshop which was launched recently. The shop was headed by a man from Odessa. He was hired as a specialist in the smoking of fish when Sasha and his partners bought the plant. He showed his equipment, the process of smoking itself and treated me to freshly smoked fish. Judging by the labels, I remembered that I had seen canned and smoked fish of this plant in many stores in Johannesburg, even before arriving in Chile.

In the evening, Pat and I had dinner at the restaurant. He ordered dishes and paid for it. On his recommendation, I tried many local dishes, one of which was a shark steak. Often at our table was his girlfriend - a young local woman. Once there were two women at the table, and Pat said that he had invited her to be my partner at the table. Returning home after dinner, I explained to Pat that in my life a woman already exists and I do not need new acquaintances. Seeing that I am not asking about his family, he said that his wife in Johannesburg is very sick. He visits her every six months. She cannot take care of herself, and he pays for full-time home assistance. He can manage this support because the contract wages a substantial.

Coming every day to the factory together, we met only at the end of the day, when he had to bring me back home. Sunday we spent in the city where we had dinner, and then his girlfriend took him shopping.

In the evening we had dinner at home and drank a bottle of wine. It was already late and, after washing the dishes, I went to my room. In the morning, having taken a shower, I went downstairs and saw my partner sitting with the legs tucked on the bed, and his slippers were floating in the middle of the room in the water. Apparently, he just woke up, because he asked in amazement where the flood had come from. It occurred to me to look into the kitchen. Crossing the room in the water with my bare feet, I saw that from the tap, under which I washed the

dishes last night, there is a stream of water, and from the overflowing sink, the water drains directly onto the floor.
A soft and monotonous murmur of water, obviously, contributed to a peaceful sleep of the host of the house. I closed the tap and explained that it was my fault that we had the problem of flooding because after washing the dishes, I did not notice that the valve was not completely closed. Having opened the outer door, I allowed the bulk of the water to flow out the threshold of the house, and with a mop pushed out the remaining water. Then, using all available rags, wiped the floor dry. Lucky, the floor was made of ceramic tiles. The water did not get into my room because of the stairs leadingd up to it.

All subsequent days, after checking the work on the fabrication of sections of the tunnel, I spent time on the rocky shore of the ocean. The coast was gray, dull, and no vegetation - some huge boulders. On the rocky and short strip of land, there were nests of gulls. They were guarding the mooring of the vessel with the catch.

With interest, I watched as the plentiful catch of sardines from the ship along the conveyor immediately sent for processing.

The day of the final assembly and testing of the operation of the unit for drying the fish has arrived. In the tunnel, filled with carts with fish, the fan pushed the air heated to a high temperature. Every few hours, the carts stopped, and the fish checked for the quality of drying. A few days later, I reported to the director that I had completed my mission, and they could take over the fish drying unit. At the request of the director, I compiled a test report, wrote recommendations on the use of the installation, and attached all the calculations and supporting materials that I used in the design.

On the day of departure, the director handed me plane tickets and an envelope in which were three thousand dollars.

On the same day, was leaving an electrical engineer, who finished work on a contract for another project. We had already met several times at the factory when he came to watch my line for drying fish. His name was Gunter. He was driving home in his car and suggested that I go with him and spend a few days in Santiago with his family. His proposal to see the capital of Chile was accepted by me with pleasure because after spending a whole month at the factory, I did not have time to get acquainted with the country.

We drove and replaced each other at the wheel. Gunter told me that he had surgery on the cervical vertebrae, and a long time was without work; the contract with the fish factory came at right time. The wife does not work. Two children. Already adults, students. He has his own house and an outhouse, where I will be very comfortable. His wife, Gertrude, met me affably. Her English with a strong German accent did not allow her to speak freely, but I understood her. There were three of us at dinner. After dinner, they showed me my room. Taking a shower, I stretched out on a clean bed and slept soundly.

In the morning, during breakfast, I met the children. Tall, beautiful, fair-haired, they spoke only in Spanish, and mom and dad among themselves in German.

With my arrival, the owners of the house have devoted all their time to me, as a guest. We spent half a day together in the famous Metropolitan Park, which was located on a high mountain, from where a view of the city covered with a blanket of an opaque smog layer, known for Santiago, was opened. On the ropeway, the cabin delivered us at one of the peaks of the park with the statue of the Virgin Mary. Strolled through the Botanical garden. Watched the Chinese, who were doing Tai Chi exercises on the green grass of the park. Walked around the pool, the length of which was longer than a football field, and tired, finally, returned to the car. On the way, we stopped at a supermarket and loaded up with products, returned home.

The next day, I was shown the city, its original architecture, which reflected the Renaissance era and the new modern buildings. Then they said that they would show me their favorite restaurant, which is located on the ocean.

Below us, the surf foamed, and through the open windows, a light breeze filled the room with the smell of sea water. We had a good time over a glass of wine and Chilean dishes. I paid, and we returned home.

The next day, I was again shown the city and neighborhoods, new areas of modern architecture, and apartment complexes. I was interested in the demographics of the population, among which, as I already understood, there were many emigrants from Germany, the situation with work, the cost of living, the possibility of acquiring housing. I was also interested in the Jewish population in the city.

In one of the shops in the center of the city, Gertrude liked a marine officer's cap with a coat of arms, and she put it on to try. There was something sentimental and sad about her expression. It seemed to me that this cap probably connects her with memories of her father, whose photograph in the marine uniform I saw at their home. Gunther came up and said that she had long dreamed of having such a cap. I decided to give her a gift, and she was happy.

We partedas good friends. For some days, completely unfamiliar people hosted me in their house and gave me a lot of their time. They showed me their new homeland, which I was leaving thankful for the attention and hospitality.
They knew that I was Jewish and had lived in Israel for many years.

Returning to Johannesburg, I received the promised tickets from Sasha and several days later flew to Minsk. It was unusual to be on the board of the Soviet aircraft, flying without a transfer to Moscow. In the cabin, one could only hear around the Russian language. Passengers were returning home tourists or company representatives after business visits. I can not say that on board the aircraft, I listened the Russian language, which I used to communicate before emigration. Instead, it was a conversation of this type of people with whom I had nothing in common - it was slang into which the words of the swearing were interwoven. The presence of women was neglected. It is necessary, however, to note that many of them had already managed to drink more than one glass of the alcohol before the flight.

My Russian, in which I wrote essays admired by my teacher at school, unfortunately, for the time of immigration turned out to be at the level that lost the literacy that I possessed before leaving for Israel.

With Naomi, we spoke, of course, only English. Most of my acquaintances and business contacts required communication only in English.

My son did not know the Russian language - almost from birth spoke Hebrew. In Africa, becoming a schoolboy, he lost those crumbs of Russian, which he had left from childhood, and I had to talk with him in English.

My daughter had a Russian at the first-grade level, but it was almost forgotten under the influence of Hebrew, which she spoke and wrote at school, before moving to Africa, where she began to study English. When she got married, she spoke with her husband and children at home only in Hebrew. Russian she understood poorly, and I had to talk to her in English because I started to forget Hebrew.

I saw myself the only one among children and grandchildren who had spoken Russian in my family. I don't even want to call it literary, understanding how difficult it is for me to remember many words in Russian that I know in English.

My thoughts were interrupted by loud talk and laughter of passengers. Undoubtedly, many of them felt well, returning to their homeland. None of them can even imagine how happy I was that I was able to leave the country to which they are now returning.

I felt alien again on this flying piece of the Russian state. It was nice to know that this contact was temporary.

In Moscow, I made a stop to see the family of my cousin Lyuba. I had their address. They lived far away from the center in one of the new housing areas of the capital. Lyuba's husband, Anatoly, was already retired, but actively continued to pursue his profession as a musician - he composed music. Lyuba also was retired.

Her eldest daughter, Oksana, with her husband Levon, and the youngest, Lena, came to their parents awaiting my arrival. I could not help but drop in on them, given the rare opportunity to stop in Moscow to change planes. Unfortunately, I only had one evening to visit my relatives. Therefore, we spent time talking, and I answered their many questions. I understood their desire to find out everything that pertained to my life in Israel and South Africa, after our last meeting in Moscow in 1973.

I did not have enough time to tell in detail about everything that happened during the period of my two emigrations and tried to mention the most essential in the chain of my endless job searches, family problems, and circumstances. There was even less time to learn about their Moscow life. To my question what they think about emigration, they said that they did not make decision yet. The next day I flew to Minsk.

Ten years have passed, and I met them in America. Their whole family settled in Phoenix, Arizona. Anatoly was in a nursing home, looked well, alert and active. He continued to write music. Lyuba lived with her younger daughter Lena, looking after her granddaughter. Oksana and Levon lived not far from them. Both worked. Fifteen years later, Anatoly at the age of 90 went to a better world.
A few years later, at the same age, Luba followed him too.

For many years I have been waiting for the day to visit my parents. This opportunity I got now thanks to Gorbachev who came to power when the Soviet Union was split and divided. At the airport, my sister and her husband were already waiting for me.

The taxi was taking me through the city of my childhood. The city, abandoned by me a long time ago, became alien to me after the grief and suffering endured by me. All the good things that were connected with youth, school, college, family life, work - all this was carried by the sediment of mockery, which separated me from my mother, father, and sister. I was looking forward in anticipation to see my old father, who after my mother's death, was under the supervision of my sister.

Boris, Dora's husband, a well-built man, picked up two heavy suitcases and we headed for the house.

My father, all in fair-haired gray hair, clean-shaven and neatly dressed, looked at me with amazement.

Probably, in his mind, I should look the same as he saw on the day of my departure to Israel. And now his son was standing in front of him, with a shred of gray hair - the trail of the life in immigration.

With the excitement and joy of the fulfilled desire, I was finally able to hug my father, cuddle up to him, feel the warmth of his hands; understand that it is in reality, and hear how he called me, as in childhood - Borik. Olga, a ten-year-old daughter of a sister, a thin and tall girl, very much like a mother, stood and waited for her turn to meet her uncle from Africa. In the father's room, there was a neatly made bed. On the kitchen table - a plate with sweet cheese - daily dad's treat. My sister began to feed me as if it was the most important thing for which I came to Minsk.

I looked at my father, and I lost the words which were in my mind. I just wanted to sit and look at him, then, not knowing that this meeting was the last. I was moved when dad said that he would give me half of his pension and all his modest savings in the bank if I stayed with him and did not go back. He could not even imagine how painful it was for me to hear this, knowing that very soon I would leave him again.

My sister tried to inform friends and acquaintances about the day of my arrival in Minsk. It was a joyful meeting for me. I was delighted to see Petya Sinelnikov, my silent and loyal childhood friend, the only one of all school friends who never stopped seeing me. In the days of my wife's illness, every month he brought collected among our school friends money to help me when I was at home without a salary. He, without fear, visited me when I applied for emigration and was under the supervision of the KGB. Lenya Ledvich and his wife were here too. I expected to see my classmates Misha Levin, Boris Gankin, Ilya Bass, Igor Minetz, and Volodya Kitaychik. I do not know how to explain, but for many years of living in one city, I did not have contacts with them.

I wanted to see Misha Rieger with his wife and children. Alas, none of them came to my first and, as I understood, the last visit to Minsk after seventeen years of separation.

The others present were friends of my sister. They wanted to know about my personal life and work abroad. I showed them examples of how living abroad can be cruel and how hard to find people who are decent and loyal. But I did not forget to tell them that I had to meet good people often too.

The next day I was invited to Vitaly and Ronya Faibisovich, where another group of a company I knew was gathered. After the general conversation and the usual questions that I answered in detail, I did not recommend anyone to immigrate to Africa. I responded positively about Israel, but during the conversation, I noticed that almost everyone was interested in the possibility of emigration to America. Even though Vitaly was the director of the Institute of Electronics at the Academy of Sciences, had an excellent salary and a good apartment, he decided to emigrate.

Returning home after meeting with friends, I saw my dad sitting alone on a bench. There were so much detachment and hopelessness in his posture that I again felt my guilt. I sat down next to him. We were together, and it would fill me with quiet joy, but it was bitter to realize that there was no mother next to us.

I was going to talk with my sister and discuss the issue of emigration of her family and to find out how I can help them. I hoped that if they succeed to immigrate, seeing them would not be a problem.

The next day I went with my sister to visit the grave of my mother, where I saw that another place was left next. Sitting at the cemetery, I returned to the past. In a few moments, the years of childhood, the ghetto, and the difficult post-war years passed in front of me. I remembered my mother's joy for my school successes and worries for the mistakes that I made. I remembered my mother's dishes, with which she would no longer feed me ... Oh, how bitter and painful I felt at this moment that she was not able to wait for me.

Then, we went to the grave of Ida. The inscription in bronze was moldy. On an oval photograph of ceramics, my wife's eyes looked at me with a smile. And I saw her gentle face with a barely noticeable blue streak on the temple, her black hair tied in a knot at the nape, snow-white teeth, and bright lips, her voice, her beautiful hands with thin fingers that did not know rest in her life.

The black metal fence brought me back to reality and to my fate, broken like a crack on the slab of the grave I was sitting at.

I wandered around the city. I wanted to be alone. Everything was familiar to me but did not cause any emotions. Here is the park where I made an offer to my wife; "Round square," as we called Victory Square, where Zina lived - a relative of Ida, whom we visited more often than others; right next to the square is the house where lives the family of her elder brother Oleg.

In the evening of the same day, I came to visit them and saw their best friends too.

I loved Oleg. His face was transformed with love and care at the sight of his sister. We often visited them, and felt like one big family. Oleg and his wife raised two sons, to whose upbringing and education they devoted their whole life. To my question about the departure of his family, he found it difficult to answer. Then, after thinking, he said.

"First I want to send the children, then Mara and I will go to them when they get there."

I met Grisha Shpaizman for a short time, but I did not have time to see the rest of the people - there was not enough time. I needed to pay attention to my sister and discuss her plans for emigration. I really wanted her to go to Israel. My soul was there, but Dora's husband had a desire to go to America, where was his daughter's family.

Dad wore a suit every day. His orders and medals hung on his jacket, and my sister said that he wore this suit regularly, even when he goes to the store to buy his sweet raisin cheese. In a conversation with my dad, I tried to find out about his brothers and relatives, but he had problem with the memory and remembered nothing. The sister said that he still leaves the bedroom and asks. "Where is mom?"

They have lived together for 57 years. Dad never been ill, looked younger of his age and remained as toned up and neat as I had known him in previous years, so I hoped that after Dora emigrated with the whole family, I would see them all in America again.

Indeed, I came to America to see them two years later, but my father was gone. He died in the hospital, where my sister arranged for him to be taken care of and nourished when she and her husband left to Moscow for a few days to get the documents for emigration to America. She was told that he suffocated in a sleep. I did not believe this diagnosis.

The day before I left Minsk, I asked my friends to take me to the forest. It was a bright sunny day. The smell of the pine resin heated by the sun brought me back to my childhood. I lay down on the grass, looked at the tops of the pines and firs, and listened to the quiet rustle of leaves. It was my meeting and my farewell to the forest, which left in my memory the joyful memories of childhood and the bitter memories of wandering in search of partisans.

The forest reminded me of the post-war years ... My first pioneer camp, a vacation time in the village with my mother and sister. The forest remained a haven for me. It accepted me the way I was, if I was a Jew, or not. It gave my soul a feeling of peace, silence, the rustling of leaves above his head, the coniferous smell of fir trees. For a few moments, it dissolved the worries and feelings of injustice with which I never parted.

I always returned home with a whole jug of berries in the summer, or with a full basket of mushrooms in the fall - a gift for my loyalty and love for the forest.

My friends did not rush me. They sat quietly, leaving me alone with my forest.

None of them knew why I wanted to come here. None of them knew that I was in the ghetto, and then with my mother, got to the partisans. I do not know why, but here, in the forest, I did not want to talk about it. They saw me as a nostalgic emigre. I had no nostalgia. It diappeared before I left for Israel. I still have a warm feeling for for many good people in this country, but not to the government which prosecuted people who not accepted the scoffing Soviet Union policy. But the air and nature they could not take away.

After returning from Minsk, I decided to buy an apartment. The money I received in Chile for the project for drying fish was enough for prepayment. The bank gave me an additional discount, and I found a two-bedroom apartment on the fourth floor of the house, which was within walking distance of the house where my daughter's family lived.

I bought the best appliances for the kitchen, modern Danish furniture and, when Naomi returned from a long trip to Israel, I bought her a far from new French-made car to go to work and not to use public transport.

Naomi resolutely refused to accept this car as a gift and paid for it every month. I noticed that Naomi was often thoughtful and sad after her arrival. She explained this condition by concern for children in Israel. Permanent acts of terrorism of the Arabs claimed the lives of thousands of civilians in the country.

I understood her because everything she was talking about was familiar to me. I was worried about my country no less - after all, my relatives and close friends remained there.

Visits to her older sister Ruth, with whom Naomi did not want to introduce me for a long time, became more frequent. We were invited to all Jewish holidays. The large table was served with beautiful plates, and dishes and the meals were excellent and plentiful. This was not surprising, given that Ruth was known for the quality and service of her business and was taking orders to preparing kosher meals for everyone who needed. Besides Naomi's sister, who always welcomed me, no one in their family showed any interest in me. But I saw that Naomi had a house here and she was in her family.

When designing their house, the husband, taking into account the requirements of his wife, gave special attention to a large-sized kitchen and dining room, where it was possible to accommodate a large number of guests. I personally did not like the dining room. Despite high ceilings and large windows, the walls of the room did not have sufficient lighting.

Naomi once told me that she did not want to acquaint me with her sister, for fear that I would think that she was also a non-poor woman. This remark convinced me that Naomi painfully perceived all that was associated with wealth, to which she had no relation.

Kevin McCain, Chief Designer of the company, where I continued to work under the contract, quit his job before I returned from Chile. His unexpected call and offer to meet interested me.

We met after work in a café, and I learned that he became a Chief Designer at the company that manufacturing machinery for the coal industry. To his regret, the group of designers under his supervision does not know how to undertake the development of a new type of machine, which is necessary for safe work at the mine. Even before his arrival, the plant tried to do this project and abandoned it – nobody was successful.

He thought about me and wants me to take over the project on which his personal position in the plant, as head of the department, depends. In exchange, he promises me a high salary, status as a project engineer, any car of my choice, and the entire department of designers to help with the development.

I immediately quit my job and came to his factory. Kevin immediately signed a document about my employment, and I was given a few days to know about the company. The plant was part of an American company with the same name. The size and weight of the specialized equipment made at the factory had my respect.

It came time to get acquainted with the drawings and documentation, and then to find out what Kevin wants to see in the new development. He set before me the task: to design a transmission with an integrated engine, on which the safety of the machine's operation under the ground depended, and at the same time to reconstruct the rest of the machine body. I sketched a diagram and, having discussed it with Kevin, I began to make calculations using the programs on the computer that I received in the department. Having the necessary parameters, I started with the drawings. Kevin often was coming to me interested in the work progress. I saw his happy face and relief that he was not mistaken in my abilities.

I worked hard, and after six months, I put the assembly drawings of the transmission on his desk. Kevin was excted, like a child who was presented with a new toy. He suggested that I select designers for detailing and ordered the heat treatment engineer to provide me with immediate support to all my needs. Making drawings for manufacture took a few more months, and the productin of the prototype took about a year.

The test results exceeded all expectations and were sent to America. Our plant was a branch of a large industrial complex manufacturing the same type of equipment in the United States. They confirmed that the results really exceeded the standard rate of the ability of the engine system of such machines.
Kevin was exalted. He was cheerful, energetic, and generous. He replaced my previous BMW car with a new one, and I was assigned a separate office for work. A team was created to oversee the prototype.

Then I got another project. The head of the technical information department suggested that I should start developing a built-in brake device for driving wheels. The current device had deficiencies and often required repair. Kevin brought me the drafts of this product, which was made by another supplier, for review. General parameters could not be changed, but I did not want just to copy and significantly altered and simplified the design, and gave the drawings to the head of the information department. Several months have passed and, being engaged in current affairs, I have already forgotten about this development.

Once, the head of the information department invited me to his office and, smiling, showed me a patent for the invention of a braking device, where his name was first, and mine was the second. The plant had all rights on the patent.

Having more free time, I decided to get acquainted with the work of my machine at the mine, which was located three hours from the city. Instructed on security measures and dressed in the clothes, like all miners I went down the shaft in an elevator with a group of workers and an attendant. A panorama of long and high tunnels with two-way traffic, illuminated by daylight lamps, opened in front of me. On both sides of the wide road, square pillars of the remaining rock stood to support the ceiling. We drove for quite a long time and stopped in front of a small tunnel with a dim light of bulbs and then walked on. I heard the hum of the engine and the rattle of the drum, which was cutting the coal seam of the rock. Under rubber boots, squished water, which was sprayed on the coal and teeth of a drum. The air was full of dust and very humid. Dust of crushed coal sat on the face and on the clothes. I had to wear a mask with a filter while staying aside and watching the process of coal mining. A car drove up with a large bucket, picked up the crushed coal and crawled back, where it loaded another another one with a conveyor belt to deliver coal to the surface. No voices were heard - everyone communicated with signs. When they waved to me, I realized that it was time to leave. I went upstairs, handed over clothes, a mask, rubber boots, a flashlight, and went into the shower. Having changed clothes, at the exit from the mine I signed a paper that I was leaving. This was my first and last visit to the mine. I visited the hell, where the workers go down every day, and where they work for years.

After returning from Minsk, I became once again a grandfather. My daughter had a girl, she was called Ayala. Now she was already two years old. The eldest, Symi, was a schoolgirl. Simi, Eitan, and Ayala liked to come to visit me and comfortably seated themselves in a seashell chair. Since my house was not kosher, my daughter allowed them to eat at my place only nuts, fruit, and drink Coca Cola.

Together with Naomi, we sometimes went to Orit on Friday evening for Saturday dinner. When Naomi was abroad, I came to my daughter's family on Shabath every week. If one of her children had a birthday, I had to buy gifts for all three, so as not to offend anyone. Thus, each of them celebrated the birthday three times a year.

Ami has become quite adult and was one of the best students in school. He was engaged in a drama club, sang in the choir, and actively participated in all events. He already had a girlfriend who was so used to seeing him ather home that when she had to go to the hospital for treatment, she insisted that Ami was next to her. She was tall and as blond as Ami.

I was interested in my son studies and sometimes asked to show me his diaries and home projects, as they called homework. I wanted to get acquainted with his school curriculum and compare it with the one I had as a schoolboy. It seemed to me that we were given much more information on similar subjects and that we were better prepared. Most of all, I was afraid of the acquaintance and influence on my son by those schoolchildren who already knew what drugs are.

My friends from Kyiv, who used the name of my company to transfer money abroad, offered me to go with them to Swaziland, a small country in South Africa, to exchange rands for dollars. They used to make these exchanges many times, and they knew the road well. I have never been to Swaziland before. It was my first trip, and I was excited to see this tiny country.

Thinking that soon, if my sister immigrated to America, I would need dollars, I agreed. Our company drove in two cars. My first car, which I used for three years, was replaced and given a completely new one and more powerful. I thought that now would have the opportunity to test it on a long trip. Naomi was not in a good mood and did not talk to me almost all the way because I hurried her before leaving and thus prevented her from getting ready for the road as she liked.

We discussed the route and details of our trip, including spending the night in hotel and money exchange, before departure. The road was not busy with traffic, the weather was good, and during the long trip we did not lose sight of the car in which drove people from Kiev, but when we entered Swaziland it was already dark, and I lost them at a crossroads.

I circled along narrow roads unknown to me, from two sides of which stood a wall of the tall sugar stalks. I knew that we were somewhere near the hotel where we decided to spend the night. Suddenly, the sky covered with black clouds made the surroundings almost invisible. The flash of lightning with an accompanied roar and a wall of rainwater completely closed the visibility of the road; in an instant, a continuous stream of water turned into a river. I tried to drive the car almost at random and got into a groove from which the vehicle could not get out. I was so absorbed in the search how to get car out of the ditch that I did not pay attention to the state in which Naomi was.

Her panic suddenly became hysterical. She poured on me a stream of curses that I did not expect from her. She began to shout and accuse me of deliberately bringing her to a place where no one could find us. I left her in the car and went out to look at the front wheels that were stuck in the wet clay of the ground. I returned to the car and offered Naomi to go on foot to reach the hotel, but this caused a new fit of hysteria. Suddenly, the rain stopped. The sky cleared and stars appeared. I made an attempt to wrest the car out of tenacious clay and succeeded.

Back on the road and having driven no more than two hundred meters, we found ourselves at the gates of the hotel. Our fellow-travelers sat at dinner and asked where we were for so long. Naomi silently, without answering their question, passed into the room. I was also angry that they did not wait for us at the fork of the road to show the way to the hotel. Naomi refused dinner and didn't talk to me until morning. The next day, after the exchange of money, we left back to Johannesburg, refusing the offer of an unconsidered couple to spend time with them on a tour of the country.

I was stunned by what happened during the rain and did not know how to react to Naomi's strange behavior. We were together for four years. Now, I saw in her a woman who had nothing in common with the one I loved and respected. I did not try to find out the reasons for her strange and disturbing behavior, and she did not try to talk with me on this topic too.

We continued our life together on the parting of the ways, not knowing where it would lead us. I decided to give her the right to choose.

A few days later, we drove along the highway to the northern part of the city. Naomi suddenly grabbed the shift knob and pushed it forward to the stop position. The car, squealing tires on asphalt, began to slide on the road, leaving behind a blue smoke and the smell of burning rubber. I pulled the handle back and pulled the car to the side. Sat and took a breath. What she did this time was life-threatening. If there was another car in the back, we might not be alive anymore.

We're back home. When her eyes looked at me, I saw in them an expression of detachment from the environment. Our joint residence seemed to be unreal. I began to reflect on our relationship, trying to figure out the reason for her behavior that I did not understand. I came to the conclusion that she lives in a world of her own problems, which have been in her life long before our acquaintance. I could see her irrational behavior as a result of hopelessness and the inability to solve the problems to which I don't have any relation. I felt sorry for her.

One day I received a long-awaited letter from my sister. She described in detail the living conditions and difficulties of the first days of immigration. The Jewish commune helped with housing, but they needed money to make ends meet. They were cleaning the houses to have additional income. It got to the point that they sold father's medals and orders to buy food. On the street, they picked up a discarded table, chairs, and even a TV. In the back of a nearby grocery store, her husband often found discarded boxes of bananas and other fruits, among which were many ripe and edible. They started to learn English without which one can not find a job.

Sister's daughter, Olga, in the school also experienced difficulties. She had to start learning English at the age of thirteen.

After reading this letter, I immediately took a vacation and flew to America. Now that small amount of dollars that I received in Swaziland and the rest which I was able to get through the bank, was useful to me. My sister and her husband greeted me happily. We arrived in Skokie - the northern suburb of Chicago.

I looked at the old apartment, which they rented from the owner, also an immigrant from Russia, and I was sorry that they were so far away from me and I could not help them when it was necessary. I wanted to hear about their life in Minsk, before leaving for America, and I learned that they had to delay to install a tombstone on the grave of my father and solve problems arising from the refusal of my sister's first husband to give the permit to his daughter to leave the country. The son stayed with his father, and the sister managed to take the daughter with her to America.

With the arrival in America, they asked for help, which emigrants received under a special program. They found a temporary apartment and were sent to free classes of learning English. When they began to understand and explain themselves a little in English, they began to look for work.

The next day, without knocking on the door, a bald man with a tummy walked in and, seeing me, turned to my sister and said that strangers could not live in this apartment. The sister looked at him frightened and began to explain that I was her brother and came to visit. Realizing that he was the owner of the apartment, I explained to him that, by the signed contract for the apartment, without my sister's permission, he has no right to come here, and now he has to get out. After he left, my sister said that he comes many times and inspects the entire apartment, and more recently, his wife told them to remove the curtain on the window, which she does not like.

I spent time with my sister's family, trying to understand the situation in which the immigrants find themselves in America. It was vital for me to see with my own eyes how they live, what is their mood, what opportunities they have, and plans for the future. I got acquainted with the school where my nephew Olga is studying. I proceeded on foot and familiarized myself with many areas of this small town.

Sister's husband, my namesake, earn some money and, for several hundred dollars, bought an old car. It was delivered to them because he did not yet have the driving license. Laughing, they said that the next day, they did not know how to start the engine, and they had to seek help from their neighbors. On this car, they were able to show me more distant places, to which on foot, I did not try to get. We visited the modern buildings of shopping centers and elite areas of the city.

After some time, my sister advised me to apply for the Social Security document that gives me the right to work and stay in America.

"Why do I need it?" I asked my sister.

"It can be useful. This is the most important document in America, she replied."

In the administration of internal affairs, the official asked me for what reason I need this document. I said that I came to America with a considerable amount of money and I want to keep them in a bank, but the bank refuses to open an account without presenting a document that gives me this right.

I didn't have any large amount of money, but I thought it would give me an "important" document, as my sister said. The card with permit was given to me, I opened an account in the bank by depositing two hundred dollars.

Having given the remaining amount of money to my sister, I left America.

I returned to an uncertain relationship with Naomi, not knowing where it will lead us.

To my surprise, she met me with joy. I saw again the old Naomi, which came into my life and became a part of it. So, time went for her good. I saw the glitter of her eyes and a smile when our eyes met. We began to talk, as if what we had passed through never existed. It was nice to see her sitting at a table with a typewriter that I bought for her because of the original font of letters.

One day, when I was sitting in a shell chair, she sat down beside her and said that she wanted to tell me something she didn't want to talk about, fearing that I wanted to be with her, only because her father is a wealthy man. Here is her story.

Her father, Nissim, was born in a poor family and mastered the profession of carpenter. The village in which he was born was next door to Arab's, and from childhood, he learned their language, although his native tongue was different - Ladino. After the marriage, he and his wife went to Zambia, where they had three daughters. His profession was highly valued. Over time, her father managed to open his own company, and the family moved to Rhodesia, where he started the business again. Income from business, he began to invest in residential property and land. Then he began to buy residential and industrial buildings in Johannesburg and leasing them. Revenues allowed him to help Naomi's husband open his own business.

Nissim's daughters were provided with everything needed. Eleven grandchildren received an education thanks to the foundation that grandfather established for this purpose. Then her father moved to Israel and lived in the kibbutz, from where he traveled to South Africa, checking his multiple properties. Naomi's divorce with her husband, whom he trusted, disturbed all his plans. After all, it was her husband he wanted to be in the future his successor, the owner of his company and responsible for business expansion, and for the good of all three families.

Father's discontent was expressed in the punishment of Naomi. At first, her father refused to support her, and then he sold the apartment in which she lived. Thus he hoped to make her return to her husband. Acquired profession allowed Naomi to ensure independence. But her stay in Israel, where her father and ex-husband were a constant reminder that she is not a part of the father's family, was unbearable and she decided to move to Africa, where she had two sisters.

From her story, it became clear to me that the past continues to pursue her. Also, the remoteness from the children in Israel always made her feel anxious. Against the background of the well-being of her sisters, Naomi felt her disarray, and her connection with me, a person with a profession, but without money, quite possibly, was also not approved by her relatives. This, as I understood, explained our unstable relations.

After hearing her story, my thoughts about leaving her evaporated. Probably, I was the only person with whom she could share her pain. She finished her story and we, hugging ourselves, continued to sit side by side, each of us, having gone into our own thoughts. They were interrupted by her question:

"How do you look at my offer to go to Cape Town, where my sister lives with her husband?"

I did not mind. I had a lot of unused vacation days. We left very early in the morning, before the sunrise. There were no cars on the highway, and the road was smooth and straight without a single turn. We flew through the air. I watched the road and Naomi pointed me to the speedometer - 180 kilometers per hour. I immediately reduced the speed. After some time, Naomi asked me to allow her to get behind the wheel, and we switched places. The first rays of the sun appeared behind our backs, and we stopped at a roadside cafe for breakfast.

Continuing the trip, we stopped after every three hours of drive, ordered food, and had coffee. During this short break, Naomi told me about the family of her siter. Her husband, an electrical engineer, became a millionaire without the help of her father. Quite by chance, finding buyers, he managed to order and to sell an entire ship loaded with metal pipes and made a deal, depositing several million dollars at his bank account. He bought in Cape Town a big house with a pool on the mountain overlooking the ocean and went on retirement. Then he bought a yacht and spent all his days at sea. He became a professional navigator and began to take part in the international regatta.

We drove into the city at night, having spent 14 hours on the road. I did not know the city, and Naomi got behind the wheel. Half an hour later, we stopped in front of the house in which Naomi's parents had their own apartment. It served them as a stopping place when they visited Cape Town. Tired from the long drive, we immediately fell asleep.

In the morning, when I woke up, I noticed a slightly open closet door next to the bed and, when I opened it, a bag of documents lying on a pile of dumped clothes fell out of the closet. I picked up one of them at my feet and, opening the cover, looked at the content. It dealt with the distribution of funds intended to pay for the grandchildren's education. Naomi, who had come to the bedroom at that moment, said that I had no right to open the closet and read what belongs to the family matters and I must remember that I was not at my own home.

She was right. We went to the kitchen, where there were glasses of tea and cookies on the table. That's all she could find. In the kitchen hung self-made work cabinets, cheap table, and chairs, aluminum dishes, and an old kettle.

Everything looked so primitive that I could not imagine how a millionaire could live in such unpleasant apartment. Naomi, seeing my puzzled look, said that everything here was done by her father. Even in her Jerusalem apartment, her father built lockers that she did not like, but he did not accept her objections.

In my home which I bought recently, I had in the kitchen the best Japanese refrigerator, all the kitchen appliances were made in Germany, on the shelves were French cast iron pots covered inside with enamel, and the saucepans made of stainless steel. On the wall were standard wooden cabinets in good condition. Light Danish furniture moved with me from an old apartment.

Looking now at the old furniture, and the outdated kitchen, I could not understand this man who could live in poverty, denying himself the simple pleasures of life, which he deserved. I recalled Naomi's words about his father's dissatisfaction with his older sister's husband, who had built a big and uncomfortable house with pretensions to luxury. With this remark, I agreed. From the architect, one could expect more practicality and a modern style.

Our visit to the younger sister was short. The conversation was mainly about family matters I had no interest to listen. I walked out onto the terrace with the view of the bay and houses scattered on the mountainside. The ocean merged on the horizon with the sky, and the sun's rays shone dazzlingly, reflecting from the quiet surface of the water, on which sailing boats glided smoothly. Fascinated by the view of the bay, I could not move and, it seemed to me, I could look at this magnificence of nature for hours. After a modest dinner, during which I found that Naomi cooked much better and tastier, we said goodbye.

The second half of the day was used for a walk through the city, which attracted tourists and foreign retirees who settled in the elite areas of the hills and in the center, where high-rise buildings of modern architecture were built.

The next day we left Cape Town early in the morning and often stopped in the places where it was possible to view the ocean along which the road passed. No wonder this road with many sightseeing places called - "Golden Route".

Naomi looked as if she had rid herself of the burden that had been in her way for a long time. She was in a good mood, and I was glad that she liked the trip.

After this successful trip, we made two more. The second was a trip to the world's largest zoo - Kruger National Park, where all the animals were in natural conditions, untouched by man, except for roads laid for tourists. We were driving in my car with Naomi's friends. She knew them for years when they were together in Israel. Amiable and intelligent couple. Former kibbutzniks, they lived in Africa for more than twenty years. I met them shortly before the trip.

The road was long and tiring. Stopped several times. On the way to the park decided to see the famous stalactite caves. And at the next stop we went to a local restaurant, famous for delicious and tasty pancakes. I tried to find out from the owner of the restaurant the recipe for his pancakes, but he, smiling, said that it was his secret and the luck of his business that he did not want to lose.

The next was our destination - Skukuza. It was the largest and most famous historical tourist camp, where all necessary services were available, including a telephone, a post office, a bank, a gas station, a restaurant, several shops, and cafes.

Precisely here were the most significant number of lions, elephants, buffalo, leopards, and hippos, not counting giraffes, wild cats, wild dogs, impala, kudu, and monkeys. From the latter, it was necessary to protect the personal belongings, because they could cleverly grab them even from people's hands.

We stayed in two bungalows equipped with all the necessary amenities, including the kitchen. The next day we went on a long trip to the North of the zoo. We refused the services of a guide, deciding to use the travel time to the places of our interest and desire. As per the rules that all park residents should follow, we drove slowly along the route, observing the life of the real owners of the reserve.

Full of impressions, at the end of the day, we returned to our bungalows and prepared a delicious dinner.

On the way back home, everyone agreed to a stop, and we visited my favorite pancake restaurant.

We made the next trip with Naomi at the end of the year. If all previous trips were short, then this time our trip was designed for a whole week.

We went to Durban, the third largest city in South Africa. Ruth, Naomi's older sister, had a vacation apartment there that all family members used to rest at their own discretion. Now, nobody was there and Naomi decided to take advantage of the opportunity.

The story of this apartment Naomi told me during our trip. Sister's husband got an offer to design a residential building right in front of the ocean. He agreed, provided that he does not take money for the design, but after the construction is completed, he will be allocated one apartment. When the building was ready, the owner refused to fulfill the terms of the agreement, wanting to pay only for the work on the project. The court awarded the apartment to the architect.

Having put the car in the garage, we took the elevator to the third floor and entered the apartment. Very spacious, three bedroom apartment made a pleasant impression. The layout was great. I was particularly struck by the balcony. The entire facade of the building, facing the ocean, had a step-like shape and huge balconies, the width of the apartment, distinguished the building with its original architecture. We must pay tribute to the design - the architecture of his building differed from its neighbors in its unusual shape and attractiveness. Humid air and high temperature outside forced us to turn on the air conditioner, and we did not turn it off until the last day of our stay.

The kitchen, in addition to the necessary kitchen utensils, had all sorts of food stocks, the presence of which was known to Naomi before our departure. It was understandable, taking in the consideration the sister's favorite and professional occupation. Regularly, every morning, we appeared on the beach and, having received the sun's rays, we could withstand, hid in the cold house. We went to the store only for the purchase of fresh vegetables, fruits, and bread products. We made several breaks from the apartment to visit crowded bazaars, where trays of Hindus, Greeks, Chinese, and Arabs were mixed up in the colorful colors of fruits, vegetables, and fish products. Naomi was a big lover of pickled and marinated products, and at this market, one could try everything and make a choice. To go around the city in this heat and humid air was a bad idea. We traveled to different parts of the town only in the car, cooled by air conditioning.

The area where the Hindu population lived in a completely isolated manner was striking in the size of the buildings, many of which were real palaces of oriental architecture. They also symbolized the wealth of their owners. The apartheid law here lost its rights. City demographically was like one of the cities of India or the Middle East.

A short stay in the sun turned my white skin into red, but there was no burn. Without a skin protection cream, we did not appear in the sun.

On the last day of our stay, we took care of washing the bed linens, washed the tiled floor, cleaned the kitchen, closed the windows, checked and turned off the appliances. Everything was done following the instructions hanging on the wall in the kitchen. With relief, we left this burning heat city, where the air had a peculiar smell of the sea mixed with the scent of spices.

Both of us again plunged into work, but our joint visits to the family of Naomi's sister and her acquaintances did not stop.

Naomi's girlfriend, who moved with her husband from Rhodesia, invited us to dinner at a restaurant owned by her husband, where a musical group of three Russian émigrés performed Gypsy songs. Having talked with me and after learning that I was a design engineer, the husband of a friend turned to me with an offer to visit his factory, where he wants to consult with me about the problem that he needs to solve. We met. He had a small plant of weaving looms, and he needed to be able to bring and place on them the drums weighing several thousand kilograms. I made the drawings, and according to my order, the device was made. I delivered it to the factory and showed how to use it. He paid off all my expenses for the work and thanked for help.

Soon, Naomi and I were invited to their home. After lunch, we went into the living room. In the corner of the beautifully furnished room was a grand piano. From the conversation, I realized that Naomi's girlfriend, a professional singer, often takes part in different performances, and they conversed about her next ones.

Already saying goodbye, a friend asked Naomi when she was going to leave. Naomi, apparently not expecting this question, hesitated and said that she had not yet decided. On the way home, to my direct question, when and where, Naomi, without embarrassment, said that she received permission to immigrate to Canada and leaves in two weeks.

Only now I began to realize that Naomi was not frank with me and her active participation in joint trips was, in fact, a kind of farewell.

Her frequent trips to Israel and uncertainty in the relationship made our life together so unstable that she made her decision to leave me for good.

After Naomi left, I had a lot of free time, and I began to pay more attention to my family. I needed time to see myself in this vacuum, before thinking about how my life will develop in the future. I had no plans.

Visits to the Sabbath dinners at the daughter's home became regular. I loved her Moroccan cuisine. Fish dishes and salads burned my mouth, but it gave me pleasure. Zion crunched green pepper, from a small piece of which I could not catch the breath. Children tried to imitate their papa. Here, among my family, I forgot about everything and was glad that my daughter has a husband and children, that he is a good family man and provides the family with everything necessary.

He was always calm, restrained, and a smile appeared on his face as he looked at the pranks of his children. The eldest daughter Simi looked after the younger ones, and they obeyed her.

The burden was on the mother. She prepared for them snacks for school, drove them to and from the school, forced them to do their homework, and checked their homework. Then she fed them, washed them before bedtime, forced them to brush their teeth, and sent them to bed at the same time. In the house, it was always ready dinner, and the whole apartment was kept clean. I have never seen scattered things or toys, as could be seen in the homes of wealthy families. In me, her children always saw a grandfather who would never refuse their request, and I was glad to see their happy smiles.

Meetings with the son have become more meaningful. He was already finishing school and was taller than me. His youthful passion with a girl turned into a friendship. I hoped it would be reliable. Discussing his plans for the future, my son admitted that he wanted to study language and literature, he likes to write school essays and dreams of becoming a writer. Surprised by his choice, I remembered my writings that had been read at school for years, after I left it, and thought about the coincidence of our common interests. My only objection was, and I explained to my son that to write, it is necessary, to have a life experience. It will allow describing the chosen theme correctly and will show the depth of human relations.

Nevertheless, I was glad that my son was thinking about the future and did not connect himself with the desire to have something material, but, on the contrary, he was thinking about using his abilities.

I had a change at work that I did not expect. My immediate superior, having earned the authority of a talented leader, found another job with a higher salary and quit. He became the chief designer of the plant, which manufactured the braking devices. The ones for which I had a patent. He was offered this position as the head of the department who worked on this patent.

Only now I realized that he was preparing his transfer to another job even when he brought me drawings of the brake device in order to improve the design. He called me and offered to work together in a new venture. When I learned in which area the enterprise was located, I realized that a trip to work from my place of residence would take more than an hour.

I refused. As always, I made a mistake, and as always, later regretted it. Working with Kevin, with whom I had the authority of a designer, and on whose aid he could rely, I did not take into account. He would be my defense in any situation.

I got used working not far from home. For many years at six in the morning, I drove to a sports club, located five minutes from the house, worked out for about an hour, swam, took a shower, shaved, returned home, had breakfast and was at five minutes to eight at work. I was so used to this regime that I didn't want to break it.

After Kevin's departure, I went to the factory director and said that, given my experience at the plant and the achievements in design, I can confidently replace Kevin as Chief Designer. After listening to me, the director, as I understood it, did not expect such a statement from me and said that he needed to think about it.

After a while, the director called and said he wanted to see me. I was sure that this call was connected with our previous conversation. But I was wrong. It was about the fact that a young engineer who had just graduated from the university was hired, and the director asked me to familiarize him with my projects and responsibilities. I guessed that the director employed the "national cadre," as they said in Russia. He was less than half of my age. No one was interested in the fact that he had no idea about production and design.

Six months later, the director called me again and said that I should give up my position, the office and my car to a young engineer, and I was transferred with the same salary to the technology department, especially since I know this job well. I bought myself a German model, seven-seater Volkswagen. It had a powerful engine and was a pleasure to drive. These cars for the transport of passengers used by taxi drivers.

I did not like my new job. The head of the department knew about my demotion, like everyone else at the plant. I looked at my primitive work, the neighbors of idlers, who spent half a day in constant conversations when the head of the office was out, and thought that I have a lot of free time and need something to do.

I came to the conclusion that it is necessary to open my own cafe and spend all my free time there.

I remembered one of the acquaintances, whom I had not seen for many years. Her name was Jenny Aranovich, whose dad, the owner of several bakeries in Rhodesia, helped her to set up a bakery business in Johannesburg. Her bakery was not far from my house, and I often went to buy fresh, delicious buns right after baking. The black-haired beauty lived with her son in a small cozy home, and I sometimes visited her with my son. Children were the same age and spent time in games. Jenny loved to cook and, treating us with delicious meals, asked about my affairs, acquaintances, work. Often at her place, I met her friend, with whom for many years she had a close relationship.

I was interested in her new business - a cafe which she opened recently.

After the robbers broke into her bakery and after tieing up her and two assistants, cleared her cash register, she closed the bakery. About a year she was in distress, before opening a cafe in a safe place.

I explained my interest in her business because I wanted to know what she thought about my desire to buy a small cafe. I was not going to leave my job at the factory, but only to devote my free time to this business.

My son no longer could find time for our scheduled meetings. He preferred to spend time in company of his constant girlfriend. I visited my grandchildren every week on Fridays. No inventions interested me anymore. True, I somehow made a device for making donuts and showed it to Naomi in my kitchen. It was a long time ago when I bought an apartment after arriving from Chile. But then left this idea.

As I had foreseen, Jenny gave me a lot of useful advice and promised to help me when I find something I like.

In search of a suitable place, I began to drive around a lot on weekends, and accidentally drove to a constantly operating fair in a huge amusement park for children. There were many small shops and cafes, thousands of people walked along the avenues, and stood at counters to buy sausages with a roll. Only the car parking area, where it was not easy to find a place for the newly-arrived, made me understand that I did not need to look for anything else. Having found an office that was in charge of this busy place, I asked what the possibilities to open here another cafe are. The manager explained that she had only a few spots left, but the owner had to deal with the construction of the unit by himself. There is a specific size of the room allowed, but you can do the planning yourself. Electrical work must be carried out according to the appropriate standards and, if I need help, she can give me the name of the company that was involved in building of the other premises. Then she gave me an application form, which I immediately on the spot, in disbelief of my luck, signed. The manager announced that new business owners should sell only those products that others do not have in order not to create competition. I assured that my cafe will sell only products of Russian cuisine. No one has this.

A month later, the construction company built the café according to my drawings. The hexagon shape, with a conical roof and wide windows of the attracted many visitors. The sign reads - "Russian food." Buyers liked the white tile floor, the only one among all such units, and delicious natural burgers. I hired two unemployed immigrants - a husband and a wife, both without English and a particular profession. Husband, former champion of Moscow in rowing, tall and broad-shouldered man, and his wife, tall blonde, they didn't live far from me, and I decided to give them an opportunity to earn some money

The first day of opening the cafe struck me – before noon time we sold out all our products. We arrived home, sat, and counted our income from the sale. All the workers I paid off at the end of the day and gave them all the remaining products.

Three black women worked for me in cooking place. Without one-time rubber gloves, I did not allow them to work. I used them too when serving meals to buyers. No one except my site used it at the fair. I was pleased when I caught the approving looks of the buyers. All cooking appliances and kitchen counters were made of stainless steel and designed by me.

At work, sitting in my office, I ordered all the necessary products directly by phone. I got up at 5 o'clock in the morning, and in my car, which was very useful for me now, I stopped at a meat factory to get bags of fresh sausages and meat. I bought the highest quality meat. Then I collected bags of potato chips, vegetables, and fresh buns from the bakery. The cake that one housewife made for me was the last product before I drove to my café.

Jenny supplied me with ready-made salads, which she bought for her cafe and delicious muffins, which she baked.

One of my friends, leaving engineering work, bought a cafe in one of the city's shopping centers. Before I got my business, I sometimes visited his café to have a cup of coffee. He was well organized. Had own apartment and his own business, always in a good mood - no pessimism.

I came to tell him about my cafe and about what I am selling. Hearing that I am selling hamburgers that were listed on the menu as Russian cutlets, he explained how to make them juicy. At his suggestion, the hamburgers necessary to put in the pan, pour the ready-made mixture of tomatoes ground on the mixer and keep it on low heat. I followed his advice. The result was amazing. Having the hamburger, people looked in surprise towards my café, and after a while returned for a new one. My Russian cotlets became popular, causing the envy of other traders at the fair.

I was bringing a loaded car to café at seven o'clock in the morning and unloaded the products in the cooling boxes. The workers started immediately to prepare meals that my neighbors ordered every morning for breakfast.

The German, the owner of a jewelry shop, ordered eggs with ham and strong tea. A neighbor in the kiosk that sold clothes, a young woman, got her sausage sandwich and a glass of coffee.

Before opening in the morning, in the front of my cafe was already a waiting line.

The former Muscovites had little interest in their work. I always had to look for them, somewhere at the fair where they stood with their open mouths, at a time when I needed their help. The rower's wife, stating that her husband had a back problem, did not allow him to lift anything heavy. At home they, had plenty of food, even their dog no longer wanted to eat a sausage that lay before it nose. I had to part with them.

Soon the other cafe owners began to complain to the park manager that I did not follow the rules and they were losing business because of me. This was especially evident when the flow of cars and visitors decreased.

One day, two visitors ordered my famous cutlets, then walked nearby, watching my stall. A few hours later, they appeared again and one of them said that he wanted to buy my business, asking for how much I could sell it. The offer to sell suited me entirely and even pleased me.

I was exhausted. It was necessary to wake up very early. Buying the groceries, delivery, unloading and working long hours, - it was not what I expected when I wanted to use my free time. The fourteen-hour day was, despite my proper physical form, was quite a load.
Besides, I was so annoyed with the complaints of my rivals. The decline in income was a worry, and I was going just to leave my kiosk and put up with the loss of costs.

Thinking a little, I called the amount in which I included funds spent on the construction and all the equipment. The buyer shook my hand and said that this amount suits him. He took out a checkbook, wrote a check, and handed it to me. Trying to hide my joy from luck, I said: "From now on, it's all yours."
The new owner said he had retired and was looking for doing something. He received a substantial amount from the pension fund and decided to invest part of it in the business. Showing at his companion, he said that he was a cook of French cuisine and that he liked my kiosk more than others, especially the cleanliness and tiled floor. Wishing them success, I left, happy with the thought that I no longer need to come back here. Depositing the check in the bank, I returned to my usual routine – early morning health club, breakfast, tedious office hours, and back to my clean, empty and quiet flat.
My happy mood did not last long. A few months later, unexpectedly, I received an official letter. The management of the factory praised me for the contribution that I made to the work of the enterprise and sent me to a well-deserved retirement.
Then the following letter came from the accounting department with a request to fill in the papers for an earned pension. The worker who had my file, advised me to ask to be fired. Because in that case, under the terms of the contract, I would be paid a large amount of money, and this is better than

receiving a small pension. I went to the director and asked to be fired. He flatly refused, saying that he had no reason for that.

With severance pay in the amount of my salary, I found myself out of work. It was unpleasant, but I did not feel any worry, as it was before, when I was losing jobs.

My children were well and independent. There is an amount of money in the bank, which makes me feel confident. I turned to Sasha, but he told me that he had nothing for me and, by the way, told me the story of the installation for drying fish. It turns out that the line I designed took so much energy that the plant began to experience interruptions in the work of the production shops. In this regard, they had to abandon it. Later, the plant in Chile was sold with high profit, and the partners switched to business in Israel.

My contacts with Naomi were not interrupted. We often talked over the phone. She immediately found a job in Canada, but she felt very lonely. Six months later, when mass shelling of Israel with rockets from Iraq began, she could not stay in Canada and returned to Israel, to be near her children and parents.

We continued our long telephone conversations, of which I had an idea of life in Israel, which I left fifteen years ago. I knew the details of the affairs of her eldest sons, engaged in business with their father. I knew that all three sons, except for her daughter, regularly visit their mother. I knew that Naomi's younger sister immigrated to Israel, and Naomi's cousin persuaded Naomi's father to buy her an apartment. I was happy for her. After years of wandering around the world and uncertainty about the relationship with me, finally, she had her own roof over her head. And most importantly - the children were close.
Unexpectedly for myself, I asked:
"What do you think if I move to you in Israel?"

I was ready to go to America, where my sister wanted to see me. Remembering Naomi's refusal to see me in Canada, I expected the same answer and was surprised when she agreed. Now my plans have changed.

I did not see for myself any perspectives to find a job in South Africa, where the economy began to decline.

After the release of Nelson Mandela from prison and the amnesty of all participants in his underground movement, tens of thousands of young people who had learned to hold weapons in their hands but did not have any useful occupation were out of work. Robberies of people and the banks have become the daily reality of life. Reports of the murders of shop owners and city residents have led many to leave the country. Businesses sold for nothing. There were cases of attacks on people who tried to take money from the machines installed at the entrance to the banks. People robbed of their cars and murdered.

President Mandela called for cooperation in building a new society without apartheid, but most people did not have a job.

Government positions were distributed among only Mandela people. Power was in the hands of the black majority. But hunger and deprivation of the poor population of the country could not disappear in an instant, as it seemed to the winners.

My daughter and her family moved to the area near the synagogue. There was the Jewish religious population. The area was safer and not subjected to violence and robbery, like at the rest of the city.

The attempted robbery in my son's house ended in a dog holding the robber against the fence wall until the police arrived. In the second robbery attempt, the dog bit the guy, but was injured with a knife.

In the house where I lived, the central door had a code, but the robbers entered the garage, making a passage in the brick wall of the building. They teared up the whole panel of a new neighbor's car, pulling out a costly radio installation, which they may have sold to buy food.
My old car was not touched.

I didn't want to be a burden for my daughter's family. And I didn't see an opportunity to solve the problem of my lonely life too. An elderly pensioner, without work, I could not be a gift to anyone. It seemed to me that with the knowledge of three languages and with my profession, I could easily find a job in Israel and began to prepare for departure.

The transport company provided the necessary services, including the manufacture of boxes, the preparation of all required documents, and taking care of the rest. I decided to take part of my furniture with me and leave the rest to my daughter. My daughter refused to keep my kitchen appliances and expensive French-made saucepans - her husband did not allow it because they were not kosher. I gave some of them to my acquaintances. An unusually beautiful floor lamp, I did not manage to pack in a box, and I went to see Sasha's sister, who was leaving for Israel with her husband, and they agreed to take it with them. They had already sold their large two-story house, where I had been more than once, and were ready to leave.

I only had to sell my apartment. I advertised in the newspaper and the next day received a call. A Chinese man, a business owner in a nearby street, inspected the apartment and, entering the kitchen, nodded his head in satisfaction. Pointing to the refrigerator, the remaining gadgets and appliances he said that he was buying everything the rest as well, and asked me to name the amount. I mentioned the amount for which I bought my apartment, knowing that I sell it much cheaper. Taking out a checkbook, he wrote a check and handed it to me. Seeing the check with the total cost of the apartment, I asked if he would like to give me only the deposit, he smiled and said that he had nothing to worry about me. Then asked what day and time he could move in, wrote down in his notebook and left. He never called but appeared precisely at the appointed time. I handed him the keys and thanked him for the trust. He laughed and wished me luck.

Before flying to Israel, I spent a whole week with my daughter at her home. My baggage has already been sent to Naomi.

When I met my son, we were both sad. He was aware of my job loss. He understood that my decision to go to Israel to Naomi, with whom he was familiar, was logical. He had already finished school and entered the university. Six months before school graduation, he was chosen by theadministration and recommended to a representative of the British insurance company as a candidate for a future employment. The insurance company provided the scholarship, subsidy to all costs of the study in the university, on condition that Ami would finish the faculty of Law and worked for the company's President in England.

My son did not like this faculty, he wanted to enter the faculty of English language and literature so that after graduation, he would work as a teacher and write. I tried to convince my son that such opportunity would give him financial independence and a career that one can only dream. No one will take away from him the desire to write, working as a lawyer. I gave him the example of a famous Soviet writer, Scheinin, who, as a lawyer, worked as an investigator at the prosecutor's office for many years. Based on numerous crimes uncovered, he collected the information that he presented in his book in the form of stories which I could not stop reading.

Unfortunately, Joseph Stalin did not take into account the talent and recognition of the writer and lawyer Sheinin. As one of the members of the Jewish Anti-Fascist Committee, he was shot in Lubyanka in 1952.

I tried to explain to my son that there is nothing more reliable than working in the office of a world-famous insurance company. Money has always ruled and will rule the world, and everything else is changing, bought, and sold over time. I saw that I did not convince him with the example given, but persuaded him.

The son studied at the faculty of law only for one year and transferred, at the same university, to his favorite faculty. It upset me. I dreamed that he would achieve more in life than me and that he would not have to go through the trials I went through. After talking with my son, I thought that I, myself, was also not an obedient son. Perhaps this is the eternal problem of fathers and children.

Children always see the world with different eyes and lways will do. And they will repeat their mistakes, as their fathers did.

When parting with my son, I did not know that our next meeting will take place many years later in America. He graduated from university. Tall and broad-shouldered, a head taller than me, with a short beard and long, dark hair shoulder-length, he looked like an actor who prepared for the role of Jesus in the film.

Parting with the daughter's family was even more painful. They have been a haven for me, where my tormented soul, which re-endured many deceptions and continuous experiences, found peace and joy.

Every Friday, I met with them the Sabbath. I rejoiced this Jewish religious custom, the taste of Moroccan food and joyful mood at the table.

Even though they lived in the area of the Jewish religious community and communicated with families like their own, I was worried about their security in the prevailing situation in the country. The only consolation could be the realization that we will always have the opportunity to meet.

At the airport, Zion was quiet, my daughter cried, and my little grandchildren could not understand why I leave them and looked at me with a sad surprise.

Destiny is unfair to me, I thought. I always leave those who are dear to me, causing them the pain of separation. Kids will not be able to pronounce the word "Saba," in Hebrew - grandpa. After all, I'm their only grandfather, and they have no grandmothers. And my daughter cannot call me "Papa" when she needs me.

How happy I would feel if I had the opportunity to say the words "dad" and "mom." But this will never happen. They remained only in my memory.

From the first days of my arrival in South Africa, I met a lot of people who left a particular trace in my life.

I had a chance to meet people who showed sympathy to me from the first days of arrival. I felt the participation from many families of the Jewish community, of which I described only a few. The respect to myself, as an engineer and a worker, I saw from employers. I experienced favors from many individuals who helped me to survive during difficult times

Despite individual acquaintances with women, I felt very often alone.

My loneliness was interrupted by unexpected visits from people who were not my friends or acquaintances. Basically, they appeared with recommendations. They need my help. I did not refuse anyone. We were all immigrants and I understood that people who by themselves had the difficulties during the absorption, could be helpful. I was approached by people I never knew. They found refuge and support in my house. To some people I helped to get a job, others lived with me for months.

To my sorrow, in spite of my hospitality and help, these people left an unpleasant impression.

Sadly, but I also knew those who used my knowledge, my time, my devotion to achieve personal interests, and then betray. There were people whom I did not immediately understand, but then I left them, realizing that I have nothing in common with them.

Fortunately, I knew those who were my real friends and supported in the difficult days. Such a man of honor, conscience, and the word were Sasha Goldman.

There were people to whom I came to heal my wounded soul. For many years, such a person for me was the unforgettable Rola. Many were real friends of mine. I did not consider a necessity to tell about everyone I knew, because I would have to add many chapters to this book. I have indicated only those episodes of my life that can give an idea of the conditions in which I found myself as an immigrant.

Possibly, reading this book, many will see themselves in one of those situations that I have described. They will see people with whom they have lost their friendship because of the dishonest behavior, the one who called himself a friend. They will see themselves helping someone who has been deceiving them, presenting himself not as who he really was. They will look at themselves from the outside and will think that they believed and trusted the person who betraded them. They helped people in an awkward moment, and received in response, not gratitude, but alienation. They gave people the time of their personal life - something that never comes back, and can not be returned.

Attempt to return home

An enthusiastic start.
Job seeking. Disappointments.
Naomi's parents.
Baggage from Africa.
Refusal to my proposal.
Final decision.

At Ben Gurion airport, I saw Naomi from afar and happily waved to her. There were no joyful hugs and conversations. She always kept herself reserved in public places. We left the building and instantly found ourselves in the embrace of hot air. As we walked to the parking lot, Naomi's face immediately became covered with drops of moisture. I probably didn't look any better. We went to her car. With the surprise, I looked at what supposed to be in a landfill. The sun burned a plastic coating inside the vehicle at the windshield and rear window. The torn seats and a foam rubber filling emerged from their bottom.

"This is father's car," Naomi said, warning my question. "The main thing is to start because the first gear does not work," she interrupted my stupor.

We were lucky. From the second gear, slowly but surely, the car started to move, and we were off. Heated by the sun, our mobile sauna did not cool down, and the open windows did not help. I noticed that Naomi was driving intently, and I tried not to distract her with the conversation. When we arrived home, she sighed with relief, saying that she was worried that the car could stop on the road. It was her first long trip in this car.

Her apartment was on the second floor of a ten-story modern building. Large bright living room with two windows and a balcony, two small bedrooms and a cozy kitchen with a high narrow table in the form of a bar and two high chairs. Except for two beds, no furniture. No bath, only a shower in one of the bedrooms. I unpacked my suitcase, hung my shirts and pants. After taking a shower, we went to the kitchen, where I sat down on a high chair by the table, and Naomi put on the table a few cans of pickled vegetables and salad - our both preferred food.

Without delay, Naomi proceeded to discuss the first and necessary steps in the formal procedures, which I needed to do without delay. She already had for me prepared information about government offices I should visit and their addresses. Thanks to Naomi's organized activity, I managed to get all the necessary documents, including a passport, medical care, and opening a bank account, within a week. I even managed to visit an employment agent. Then start shopping for a car. Having no income, I decided to buy an old car. Riding on public transport was not a problem. They were on schedule, had air conditioning, and could get me anywhere in the country. But for more productive job searches and visiting the right places, the own car was preferable. A car in Israel is a luxury.

After going through a few cars that did not start, I stopped at Volkswagen. The "beetle," as we call it, started right away. I paid off and left. I did not know then that it would not serve me, but I would be at serveice. Every week, it did not start, and I had to guess what the reason for its disobedience is. I often had to feed this "bug" with money, which this metal creature swallowed, without promising that it would provide reliability. Sitting in a car, I always felt that mat was flrxible under my feet and it was only when the rains started, passing through a groove on a road filled with water, I decided to check why my legs were in the water. Lifting the mat, I saw a rusty metal sheet with many holes. Fearing that my feet could touch the road while driving, I put a sheet of plywood under the mat. The problem with legs was solved, but the problem with water remained.

I also could not solve the problem with employment. Young girls in the personnel departments, reading my documents, were laughing. "Saba, why do you need to work, you already need to rest."

One of the offered a job of assembling products at a precision instrument factory. Good salary, food. I understood that this was a reliable offer and a stable income. I refused. I refused not because I have to be a worker. I kept the tools in my hands all my life and used them no worse than a pencil. In Israel, I was ready to do any work. The reason was different. I did not want Naomi to be uncomfortable with her relatives that I am working as a simple worker. She was sure that I would find an engineer's job faster than the rich husband of her younger sister.

In search of opportunities to use my patent, I began to look for organizations that may be interested. One of them, by happy coincidence, was in Raanana, the city where Naomi lived and located in a small house where, judging by the sign, it offered help to those who have patents or projects useful for production.

Indoors, I sart reading handwritten or printed ads and sentences that had nothing to do with sign on the door.

The man at the reception office explained that their organization connected with many enterprises and people who are interested in investing money in projects and ideas which are reliable and cost-effective proposal.

I began to tell him about my grill, but his face showed no interest. He wrote down my name in the book opened before him and asked to call in a week. I got up and headed for the exit. A person standing nearby and reading ads and posters approached me and said that he would like to talk with me. We left the room together. He introduced himself; his name was Moti. He asked if I could tell him what the essence of my patent was. He listened and said that he was looking for investing money, but what I told him was too difficult and expensive for him. He would like to invest in a business that produces what people need in their daily lives. He has some ideas, but he still cannot make a decision, because he doesn't have much money.

I invited him to come to my house right now and discuss what we can do together. Naomi was at work. We sat outside on the balcony. I put a glass of juice on the table, and he told me how he managed to earn a million dollars through a construction project in Africa. After returning to Israel, he bought a house with pool, and decided to invest the remaining money in a business that would give him an adequate income for a family of four.

I agreed that my patent is not a good idea because it required a significant contribution of funds. Then I asked about his ideas. Moti said that he was thinking about solar water heaters. Now I was interested. He has two people in mind who have been in this business for many years. One of them wants to sell his production shop, and the other is looking for a partner investor. If he goes into action, he could take me as his partner, so that I would be engaged in production, and he would be involved in installing panels for customers.

During our conversation, Naomi returned from work, and I introduced them. Moti apologized and said the wife is waiting for him at home for dinner. I went to accompany him to the car. We exchanged phone numbers, and he left. A few days later he called and invited me to his place, saying that he would pick me up in the morning. I liked his house - spacious, bright with a large white kitchen and the most modern kitchen equipment.

Moti said that he refused to buy the business because the owner more than a year did not pay for the premises and he was not sure that there were no other debts. The second owner refused to sell 51 percent of the shares of his business, which means that he, without the knowledge of Moti, could sell his business, and as a result – Moti could lose the money invested, as a lawyer-consultant explained to him. He looked at me, waiting for my advice.

I said that I like his idea of investing money in solar energy. But it's best to have a small, own and reliable business.

The production of installations for water heating, the payment of premises, materials, wages, insurance of workers, and manufacturing require a lot of money. Even if he has enough money to start such a business, then any non-payment for several installations can put his business on the verge of bankruptcy. "I am sure, - I said, - those two people who wanted your investment in their business, experienced the problems, I have mentioned."

Having seen his distressed face, I said that we should better imagine how, based on this enormous industry, which embraced every family in the country, to make an installation that would improve the work of all the panels already installed.

"Why improve them if they work for decades, and no one ever complains?" asked Moti.

"They do not complain because they do not know that the effectiveness of the solar panels could be improved."

And I began to tell him about my work experience with the use of solar energy. Due to dust and air pollution, solar collectors lose up to 40 percent of their efficiency. If we do an improvement which will automatically regularly clean the surface of the panels from pollution, we will be able to start producing such devices for very low investment, and we will have our own business. Moti was silent, pondering. It was difficult for him to imagine what I had in mind. Then I asked for one day to make a sample and show him my idea on a model.

The next day I went to the local building goods store. I chose the plastic parts I needed, which are used everywhere when irrigating trees or greenery. Everything was standard, affordable, and not expensive. At home, I assembled the parts with pipes, drew a diagram of the connection to the panels on the paper, and went to my new friend. I connected the model to the tap, and thin streams of water splashed out of the pipes.

"That's all," I said, "the water supply automatically turns on, and dust and dirt removed from the panel.

Then I offered to start with those enterprises where there are many panels installed. After signing the contract, we buy the parts and do the whole assembly on-site, using the cheapest tools. Moti agreed, but before taking up with the business, he suggested I test this idea on several objects.

I started from the building where Naomi bought her apartment. It had centralized hot water supply. I went up to the roof. There, I saw a frame with the rows of water heating panels connected to a large tank, from which hot water distributed to the apartments.

It was a good idea to start here and show future customers as a example.

I knocked on the house committee president's door. An older woman opened the door. In Hebrew with an English accent, she asked about the purpose of my visit. Having introduced myself, I said that I lived on the second floor and gave the name of the owner of the apartment. She invited to come in. After listening to me, she sympathetically said that maybe this is a good idea, but there were never problems with hot water in the building. There are problems with the repair of the panels, which is costly. The most urgent expenses for which she should always have a stock is the repair of the elevator. Therefore, she can not now allocate money to my offer.

I made several visits to various enterprises and appealed to private owners of the panels manufacture. The answers and the reasons for the refusal were the same everywhere. I saw that Moti was right - no one was interested. Our cooperation was over.

Twenty years later, I learned that many European companies engaged in the manufacture of solar cells and heaters concluded that cleaning the surfaces of the sun collectors from pollution is necessary to increase the panels' effectivity. The idea of cleaning with the use of thin jets of water accepted as the cheapest and reliable.

Naomi watched with interest in my job search, and even several times attended my conversations with employers, saw my enthusiasm in search of investors and attempts to cooperate with Moti. She believed that I would be able to find an application for my profession.

The family of her younger sister bought an apartment in the same city. We went to visit them. The place required repairs, and I offered my help. During the week, I helped to repaint all the rooms, and we brought the neglected apartment into a decent look. With this gesture, I wanted to slightly improve the cold attitude towards me on the part of her sister and husband, facilitating the position of Naomi, in which she placed herself because of me.

Once, we visited Naomi's aunt, her mother's sister. After the death of her husband, she moved to Israel and settled in Tel Aviv, where she had her apartment. Naomi loved her more than all the other relatives. From her aunt, she felt the same warm relationship. We visited her more than once, and I noticed that she talked to me very friendly.

One day, Naomi decided to visit her parents in the kibbutz. We went in my car, fearing that Naomi's car, which could have moved off only from the second gear, would not be able to overcome many hills during the long journey.

The highway ended, the road began to wind over the hills. My "beetle" coped with long-haul flight without any problems. The engine knocked steadily, the car climbed up all the hills, trying to convince of its reliability, but still left behind drops of engine oil, on which we could easily find our way back.

We drove through a few Arab villages, and finally got to the kibbutz houses.

I met with Naomi's father in Johannesburg at the house of his eldest daughter Ruth, but never introduced to him, and he, in turn, never spoke to me. One day, when I tried to enter into a conversation, he ignored me - no more attempts on my part. But after Naomi left for Israel, I met with him to transfer through him the money I received after selling her car which she paid off. He refused to take the money, saying that he had nothing to do with it.

And now we had to sit at the table face to face. Fresh orange juice quenched the thirst after a long journey. On the table, there was a meat dish directly from the stove. The fragrant bread baked by the hostess reminded me of those years when my mother brought bread from the peasant market. Appetite broke out, and I gladly took up the food. The parents did not eat; they probably had the meal before our arrival, which, of course, they knew. I understood they wanted to see the man trying to become a member of their family for so many years. Naomi's mother, I saw the first time.

From Naomi's stories, I knew her mom had to endure a lot of humiliation from an overbearing husband who, along with business, spared a lot of time outside the family, to women. Now in front of me sat an older man who did not care what was happening outside the kibbutz. His business had a solid foundation of invested funds and was in the hands of the heirs. Grandchildren received education at the expense of the foundation established by the grandfather, and all were well of. Naomi's, two eldest sons after graduating from the university opened in Moscow a branch for the import of goods into Israel. One of the eldest sister's sons became a doctor, and the other one is an architect, like his father. In short, all eleven grandchildren had professions and jobs.

Naomi's mom watched me enjoying the food she cooked. Naomi barely ate and exchanged words with her mother in general phrases about children, sisters, work.

Seeing that I had finished with the meal, Naomi's father chatted with me. He asked me how I feel in Israel, what I want to do, whether I have relatives and friends. But it was only to keep the conversation going. I was sure that he knew everything about me from the words of his daughters and, perhaps, from the words of the former husband Naomi, whom I had never met again. Mom continued to treat me relentlessly, seeing with what pleasure I eat, and in her eyes, I saw participation and warmth. Naomi decided to show me the kibbutz farm, and we went outside. Grape clusters on one slope, alternated with fruit trees on another. Vegetable gardens, cows, chickens, sheep - everything that made kibbutzniks independent in nutrition.

Being two hours drive from the nearest town, the residents had the most necessary products.

When my daughter was in a kibbutz, I was offered to stay in it. But I could not imagine that I could get used to and be satisfied with the conditions of life in the kibbutz. Perhaps I was wrong. Kibbutzniks have always earned my respect. They supplied themselves with almost everything they needed and provided the country's market with products. I had to meet people from the kibbutz, and I found that, first of all, they were honest, hard-working, and loyal to their country. Among them there was no concept of dishonesty, untruth, deceit, laziness and everything else, which is enough in any country and any society, not excluding our Israel.

Saying goodbye, we left the kibbutz. Naomi was silent all the way. I guessed that her attempt to get her father's approval was unsuccessful. Her father could not forgive his daughter's replacement of his favorite man, a prosperous businessman, with a poor immigrant from Russia.

Getting my baggage from Africa transformed Naomi's apartment. Danish light furniture blends in well with the pastel white color of the living room. The curved stand of the lamp with a beautiful modern lampshade and a coffee table with chairs gave the apartment a residential appearance. At the far wall of the living room, two chairs of the hand-made work of one of the African tribes immediately attracted the attention. Each chair consisted of only two parts of a very durable wood, which were not tied together. Strange as it may seem, it was extremely comfortable on them to sit, and all visitors tried their reliability. A small desk now made it possible to sit down and write a letter. A typewriter used by Naomi in Africa came along with the furniture. Naomi was delighted with it more than anything else.

We sometimes spent weekends in Tel Aviv, where we preferred Old Jaffa to the rest of the city. The narrow streets of this ancient city, where, in the past two donkeys with harnesses could not easy to cross, were restored. The houses were repaired, painted and artists, sculptors, and jewelry manufacturers settled in the small apartments of these houses. They sold their products and paintings on the "flea market" located nearby in a small square, always filled with tourists. It was exciting for us to visit their working studios and museums, to buy a tasty fresh bun from an Arab merchant, then, tired of a long walk, we sat down at a table in a fish restaurant right there in Jaffa. Before returning home, we took a walk along the sandy shores of the Tel Aviv beach.

An unexpected call in the middle of the night woke me up. It was a call from the Tel Aviv police. They asked if I was the owner of the Volkswagen car. When I confirmed, they said that the "beetle" is in their possession and I can come to pick it up. Looking out the window, in the light of the lanterns, I saw that there was no car in the parking. In the morning, I arrived in Tel Aviv and saw it with a crumpled buffer. At night the police noticed a suspicious car with three teenagers, and when they stopped her, it turned out that the car did not belong to them. There was no other damage besides the torn wires on the steering column. I was lucky; it could be worse. I got into the car and returned home.

My job search continued. I found in the newspaper the announcement of the hiring the kitchen designers. The woman said that she represents a private company and recruiting people for work. She invited me to test my drawing skills. It turns out she worked from home. She had a room equipped with a real drawing board and her kitchen was made by the company which products she represented. After checking my skills, asked to come to the place in the industrial areas near Ashdod. I began to study the design of kitchens. I bought a book and got acquainted with the requirements and standards related to the design of the kitchens. A long trip in the exhausting heat was justified only by my desire to bring money home. After a month of work, I was expecting payment as pomised, but the women who hired me said that the owner of the business does not want to pay me for a work done. When I met with the owner of the company, I found that he didn't have any application for employment and I am not a company worker. He advised me to see the person who hired me and let her pay for the work. He was right. I never saw him and did not fill out any documents. When I gave him the name of a woman, he said that she, too, was not listed as a company employee and worked independently. They pay her only for work she delivered. It became clear to me that I had fallen on a swindler who used my time and work.

Designing kitchens interested me, and I decided to work independently. In the baggage delivered from Africa, among my personal belongings was a small drawing board and a set of drawing tools. After a few ads in the newspaper, the first customers appeared - a young couple of professionals. I saw them at my place. They bought the first house and wanted to have a kitchen according to their likes. I wrote down all their requirements, came to their home, and made the necessary measurements. When I finished the design, they came to see the drawings. They liked it, and they immediately paid me for my work. The next client was Naomi's acquaintance. Then I was approached by a builder who wanted to make a beautiful bathroom for a wealthy buyer. He also liked my work. He paid and asked if I could make him the layout of the apartment in the house, which he was going to builds for himself. With a short break in the orders for design, I was busy. I had a problem in one family only where the husband and wife argued and could not decide which of them should cede. I tolerated all changes, but they did not come to an agreement and, of course, did not pay.

The arrival of my daughter's family to Israel was a joyful event. Naomi and I bought presents for the children and came to visit the hotel where they stayed. The joy of my grandchildren knew no bounds. Simi, the oldest, behaved like an adult and. Eitan and Ayala could not be calmed down. Ayala, thin and raised, tirelessly tumbled over and did a headstand against the wall on the sofa. Our visit ended when they gathered for a visit to the numerous relatives of Zion.

I met them again before they returned home. My daughter clung to me and could not speak; her eyes were full of tears. Yes, I understood her. She was already a mother of three children, tirelessly devoting herself to the care of the whole family, but she missed me, her father. Her husband was born in a family where the duty of the woman was to give birth to children, to prepare food and keep up the household. Zion was a good husband and father of his children and did everything possible to feed, clothe, and give children an education that he did not have for himself. He observed Sabbath and kosher house; every day, he began with a prayer in the synagogue and a cup of coffee. But I never saw from him that kindness and attention, in which, like any woman, my daughter needed. It did not exist in the family of religious traditions, and I saw it in my daughter's eyes.

Therefore, I understood Naomi, who deprived her children of parentall participation during her refuge in South Africa. Is it possible to compare a written letter, or a telephone conversation, with the feeling of hugging hands, warmth, and love in the eyes? No, you can not. Our fates, to some extent, were equally broken and our relationship, most likely, also had the character of a fractured past. Naomi never discussed her thoughts with me. Lying in bed, she smoked a cigarette, and her gaze directed to nowhere.

She often visited her children without me; also her sister and her cousin. In our joint visits to her acquaintances, she was embarrassed, not knowing how to present me to people I did not know. It made me remember our recent past.

Having come to the concluded that we need to figure out how she sees our relationship, I and chose the right moment and offered her to marry me. She did not expect this and was silent for a long time, and then said that about this is too early to talk. I explained to her how humiliating it was for me to feel as a tenant in her apartment, not seeing the future. A few days later she said that she was leaving for her nephew's wedding in Johannesburg and asked if I also wanted to go with her. The question was in such a way that it sounded more like she had already decided to go without me, but she still can, if I insist, to take me with. She accepted my refusal with relief. On the day of departure, she asked to clean the apartment, which was full of the dust after installation of the central air conditioning unit. I took her to the airport and began to get ready for the road. My decision was final - I am going to my sister in America. I ordered a ticket, coinciding with the date of my departure a day after Naomi's return from Africa, got a visa, and closed a bank account where only four thousand dollars remained of the money I brought to Israel. Then sold the car and packed my personal belongings.

Having met Naomi at the airport, I didn't tell her anything about my decision. Upon entering the apartment, cooled by an air-conditioner, she thanked me for cleaning out the dust, unpacked her suitcase, and took out a denim shirt - a gift for me.

She always gave me amazing gifts, with better quality and, most importantly, necessary and practical. In Africa, she presented me with a Japanese camera, a Japanese blood pressure measuring device, a shirt made in Italy and a beautiful wool sweater. They have remained with me to this day. She always refused my gifts, just as in restaurants she declined to order a dish for herself, considering that she was saving my expenses. She ignored my help to pay for the surgery when we lived in Johannesburg and, for the first time, she turned for help to her father, who did not refuse and came to follow up her recovery in the hospital. I saw her refusal, as a desire to be entirely indebted to me and not to feel the guilt, in making the decisions she needed. Her frugality has reached the point of absurdity. Taking a walk in Jaffa, she bought a fresh roll from a merchant and divided it into two halves. No less was her modesty in clothes. Perhaps, she inherited it from a father- millionaire who rode a car in which the first gear did not work and which he then presented to his daughter, instead of getting rid of it.

I treated with the respect Naomi's rational spending and unpretentiousness, but I was sorry for her constant refusals to herself in the most ordinary and necessary things. Jewelry, rings, or earrings were alien to her. I thought it was her form of protest against the unfair decision of her father, who had deprived her of support.

Accidentally turned my attention to the healed scar on the skin of the inner side of the hand. Naomi was silent and did not answer. The sisters never defended her against her unjust father.

Only Naomi's cousin, who lived in Israel, found the courage to say to her father, his uncle that his daughter, having arrived in Israel, wanders without a roof over her head.

Waking up in the morning, we had breakfast, and I told Naomi that I was leaving for America. It sounded so usual that she asked when I was going to go there. Hearing that I needed to leave for the airport in two hours, she said meekly and quietly.
"I'll take you there," and began to gather.

In the car, already on the road, she asked when I made this decision. I answered, "On the day you left for the wedding. Here in Israel we have been together for a whole year. Since we first met ten years ago, it was the best period of our life together. If you could not decide whether you want to be my wife, I have no other ten years for you."
She walked me to the escalator. I turned to her and said. "I never stopped loving you." When I put my foot on the moving up steps, Naomi suddenly asked.

"When will you be back?"
I answered - "Never."

America

Mother's will. New family.
Job seeking. Start a new career.
Friendship with Dr. Dovzhenko.
My son's visit to America.
The search for relatives.
Moving to California.
Two weddings.
The end of my career.
Retirement.

At night, on the plane, I could not sleep. After all, I left not only Naomi, I left Israel, my country that always was in my mind and in my heart. The emigration from Israel to Sout Africa was not by my will, but now - under different circumstances. This plane, a tiny part of Israel, takes me to America where I will meet with my sister, but what I am going to do after that, I did not know. Africa did not become my homeland, but only the country where my daughter and my son live. I came to Africa as a young and full of a confidence man who, like immigrants from Lithuania and Russia fleeing the pogroms and revolution, came to succeed and to build a future for their children.

Now, it's all in the past. I made many mistakes, not because of stupidity, but of gullibility and the desire to help. Will they be repeated in the future? I do not know. Errors are not planned. There are always, and will be people who know how to use others for their own purposes. To avoid mistakes is not everyone's luck. Cheaters, unfortunately, can wear expensive suits, sit in cabinets, live in expensive homes and ride expensive cars, personify nobility and genuine interest. Some of them, on the contrary, cause pity for their helplessness and need for help. All of them, having received what they need, show their real face.

Most often, these are people without a twinge of conscience or even a hint of gratitude. I thought about myself - "Why did I find myself in the position of a person who, in most cases, gave people the knowledge and time for nothing?"

Since childhood, I responded to somebody's need. I remember, I gave my gloves to a friend whose hands suffered from the frost.

This human sense of concern remained with the old Russian woman believer who sent her granddaughter with a paper bag in which potatoes and onions were wrapped when our ghetto column passed by their house.

This human feeling is probably preserved by those Germans who saved my mother and me from being shot. This human sence of concern never left Russian Ivan Bakhmetov, who saved me from a pogrom in the ghetto.

It was also preserved by those peasants in Belarussian villages who gave us, survivors from the ghetto, a piece of bread and a glass of milk, and did not refuse to stay overnight, knowing that they could die if the neighbors give them out to the Germans.

Late night, almost all passengers sleep peacefully. I went into my thoughts about the past, trying to understand my mistakes, tried to analyze their causes and, not finding the answer, I began to think about a future that wasutterly vague and unknown. I flew to America for the third time in my life. This time, a three-month visa will allow me to get to know this country better and be with my only sister.

Her joy at meeting with me and the hope that I could be with her for a long time convinced me that I did the right thing.

At home, was, of course, a plentiful lunch. My niece, tall, slim and beautiful girl with big black eyes, very similar to her mother's, was already in high school. Dora and her husband had a job, and it was felt that they had the hardest days behind them. It immediately took away the anxiety with which I feft three years ago when I saw the conditions in which they live. They left the dirty apartment of impudent owners and lived on another street in the same area of the city. The next step - to visit the bank. My sister reminded of her advice to open a bank account, and now I saw that she was right. Depositing the cash in the bank, I felt more comfortable and I was not a burden to the sister's family.

For several days I walked around the city, trying to remember the routes and places I had come to know in my previous visit. Sister preferred to take me shopping. From the groceries I saw, I preferred made in Israel. Trip to the clothing stores caused bewilderment to the poverty of styles, faded colors, and the unpleasant smell of fabric's paint. I wanted to find denim pants and could not find a single pair with the brand - Made in America. Everything was made in China. I had nothing against China, the country of ancient culture and traditions, which evoked respect, but buying denim in America with a brand - Made in China, was ridiculous. In Africa, I wore clothes and shoes with a brand - Made in Italy, because in the shops you could find goods from any country in Europe.

I refused all the shirts that my sister had suggested me to try on until I accidentally saw a T-shirt with the emblems of the inventions of Leonardo Da Vinci.

To my satisfaction, it was made in America, and I still got it.

My school friend, Ilya Bass, moved to Rochester, a small town on the border with Canada, and I decided to visit him. It was my second meeting with Ilya in America. The first occurred when I came to visit Dora in America two years ago. When I learned that he lives two hours from Chicago, I arrived in Richford, the state of Wisconsin on a bus. Ilya worked as a consultant at a private enterprise for the manufacture of gears which required quite complicated calculations. They paid him for this responsible job well, considering that there were not many specialists of this kind. His wife tried to pass the exam for the right to work as a doctor, their daughter finished school.

Ilya told that in Milwaukee, the capital of the state, lives Yakov Kapul the former head of the department where I worked before the immigration to Israel. Lenya Dukhin - head of the design bureau of the Thermoplast plant was in the same state too. Two friends, having worked together for many years, spent many hours in battles at the chessboard. They immigrated much later than me. Before I left to Israel, I told them they have no future in Russia.

Naturally, I could not leave the town without seeing them. We were first to visit Lenya Dukhin and came to his home. When I learned that he was the head of the design department, I immediately asked if he could help me to get a job.

"With the pleasure," answered Lenya.

"By the way, what is your status in America?"

"I just arrived."

Learning that I had come only for a visit, he spread his hands with regret - "Sorry I can not help you."

He looked very pale and sad. To my remark, replied,

"I have a lung cancer."

I remembered how he and Yakov Kapul, two friends, sat for hours at the chessboard, dipped in tobacco smoke, holding cigarettes in their fingers.

The next visit was made to Jakov Kapul. After arriving in America, he became the owner of a grocery store and alcoholic beverage products. He looked very well and friendly. Met us affably. Business brought great profits. His eyes show the satisfaction and contentment of life.

Having made some pictures with the camera, we said goodbye.

I flew to Rochester from Chicago. Ilya was waiting and met me at the airport. We have not seen each other for ten years, and I wanted to know how his family is doing. I found that after graduating from college, his son got married and moved to another state. His daughter finished medical school and works. His wife, Sophia, a doctor, works too. They live in a two-story house with a small plot of land.

In the memories of the days of our youth and friends, we spent hours, feeling the warmth that can manifest itself only among those who passed through the difficult and hungry post-war years of childhood.

Ilya remembered how we together took part in a drama group that was led by a former artist of the Jewish theater, Lev Kravetz. In those years, we did not pay attention to the fact that the same group of students took part in the composition of the drama circle, as well as in all school events. Now, listing the names of participants in school events on those distant days, Ilya noticed, to his and my surprise, that for some reason, among all these activists, there were mainly Jews. Ilya reminded me how we took part in the dramatization of a passage from the book by the writer Mikhail Zharikov "A Tale of a Stern Friend." The play, which our teacher, former artist, staged was called "The Battle on the Kalmius River" - one of the chapters of the book mentioned above.

The essence of this play is a battle between the poor, dressed in a torn clothe and always hungry boys from the village, and a group of children, the sons of the wealthy dignitaries of the city. The time of action is July's Sunday of the year 1917.

Ilya played red snotty Ilyukha. I played a Greek boy Ucha - a cripple with a hunchbacked nose. My face was smeared with a dark layer of washable paint and on the head I had a bucket to protect the head from the cadet stones. Seeing my appearance in this image, Illya forgot that he was on stage and began to laugh. This caused an explosion of laughter among the school children audience and the teacher seeing the disturbence on the scene, began to bite his fists in frustration.

I remembered how he reacted in the same way when somebody of us did not read the poem correctly in spite of all his teaching efforts to tdo it right. Now, recalling the episodes of our school days, we experienced almost related feelings to each other.

Ilya decided to show me Niagara Falls, which were two hours away from his house. Leaving the car in the parking lot, we approached the fence of the observation deck. From here there was a beautiful view of the cliffs, from where a wall of water plunged down, forming swirling bursts of high ejected streams, scattering in small droplets in the air. We walked along the barrier and looked at the ship with tourists, coming close to the waterfall. From the height, they looked like children's toys. On the opposite clearly visible side of the Canadian territory, we saw many buildings. No description and photographs of Niagara Falls can replace the real image of this miracle of nature.

Ilya offered me a boat trip to the waterfall. All passengers were given yellow plastic raincoats to protect them from splashing water. Being on the deck of a small ship, next to the roar of the overflowing wall of water, I was at an admiration of a suddenly appeared rainbow.

The next morning, I watched Ilya mowing the grass on the section of his house, explaining that if he did not do this, he mightreceive a fine. After the lunchtime, Ilya had a visitor, and we conversed about ordinary matters, when his quest, finding out that I am a single man, said that his sister is divorced. She lives in New York, and he would like me to contact her. Before leaving, he gave me her phone number and asked to call her.

I was glad to see my friend and I flew home with the hope of future encounters.

Returning to Skokie and having lost many hours in the wating for the buses, I decided to buy an inexpensive car. I looked through many dealers of used cars, and saw that the cheeky sellers tried to sell vehicles which required expensive repairs. Finally I saw a car very dirty inside. It was unpleasant to sit in it, but after examining the engine, I asked to drive. Satisfied with the condition of the engine, I paid and drove away. I washed the dirt with a brush and soap for two days. Only after that I saw what color the seats and body paint were. The car was reliable and served me for many years.

I was at home alone, studying the map my sister's husband gave me to explore the area. The phone rang. A female voice asked for Dora. I replied that she had not come home from work, yet. The woman asked to tell Dore that Larisa called her.

Finding out who was calling my sister was delighted. Then Dora said that our mother, before she passed away, assured her that in the future, we woud be together.

"You are my only brother. Therefore, I want you to stay in America," said my sister. "This is our mother's will and my wish too."

Dora never told me about it before. "If mother said so, I would fulfill her will, but I don't have any idea how we can do it, because my visa ends in two months."

"I already thought about this before your arrival, and I want to introduce you to Larisa. If you like each other and get married, you can legally stay in America and have the right to work. I want to tell you; I liked Larisa very much."

My sister's recommendation was enough, and I called Larisa. We agreed to meet during the lunch break not far from her work. I did not ask Larisa what she looked like, but told her about myself that Iam an old man, and wearing glasses.

Sitting in a bookstore, I watched all those entering and, when a woman appeared in the doorway in a blouse embroidered with a Ukrainian pattern, I realized that it is Larisa. We went to a cafe, in the same store, and sat down at a table. Only now, sitting opposite, I could look at her attentively.

In the brightly lit room, her light gray eyes looked blue, her face with bright lips looked at me questioningly and with a smile, and I noticed her patterned blouse, gorgeous breasts, and hands folded on her knees. Knowing that she was using her breakout at work, I offered something to eat. She refused. Then I ordered two cups of coffee, and we started talking.

Larisa briefly, as is usually the case with strangers, told about herself, her work, her family. Unnoticed, her break time came to an end. I suggested to meet for another day, and she agreed. The day of our next date happened to be a weekend.

We went to the Botanical Garden and spent the whole day walking through the alleys and talking. We sat on benches in the shade. We had lunch at the restaurant. This day she told in detail about all her life. Her story about what her family and she went through during the life in the Soviet Kyiv could be a separate story, which I can only mark with a few lines, beginning with her post-war childhood.

It began without a father who returned from the war and unexpectedly died in the hospital during the surgery, several months before her birth, leaving without support his wife with two children and a blind grandmother. Old apartment, where everyone huddled in one room. One kitchen for three families and one toilet.

Mom worked as a simple worker in a foundry at the factory. Sympathetic neighbors were lending her mother money to buy food. The blind grandmother whom little Larisa led through the streets of the city for shopping. Constant poverty and shoes with a hole in the worn soles. Youthful years at school, where she, half-starved, sat next to the children who had everything they needed.

The poverty, nevertheless, did not prevent her from being one of the best in academic performance and going to the college. The older brother was in a military school.

The unexpected visit of her grandfather, mother's father, from America, who had been searching for his daughter for many years and not succeeding to find, considered her dead.

Marriage. Birth of a daughter. Husband's illness. Failure in the application for emigration; and, as a result, dismissal from work. Husband's disability. Work on cleaning the streets. With the friend's help she got temporary employment. Chernobyl disaster. Help from Siberian friends in saving her daughter from the threat of radiation. The decade's end of KGB refusal to permit the immigration. The loss of a seriously ill husband. Emigration of the whole family to America. Support by American relatives. Language learning. Studying in college. Job. The buying a first car. Even before Larisa arrived in America, her grandfather, who had no savings, and no medical insurance, sold his business to pay for the treatment of his wife, whom he could not save. Soon grandfather passed away too. Four of her mother's brothers were all already elderly. They could not afford to retire and continued to work.

But mother's brothers did not leave their sister and her family without attention. They regularly visited their immigrant relatives, helped with useful advice, often took with them on various trips around the country, treated them to restaurants, and helped them with finding a job.

After learning about Larisa's life, I felt great respect for this woman who courageously fought for survival in anti-Semitic Kyiv.

Now here in America, at her age, she went to the college to become a computer programmer.

We rose from the bench and went to the exit. Larisa took my arm. This gesture of trust touched me with its immediateness. I wanted to support this woman, and I thought that we both, who had many difficulties and losses in our lives, probably, could be a suitable pair.

I remember that Naomi never took my arm anywhere, and always left me alone in the company of her friends and relatives as if emphasizing the uncertainty of our relationship to others.

The next day Larisa and I met again and went to the music festival held in the park of Ravinia, near the Botanical Garden.

Thousands of people sitting on folding chairs, or on the bedding, comfortable on the clipped grass with wine glasses in their hands fell silent with the first sounds of a symphony orchestra - the park full of people immersed in a world of magical sounds. We sat next to each other, Larisa against my shoulder. I felt the warmth of her body and realized that this woman would be part of my life. The next day I was invited to her house for lunch. Her daughter Lena, a very nice and beautiful girl with big brown eyes and great hair, sat at the table with us. At her age of twenty-five, she seemed like a schoolgirl. Another creature that felt like a host at the table was a parrot. He sat down on a glass of wine with the intention of bathing, tried all the dishes, sat on Larissa's shoulder, tugging at her ear, took off to a lampshade, hanging over the table and from there landed on her haircut.

We met every day. At the end of the week, I offered her to marry me. Larisa agreed. Having registered our marriage officially, we became husband and wife. I moved to Larisa. There was no wedding. We celebrated this event with a trip to Las Vegas and stayed at the hotel where Larisa's uncle Abe worked. Having retired after serving in the police, he bought a house in Las Vegas but needed to work for additional income.

We spent three amazing days in walks around the city, swam in the pool, and indulged ourselves with delicious dishes in the hotel restaurant. In the evening, we visited all sorts of presentations, moving from one hotel to another, and watched the thrill-seekers rush to the casino to fight for good luck and hope for a big win. I don't know how the playing machines could predict, but judging by the coins that I left in their slots, they understood what kind of a fortunate person is sitting in front of them. Larisa won twenty dollars, and we had something to rejoice because it was the price of four breakfasts in a restaurant.

We took the time to visit the house of her uncle. Unfortunately, his family life with his second wife was unsuccessful. His former partner in the police and now also retired, she showed no concern for her husband. They lived under the same roof, like neighbors tolerating each other. Uncle had free meals at the hotel where he worked because his wife never cooked at home. She spent many days at the casino, leaving her entire pension there. He never talked about his lonely life, but when we came for a visit and found him with a cup of tea and a piece of bread on the table, and his wife in the next room, watching TV with a sandwich in hand from Mac Donald, we did not need explanations.

Two years later, he died of a heart attack while sitting at a table by a glass of unfinished tea. With military honors, he buried in Chicago, where he served as a police officer for many years before he retired.

Larisa decided to sell her apartment and began to look for another one - closer to the place of work. Having a lot of free time, I took an active part and soon Larisa managed to buy a two-story house in Buffalo Grove, the northern suburb of Chicago. After moving to a new place of residence, I began an intensive search for work. I was trying to alleviate Larisa's workload to support our family and had to accept completely unexpected suggestions. At first, it was a small workshop, where for two months, I designed accessories for machines with programmed control. After explaining to the owner that his idea of fixing the machining part was wrong, I lost the job. Then was the sale of meat, walking with the box of the frozen meat from one house to another in the company of young drug addicts. I earned for all-day only eleven dollars instead of promised by the ad in the newspaper twenty dollars an hour. Then I replied to another ad in the newspaper about assembling the furniture.
I bought a box with tools and with my knees on the cold cement floor of the shop's utility room, assembled the furniture exhibits. After three months of work I got a hundred twenty dollars. In both cases, I was a victim of the crooks, who made money and paid me pennies.

I was luckier designing kitchens in small private companies, where the owners wanted me to pay more attention to the art of selling, rather than to design. I worked as a glass cutter and assembled picture frames. The longest was the work on the design of kitchens at Home Depot.

In between work breaks, I did not give up hope of finding a real job. My age was an obstacle. Even where specialists were needed, having learned that I was already over 60 years old, all the conversations boiled down to the fact that I had more qualifications than they needed. I was surprised at the ingenuity to refuse, explaining to me that I know more than they need.

Seeing my problems in looking for work, one of my acquaintances advised me to become an agent for the sale of houses. As proof of the acceptability of his ideas, he stressed the possibility of being independent, having good income, managing time at my discretion, having a lot of contacts with people, and most importantly - there is no limit to the age when applying for this work.

He convinced me. Having passed all the necessary steps to obtain a license for the right to work as an agent, I was hired by one of the companies hired me. But not everything turned out to be in pink color. I had to attend all general meetings, seminars and improvement courses, pay a monthly fee for using the workplace and a computer, and for membership in an organization at different levels — the country and the state. And the most critical thing in this work - to find clients - was my concern.

Plunging into the search for clients, I faced the fierce competition of hundreds of agents from different companies and realized that earning a piece of bread in the field of housing sales is not easy, and even if you find a client, someone from other agencies can easily lure him away. But it did not discourage me. I saw that agents with extensive experience had reliable contacts and a steady income from the sale of houses.

Therefore, I need to follow their example. I began to like my work. First customers and sales strengthened my desire to continue and achieve success.

The company where Larisa worked was close to home. Every morning, the two of us went to a sports club, where after exercising and swimming in the pool, I returned home, and Larisa went to work. This routine has become customary and necessary for both of us.

One of the constant worries of Larisa were frequent trips to the nursing home, where her mother was. Small, but physically able, due to many years of work in the factoryt, and very active in her eighty-two years, she took part in all events. She helped in the kitchen, fed those who could not do on their own, cleaned the tables, and did not forget those who could not visit the dining room. Larisa always brought her something tasty and some pocket money.

The call from the police with the message that her mother is in the hospital was unexpected. Then we got a call from the younger brother Ilya who said that he would come to take us with him. On the way, my brother did not say anything to Larisa. In the police station, we saw her older brother, Grisha. Larisa asked the police officer what happened to her mother. Without answering, he gave to Larisa's brother a piece of paper and said that we should all go to this address in the hospital.

We were met and brought to the next building, on which it written - the morgue. Only here Larisa realized that she had lost her mother and wept inconsolably. The brothers knew earlier, but they did not want to tell her until the last minute, remembering how she was attached to her mother.

It turns out that we carried out the prescribed order of identification at the request of the police. I did not advise Larisa and the brothers to look at what happened to their mother as a result of the accident, saying that it is better for them to remember her as they saw her in life. Together with another relative we confirmed that we do recognize her.

Later we became aware of what happened. After dinner, the mother was going to bring food to the person she was taking care off. She stood at the elevator door, and when the door in front of her opened, she stepped into the void - the elevator cabin was not there. It stopped above her head and the little woman did not notice it. She fell into the elevator shaft from the nineteenth floor. This terrible death shook us all. My wife could not reconcile with the fact that such a terrible fate fell to her mother. Mom buried next to the grave of her father.

Unfortunately, the legal problems associated with the death of the mother broke the all family ties and for many years became an obstacle in our communication with the family of the older brother.

I decided to change the agency where I felt uncomfortable and joined a Russian-language agency founded by Zhana and Misha Goldman.The experience in previous companies helped me quickly master a new market, and soon, I had clients and income. One of these clients was Dr. Dovzhenko. He called our agency and said that he needed our services. Despite the problem with my back which I could hardly straighten after another bout of pain associated with my old spinal injury, I decided to the meet a potential customer - the business matter prevailed over my pain.

I entered the waiting room and, seeing the man in the white coat coming out of the office, introduced myself and said:
"I came at your request, and I am ready to offer you my services with the hope that you will be my client."
Looking at my bent back and the expression on my face, he smiled.

"In my opinion, namesake, you are my client. Come on, go into this room, take off your shirt, and lie down on your stomach," he said, pointing to a high narrow bed with a clean sheet.

His fingers, barely touching my skin, ran along my spine and stopped at waist level. I felt it, as in this place, his palm stopped for a while. He asked me to sit down and, standing in front of me, said:

"You now have inflammation as big as my palm. It is very dangerous. If not cured now, you can remain disabled for life. Tell me how it happened."

I told him about my arrival to South Africa twenty years ago, and about my attempt to lift a heavyweight at the sports club. The treatment of damaged vertebrae was not successful. Since then, from time to time, I suffer from pain in the waist area.

"I can help you," he said, "and heal you in seven daily sessions. Do you agree?"

I nodded my head. "And how much will it cost me?"
"For everyone, the price is $ 2000. But now let's not talk about money. Let's start the treatment."

He led me to another room with special equipment. The assistant brought me a robe and asked to change clothes. I lay on my stomach and felt his fingers wandering around my back, stopped at some point, rubbed it with alcohol, and then followed a tolerable needle prick. Having asked me to lie down for half an hour without rising, the doctor went into the next room, where the patient was waiting for him.

Before I left his room, he warned me to go home and lay for at least two hours, resting and not strain my back.

The other day the procedure was different. Instead of needles, he glued to the points marked by him on the back attachments with wires

I felt tingling at all points, but tolerable. Then another procedure followed. Candles with a copper dotted base he placed on the same locations. When the lit candle became hot, I began to feel a burning sensation on the skin, which intensified and disappeared when the candle extinguished. This procedure went on for seven days.

Before each session, he applied his hand to the spine, checking the amount of inflammation. I carried out all his instructions, but the pain was still there. That's when I came to the last session, and he said I would be forever free from pain, I could not believe. After the usual procedure and the removal of all the candles, he rubbed the entire back with massage oil and began to gently massage and smooth the back muscles. When he finished, he succinctly said:

"You're cured. Go home and be careful with your back. You had a serious injury."

Still not believing and feeling the stiffness in the movements that accompanied me during the entire course of treatment, I carefully got into the car and drove home. Arriving home, I did not immediately pay attention that I got out of the car, without resorting to the usual caution. I walked to the door of the house and noticed with surprise that the pain had disappeared. I rushed to the phone and happily told the doctor about my recovery.
"I saw it and told you after the end of treatment," the doctor replied, "and do not forget that now we can start looking for premises for my business."

The next day, I went to the doctor and asked him to allow me to pay the debt in installments since I do not have such a large amount of money in my bank. He agreed and said that I could only pay him half of the original amount.

Then he invited me to his home. Sometimes I received such invitations from my clients. A large, modern building in which the doctor lived for two years with his family was in one of the expensive areas of our city. He recently returned from work and had dinner. When I appeared, I met his wife and his daughter, a little girl of about the age of five. Then he invited me to dinner together.

We, the agents, usually always refuse such proposals, which go beyond our official relations, but, taking into account that he was my doctor, I agreed. The wife, a tall, slim and beautiful woman, brought another plate and poured a mashed thick vegetable soup. Watching them at home, I noticed a significant difference in their age - the doctor was no more than fifty, and she was no more than thirty-five. After dinner, he invited me to his room and explained the essence of his business. He is going to open the treatment center, and he needs to find a place that is twice the size of what he has. Also, he is looking for a person who will take over the administrative functions of this institution. In the new facility, he will install devices invented in Russia.

These devices are unique and give good results in treatment, but they are expensive and costly, so his second task is to attract capital investors to the business. Early in the morning of the next day, I started checking the market. My colleague in the office, Laura Kramer, asked about my new client and I told her about Dr. Dovzhenko and his idea of a new treatment center.

Laura came to our agency after selling her business in a trade where she worked for several years. She began her working day at five o'clock in the morning and returned home at eight o'clock in the evening, sacrificing life with its benefits and pleasures for the significant income. She managed to develop her business successfully. Then, successfully selling it, no less successfully manifested herself in the sale of the property.

After hearing about the treatment center, Laura said that she had in the past managed a similar department and she would be interested in talking with the doctor about his idea. I gave her Dovzhenko's phone number. They met. Laura Kramer gave him a loan of ten thousand dollars to buy one of the new devices, which he was going to order in Russia. Finding a few places that could be of his interest, we went to see them. On the road, while driving to preview the property, I asked to tell me about himself. Here is the story of the doctor's life.

He was born and lived most of his life in the capital of Moldova – Kishinev, where he received the profession of a medical doctor. He had contacts in some government structures, which allowed him to make trips abroad. In one of these trips, he stayed for a long time in China and Tibet, where he learned the art of acupuncture and spine treatment. When he returned to his homeland, he began to apply his knowledge, and started to heal people suffering from the pain in the spine. The treatment was successful. Doctor Dovzhenko became popular among the population; and as a result, his healing practice brought him considerable income.

Having money, he decided to find a way to use them for investment. Somebody gave him an idea to invest earned money on the farm for growing vegetable products. Then he saw the demand for his products in Moscow and began to supply the market.

Money also brought him contacts among influential people in Kishinev who often gathered at his home, where were beautiful young women invited for the company.

He liked one of them, and they started dating. A ballerina, abandoned by her husband, had a daughter. Dovzhenko was an old bachelor; at the age of forty, he was not married. He was not going to marry again, but when she said that she expects a child from him, he decided he would not abandon his child. They married.

Dovzhenko had long thought about moving to Moscow. He began working in the emergency room at the Sklifosovsky clinic. Tired of constantly intensive labor hours and blood-filled gown, he decided to open his practice. For this purpose, he chose one of the protected buildings in the city, where people could enter only by invitation.

His practice of treating people with spinal problems became well known and brought him a substantial income. He bought a cheap apartment in the center of the city, because the son of a minister, a drug addict, who lived in it, set the fire there, making the apartment uninhabited. Dovzhenko invested a lot of money completely refurbishing it. He used the highest quality materials and made from this apartment a model of modern housing.

His ability to heal people with back problems has become very popular.

Because of his healing skill and popularity, the leader of the Dagestan gang, which collected tribute from all the neighboring businesses, asked Dovzhenko to cure his mother, who suffers from pain in the spine. After her recovery, he, in gratitude for the treatment, promised to fulfill any doctor's request, if he would need it.

Dovzhenko did not need any help from the gang leader and even forgot about his visit. But the unexpected case brought them together again.

One day, the door opened, and three people of an unknown gang entered Dovzhenko's office. They put their Kalashnikov rifles on the table and ordered to get all the money he had in the safe. Taking everything, they asked for the key to his Mercedes and left, saying that they would revisit him again when they need it.

The only thing that confused Dovzhenko was that he could not understand how these people entered the building. It was guarded, had a unique code on the door and a security camera. Without thinking twice, he called his patron Dagestani and told about the robbery.

The next day, the same robbers came to him with an apology. They put the keys to the Mercedes on the table and said that they were ordered to deliver an additional twenty thousand dollars. Calling Dagestani gang leader and thanking for the help, Dovzhenko asked why they brought such a large amount of money that he did not have. He replied that it was their punishment.

It would seem that he could live in peace and continue the successful medical practice. However, the robbery left a sense of uncertainty about the future, which was in the hands of the mafia. An unexpected letter from Turkey invited Dovzhenko to live in the palace with a request to cure a magnate suffering from pain in the spine for many years. The doctor immediately closed his business in Moscow associated with constant danger and accepted the invitation.

The problem with the rich man's spine required a long time treatment. But the doctor has achieved a successful cure even in this challenging case. The grateful Turk asked Dovzhenko to become his private doctor, offering him a separate house on the territory of the palace with a hefty monthly payment, full maintenance, and care. But Dovzhenko could not see himself as a doctor-servant and did not want to give up his medical practice. The whole family flew from Turkey to America as tourists. The right to work as a doctor he could only obtain by passing the exams in English, which he did not know.

Buying a car, renting an apartment, purchasing furniture, computers, daily living expenses, and paying attorney fees for paperwork required money.

There was no income, and the savings began to dry up. Dovzhenko became acquainted with a Russian-speaking doctor who had her own practice. She offered him to work for her without his official registration for the treatment of patients with spinal problems. He worked many hours a day, bringing a significant income to the doctor.

When she paid him a small sum, compare to amount which he brought to the business, he immediately left her, considering himself humiliated and deceived. The next doctor used his skills and paid him not more than the previous one with the only difference that instead of a woman, the doctor was a man.

Dovzhenko felt that he should do something to get rid of the of dishonest people who call themselves doctors. The lawyer prompted him a way out of the situation by starting a business where a doctor's diploma is not required. Using the documents issued to him in China and Tibet as a healer, he should call his practice the natural healing. Dovzhenko did so.

The documents were translated into English and certified by notaries, after which he received official permission. To find a place to start the business was easy. Equipment and necessary materials were purchased. He hired an experienced nurse who was simultaneously performing the administrative functions. After several advertisements, the first patients appeared.

On this Sunday, we spent a lot of time inspecting the premises before reaching any conclusion.

We sat in a café, and I listened with interest to the story of his former life, travels and, finally, his practices in America. A cup of coffee cheered us up, and our conversation in a half-empty cafe, which was unusual for Sunday, allowed us to relax and to know each other better.

His story confirmed my opinion - Dovzhenko is an excellent doctor and a gullible person. With all my heart, I wanted to help him. We often met, discussed my searches, and I became welcome at his home.

At my next visit, his mood seemed to me not quite normal - he was pensive and sad. Answering my question, he said that Russian doctors, with whom he worked, complaint against him. They accused him of treating the patients, which can only be done by a licensed doctor. Besides, they wrote that he was doing surgeries that did not correspond to his status as a healer.

"As I understand it, these doctors, mainly treating Russian-speaking patients, noticed that I was successfully curing without drugs and surgical intervention, decided to get rid of my competition. Yesterday there was a commission. They searched all the rooms looking for surgical instruments. They checked the patient registration books. This intervention in my office showed how dirty doctors could be," he said with a sigh, "I haven't met such mud, yet."

"What are you going to do?" I asked.

"Continue to heal, help people get rid of pain. Besides, I have to support my family."

Having experienced his treatment, which saved me from many years of pain in the spine, I strongly recommended his practice to two friends of mine.

Rarely, it is possible to find a man in old age without problems with the spine. Older people like to talk about their illnesses. Naturally, the news about the miraculous healer spread resonably quickly and his office was alwaus full of the patients. For a while, we stopped searching for premises.

Laura Kramer, having learned about the complaint of doctors and the troubles that they brought Dovzhenko, changed her mind about working with him. She demanded to return her debt.

Dovzheko canceled the contrast with suppliers and returned her money.

The unexpected visit of my son from Cape Town made me happy.
He had already graduated from the university, received an invitation to work at one of the publishing houses, but decided before starting to work, to see me in America. On the first day of his visit, we went to the store to buy him a warm jacket: he forgot the warm clothes at home.

Together, we went to Chicago, which is about an hour drive from our house in Buffalo Grove. It was too cold and windy to browse along the streets. In spite of the cold weather, we tried to show Ami as much as possible: we visited the museum with the famous Chagall's stained-glass windows; had dinner at Russian cuisine restaurant, and after a brisk walk through the evening streets of the city, went home.

We tried to give him an idea of the place where we live and to answer his questions regarding the American way of life. In turn, I wanted to know what impression he had of what he saw, and whether he had a desire to move to America. No, he had no such desire.

Now I, in turn, could learn about all aspects of his life. I was worried about the situation in Africa, and I wanted to know about his plans for the future. Son's logical reasoning and his confidence in the future sounded convincing, but this did not reassure me. America, by its economic sanctions policies, forced the government of De Klerk to get rid of apartheid. America supported the new President Nelson Mandela. But there were millions of young people without needed skills and education, and millions of people continued to live in self-made huts and did not have a job. It was, by my opinion, the biggest problem. The power in the country transferred to the party of Mandela's people. In the ecstasy of redistributing portfolios among those who began to run this country, the promises which government gave to people, - jobs and housing - were forgotten.

In South Africa, the capitalist system has not changed, but it was not working for the people. It was in the hands of the corrupt government. During the apartheid regime, millions of black

Africans were not allowed to stay in the city after work. They had to return to their huts every day. Now they were able to walk freely through the streets of the town day and night, where they saw in the shops the food and things that they could not afford. As a result of this situation, there were robberies of the shops, banks, and people, and even murders.

A white man to appear in the city center by day time was like a car to cross the intersection on the red light in a traffic.

I remember the attack on Russian sailors by a black gang of the thieves. They took the cameras and bit the sailors up. It happened at the center of city, near the hotel the sailors stay. One day walking in the center of the town, a friend of mine almost lost, torn out of his hands a briefcase with documents. The robber was not lucky, being in good shape, my friend managed to catch up with him and got his briefcase back.

The fear of unexpected attacks and robberies gave rise to the whole security industry, and people were forced to pay for security in their own home. Seven years have passed since the government of Mandela came to power, in which there was only one white minister - the former president. But in one of the wealthiest countries in Africa the population had no work and no money.

My son had no desire to immigrate to America, because he lived his entire adult life in Africa. There are his friends and his beloved city, Cape Town. There is the ocean and his water gliding board, without which he cannot imagine himself. There is his work, of which he dreamed, and there he saw his future.

The Negro population, deprived of the ordinary conditions of life under apartheid, needed housing, work, medical institutions, accessible schools, and universities.
Not only had the well-being of the population depended on the achievement of these goals, but also the peaceful and secure environment in the country.

After my son's departure, I returned to my business. Boris Dovzhenko greeted me joyfully and said that he had found a partner for the further development of his business. His partner was a woman of indefinite occupations. She and her husband called themselves business people. Boris did not know where she got the information about his idea of the treatment center. But she assured him that with her connections, she would certainly make the business prosperous. She takes over all the advertising, patients and administrative work, leaving Dovzhenko only treatment. It was what he was looking for successful business.

To the next meeting, we went together. Their two-story house struck by the size and claim to luxury. On all walls hung the paintings in gold frames, and I paid attention to the skill of the artist. By style and performance, it was clear that all the paintings belonged to the brush of the same talented artist. On the floor were porcelain vases with artificial flowers. Expensive carpets lay on the floor, and in a large room with a two-story ceiling, there were leather armchairs and a coffee table. The woman's name was Nellie. Middle-aged, with a sleek face and traces of cosmetic wherever she was able to apply, she greeted us with a friendly, charming smile, as if we were the most welcome guests.

Her husband met us coldly, businesslike, and put on the table in front of Dovzhenko a sheet of paper with a partnership agreement. Knowing that Dovzhenko does not know English, they translated to him the contents of the document into Russian and then handed him a pen to sign. Then Nellie said that she had already found a place for the business in a very convenient area of Chicago, not far from the city center.

"We can go and see it," she said, "and at the same time I need to find a one-room apartment in the same area so that I can use it if I have to stay late in the city for business."

The street of the city where the future practice would be located turned out to be in the area of numerous restaurants, cafes, various institutions, and intensive transport traffic. My first impression was not the best because we had to search for parking for a long time. It was already a red flag in relation to future clients' convenience to find a parking place.

The place turned out to be small in size, and it needed to be completely reworked, and therefore invested a lot of money, having no idea about the number of future customers. While there was work on the reconstruction of the premises, I managed to find an apartment for Nelly on the adjacent street, and she bought it right away. A month later, the place was ready for business. I liked the design style, the quality of painting, the reception room, and two offices – for each owner, a massage room, a beauty salon, and several treatment rooms for Dovzhenko.

However, the choice of location had a negative impact on the income of his practice. With the move to Chicago, the doctor lost almost all potential clients from the Northern suburbs. Most of them could not go for treatment due to heavy traffic and numerous traffic jams that made traveling to Chicago tedious. Only a few people appeared because they were brought by family members. Parking for cars was almost impossible to find. This, too, alienated many who wished to use his services. Only now Dovzhenko realized that he was fascinated by the plans of his partner, he did not think that he was losing his main clients. He could only hope for the promise of Nelly, assuring him in an endless stream of patients. But they were not. Nellie appeared at work, went to the massage room, where she was given a massage, then switched to a cosmetic one. Having finished beauty, she sat down in her office and chatted with her friends, talking about her business. The new partnership did not bring any revenues. Dovzhenko was patiently waiting for the fulfillment of promises from Nelly.

Our meetings became rare, so I was delighted with his call and the desire to see me at home. His first request was to find an apartment for the family closer to work. The second request was unexpectedly strange.

"I want to ask you, as a friend, to help me solve the problem with the eldest daughter of my wife. She is 16 years old, does not want to study, and is unlikely she would graduate from school, she does not help her mother at home, and she comes home late. She has a beautiful face; she is tall, like her mother. She is skinny, which is now in fashion. I had an idea to send her to a modeling agency. If she is accepted, she will start earning, she will be busy, and we will have fewer problems with her at home."

I could not refuse Dovzhenko, especially since after several sessions, he recently cured my foot, which sometimes was painful, and I limped while walking - also a result of a former spinal injury. He refused to accept the payment for the treatment, despite the decrease in income.

I contacted several agencies and started driving the future advertising star to Chicago. In two places, she got refused immediately. In the next agency, an elderly woman, after carefully listening to me, and I introduced myself as a relative, agreed to a trial for a review. A photographer was invited, and for several hours they took pictures of the future star in one of the places in the city. Then I was billed for the work of the photographer that I paid.

About a month has passed. The owner of the agency called me to the conversation and said.

"Your girl has no emotion in her eyes, which is not necessary for working in an advertising agency, but she also does not make an impression and lacks femininity in the figure. In my opinion, she has very little intelligence, although not many of those who work for me own this quality. She does not have the feeling of the cat walking, necessary for the demonstration of clothes, and our lessons have not yielded positive results. What do you think about it?"

What could I think when she was absolutely right. I knew this for a long time. I saw and knew much more, but I could not let down my friend, whom I promised to help, and asked this smart woman to give this worthless and stupid pretender to modeling one more chance. She agreed.

With this encouraging news, I came to Dovzhenko. He looked depressed and unwell. To my silent gaze, he responded with a heavy sigh and shared his bitter thoughts with me.

The partnership with Nelly did not bring any results, except for a few of her acquaintances, she could not find any patients, and the majority of those in need of treatment came from those northern suburbs of Chicago, where he began his independent practice. Each visit to her office Nelly started with a massage and manicure. The specialists working there had nothing to do with Dovzhenko's company and paid only for the rented premises. They had their patients, and they were busy. Nellie never paid them for massages and manicures, and they complained to Dovzhenko with a request to pay for their work. Nellie was now in Paris. Checking the bank account, he found that at the expense of the company she was buying clothes, perfume, paying for a hotel and restaurants there, without saying anything to him. There was not enough money in the bank account for paying the rent. From the first days of joint work, she said that she lacked a few dollars and she would take them from the cashier. Being sure that this is really about a few dollars, and according to the terms of the agreement, she was responsible for managing the finances of their joint company, he trusted her.

Only now he realized that behind the document of the partnership, there was a scammer, who ran her hand into the company's cash, using his, hard-earned money. Their business existed only six months and brought half the income that he had before. He further explained that he had met with a patient who had told him about the family of his partners, who conducted their trade and business ties with Russia. The containers with goods that they did not pay for, were sold. But sent back pennies, explaining that they could not sell anything. They received a container of works by a famous artist, promising to put them for sale in the Chicago Gallery, while they arranged a gallery at home. This information confirmed what he was afraid to admit to himself - he was used and deceived.

I thought about my past. We, two namesakes, are so different, and our fate is remarkably similar. For me, it's all in the past, and he has it all in the present. I was genuinely worried about his loss in the business. He delivered the joy of recovery to many patients. Only those who had no morals, soul, and conscience could use and brazenly deceive such a kind doctor and man.

Nellie returned from Paris and told him that she had the right to use the company's money and does not have to report to him about personal expenses. Then followed a trial by the owner of the premises for non-payment of rent. The contract was signed for three years. There was a termination of the partnership and the declaration of bankruptcy.

In the newspaper appeared dirty article where Nelly accused Dovzhenko of having tricked her into business by deception and trying to spoil her reputation as an honest and successful woman in business. She also said that clients did not want to come because Dovzhenko does not know how to treat the spine problems.

I visited Dovzhenko often, knowing he needed to share with someone his pain and thoughts. He had to part with a house he could not maintain, and rented a small apartment in Chicago, next to which is a small room he accepted random patients.

His wife left him and went to live with another man. Wife's oldest daughter-model got married a wealthy Arab.

The last time I saw Dovjenko, he was very sick. The tragedy of his broken life resulted in the deterioration of his health condition undermined by diabetes. He returned to his father in Moldova.

The period of my acquaintance and friendship with Boris Dovzhenko lasted more than three years.

I have the warmest memories for him, as a doctor who brought the joy of recovery to thousands of patients, and as a kind and decent person.

My sister accidentally found out the family of our father's nephew Zelik lives in Chicago. Such proximity and the opportunity to see them did not make me wait long, and I together with Larisa came with the visit. Zelik's wife Galya Kapilevich, her son Fima with his wife Lilya have recently come to America from Lithuania.

I remember Zelik and his wife Galya came to see our family in Minsk when we lived on Zamkovaya Street. They stopped on their way to Lithuania, where Zelik got a job as a chief accountant. Fima was then only a few months old, and Galya was a blooming young woman with a healthy blush on her cheeks.

With their arrival, we were seven, but we managed to stay overnight all in one room.

Fima and his wife worked and were looking into buying an apartment. When they learned that I was working as a real estate agent, they were delighted and asked me to find the property in Chicago near Lake Michigan. Soon I did find a condo in an excellent complex on the shore of the lake. Galya was already retired. Our visits continued until my move to California.

While in America, I tried to find my father's brothers, who emigrated from Minsk to America in 1913. My mother told me about them before I was leaving for Israel. All my queries did not bring any results, and I stopped searching.

But the meeting with my first cousin, the daughter of my father's sibling, who immigrated to America in 1913, was completely unexpected.

Her son, Adam Brown, while visiting with the children of the Holocaust Museum in Washington, accidentally saw a photo of the small town Logoisk. Among the Holocaust victims, he saw the name Kapilevich, his mother's maiden last name. His search began with this photo.

First, he found the Kosovsky family, our relatives from Logoisk, who lived in New Jersey. By coincidence, Adam lived in the same city. From them, he learned about my sister Dora and me.

The call of Adam from New Jersey was no longer unexpected. Adam said that his entire family, together with his mother, are going to visit us in Chicago. I was glad and told him about the wedding of my niece Olga which coincided with the time of our upcoming meeting.

On the day of their arrival, we met in the hotel lobby, where they stayed. I was looking forward to seeing my cousin, the closest relative in America. Before leaving Minsk, my mother gave me the names of two fathers' brothers with the hope that I would be able to find them from Israel. In America, my search also ended without results because my uncles changed their names.

You can imagine my joy at the meeting. Having rushed to meet a tall, gray-haired woman, I hugged her and kissed her. She freed herself from my hands, stepped back, and looked at me with unkindness as if I had done something improper. Her displeased gesture struck me. From that moment, neither she nor I made attempts to be near and talk.

Her son Adam, vivacious, and friendly person continued to acquaint his mother with my wife, but my joy went out. We sat down at a cafe table, not knowing where to start. She, too, did not feel very confident, stunned by my gust of joy. Beatrice, that was my cousin's name, looked at all of us, with whom she had kind of relation, with the interest of a tourist, no more.

Perhaps 35 years ago, when my father and her father were still alive, this meeting would have been entirely different. Adam, the opposite of his mother, was thrilled. He was the connecting link that made this unpredictable event possible.

The next day we sat together at the wedding table, and Dora was able to see her cousin too, and Olga had the opportunity to know her aunt. The joy of Adam, proud that he was able to arrange such a long waited encounter, was natural.

I never met my cousin again, but I heard from Adam that they continued to travel, amusing themselves during an encounter with the relatives. They visited the family of Fima Kapilevich in Chicago and met my son Ami Kapilevich in South Africa. Then went to visit my cousin Raya Gurvich in Israel and met Zhenya Tarnorutskaya in Leningrad. They saw my cousin, also Boris, in Minsk and were going to meet with Arkady Danichev in Moscow. As a result of many years of work, Adam created a family three on the Gini, Internet program, which he dedicated to his mother.

The contacts with relatives in America could be dangerous for people living in the Soviet Union. My father understood it and, therefore, never tried to find his brothers in America. Did the fathers' brothers try to find our family in Minsk? Did their children try to find their relatives in Minsk? I will never know. Adam Brown managed to travel to Russia because the Soviet Union did not exist anymore. A lawyer by education and a successful owner of a real estate business, he spent most of his time searching for relatives to keep these contacts for the future generation. It was a work that required patience, perseverance, and enthusiasm.

I never met my cousin again. She never called me, and I never regretted. She was very wealthy. Her husband left her a multi-million dollar business in America. Naturally, most of her inheritance passed to her son, Adam Brown.

In December 1998, my wife and I arrived in Israel at the Bar Mitzvah of my grandson, Eitan. This event my daughter and her husband decided to celebrate in Israel at the Wailing Wall. The uncle of my daughter, Matvey, also came to this event.

I must pay tribute to him for the help that he provided me in Minsk and the participation that he showed by accepting us when we immigrated to Israel.

For many years after that, we did not communicate. It confirms the point of view that distance destroys family ties, and with close friends, one often feels close like with relatives.

Zion, who had successfully settled in Johannesburg, always tried to visit his brothers and sister in Israel. This important event gave him the opportunity for the whole large family and many relatives to gather together. I was pleased to see them again. I had respect for them from the first days of my acquaintance.

During our short visit, I wanted to find time to see Oleg, Ida's elder brother. But Matvey, his younger brother, said that he didn't remember the address. And he didn't advise me to go there, because Oleg is very sick and unable to meet anyone. I did not understand his advice but hoping my other trips to Israel would soon follow; I did not insist.

We managed to visit Geta Rieger and her family. She was glad to see us, but mainly she was happy to see Orit and her children. We went to a cafe and Geta was able to learn about everything related to the life of my daughter in South Africa.
After all, Sveta, she continued to call her the same name as in Russia, was for Geta the connection with the memory of her best friend, Ida.

Three months after returning from Israel, we made a trip to Spain. Why Spain? Probably because we knew from school years about the famous commander Hannibal, a talented and intelligent military strategist who fought against the Roman Empire.

We knew the name of Christopher Columbus, who carried out the first Spanish expedition, discovering the New World; the name of Magellan, who made the first round-the-world journey. Who has not read the book of Cervantes - Don Quixote and Sancho Panza? Who has not heard the names of such great artists as Goya, Velasquez, Rubens, and Picasso?

We knew about the 1936 civil war between the Republicans and the Phalangists of General Franco. We remember Dolores Ibarruri with her famous call - No Pasaran! Who does not know what a Flamenco dance or Bullfight is? We admire the poems of Garcia Lorca and the extraordinary voices of the most famous singers - Placido Domingo, José Carreras, and Julio Iglesias. It is impossible in a few words to mention everyone who made the world, art, architecture, progress in various sectors of life more vibrant and better.

We wanted to know and see firsthand how this country is living now. Without thinking and not spending time on the best acquaintance with the weather and recommendations of friends, we decided to go without using the excursion service. We were in such a hurry that I forgot the camera, without which our tour of Spain would be incomplete, and bought another one at the airport before departure.

So, we flew out of cold and windy Chicago, to awaiting us the warm climate of sunny Spain.

Spain, known in the past as one of the most significant colonial powers of the world, owned land in North and South America, Asia, Africa, the archipelagoes of the Pacific Ocean, lands in France, Italy, and Germany.

Therefore, Spain was called "the State over which the sun never sets." The conquistadors of Spain destroyed the empires of the Inca and Aztec. The Spanish fleet dominated on the routs to all continents, filling the country's treasury with goods and jewels from all the subject's lands and colonies.

In the following centuries and continuous wars, Spain lost its former status as the greatest empire and lost almost all conquests. Currently, Spain is a country with a developed industry, modern technology, and well-developed transport, combined with a well-preserved legacy of architects of the past and amazing modern buildings.

We started our first acquaintance with Spain from Madrid. Naturally, in each hotel, there is information about the city's remarkable sights and recommendations on the tourist routs. We stopped at a hotel near the Alka-la Gate on Independence Square. This place is considered the main gates of the city; built by order of King Charles the Third according to the design of the architect Francesca Sabatini. Not far from the entrance, was a large city park with a lake and a monument to King Alfons. Next to the square was Alcala Street, the longest street in Madrid.

Going a little further, we came to the central square of Madrid - the Puerta Del Sol, paved with granite slabs. The bronze plate, mounted among the tiles, serves as the starting point for road distances to all cities in Spain. In the center of the square is the equestrian statue of Charles the Third and a beautiful fountain. The first gas lantern installed in Spain on the same square, and this lantern on the pole stands on the square today. From this square began the first horse trail, and later the first trams and the first metro line. Here the first electric lighting was made, and the first car drove from here to the city streets. Continuing our walk, we reached the Main Square with the Monument to King Felipe the Fourth. It surrounded by multi-story buildings with balconies, from which residents watched royal ceremonies, knights' tournaments and public burning alive of heretics convicted by the Inquisition. Sights followed one after another. It seemed the whole city is a giant museum, and it was no time to stay on one thing only. Every street, every square, every building was an unusual combination of the art of the past centuries and modernity. Opera Theatre. King's Park. Royal Palace and the ceremony of the guards' change. Opposite the Palace is the building where Velazquez lived. There was a cafe in this building, and we sat down to relax over a cup of strong coffee. The Plaza of Spain and the Monument to Cervantes, at the foot of which are the bronze figures of Don Quixote and Sancho Panza. Cibeles Square with fountains in the form of chariots, lined with lions and panthers. Neptune Fountain. We walked around the city, tirelessly. Then we went to the nearest cafe to have a bite and rest our legs, which were not used to intense load after many years of sitting in a car.

The next day we dedicated to the Prado Museum - one of the most famous museums of art. Not far from the entrance we saw a modest bronze Goya monument on a pedestal. The ground floor met us with paintings by Raphael and Flemish artists who worked in Spain. Then we went up to the next level, where we saw the works of Rubens and Van Dyck - followed by the paintings of the Venetian school - Titian, Veronese, and the exhibition of paintings by El Greco, Ribera, Velazquez, and Goya. The names of painters from Germany, England, and France, were less known to us. We understood that such rare opportunity we should not miss, and we did not want to have a break for lunch. We could not tear ourselves away from the paintings in the semi-dark, quiet halls of the galleries. The Museum employees were closely watching everyone, forbidding to take photos with camera flashes. We made hundreds of pictures which I now looked through in the album to refresh my memory and once again see what left a lasting impression on us. When we left the Prado, it was already getting dark. We returned home and passed through the same squares, now illuminated by night lanterns and seemingly no less beautiful than in daylight.

We continued to tour the country as planned. Our next stop was in Sevilla. This city is considered the most beautiful after Madrid. "Whoever did not see Seville, did not see a miracle," says a Spanish proverb, so we decided to visit this beauty.

The Arabs conquered the city in 712, then Seville was captured by the Berbers. More than five hundred years passed, and in 1248 the Spaniards returned the city to themselves. After the discovery of America, Seville became the principal trading port of the Spanish Empire. A variety of goods brought to the port of Seville and then sent on ships to America and other colonies, returning loaded with gold, silver, and other valuables. Today, Seville is the center of art and tourism.

In small by population city, a large number of the temples complements the picture of the antiquity and the change of religions.

As in Madrid, there are a lot of squares and fountains. To this day they supplied with water from a viaduct built during the time of Rome by Julius Caesar. The impressive Seville Cathedral, created by the Spanish king on the site of the mosque, is the third-largest cathedral in the world. The palace-fortress Alcazar, built by the Arabs, later became the residence of the Spanish kings for 700 years. This palace combines the ancient architecture of the castle with flower alleys, gurgling streams, water pools, and fruit trees – all enclosed in the stone walls. The castle houses the Archives of India, which contains historically valuable documents of the Spanish colonies and conquests, as well as the personal journal of Christopher Columbus. Here, in Seville, we saw the ship of Magellan, on which he made his world tour. He seemed so small to us that it was difficult to imagine how he could make such a long and dangerous trip. Plaza De Spain, it appeared, conveyed to us the spirit of past centuries. We completed a trip around the city with a tour on a small tourist boat along the Guadalquivir River.

Our next stop was Toledo, a small city in which El Greco lived and worked from 1577 until his death in 1614. His works located in various places in the city. El Greco lived in the Jewish part of the town. In the house-museum of El Greco, we saw his famous painting - View of Toledo. His pictures are also in the Museum Santa Cruz and the Hospital Tavera. In the latter are his Holy Family and the Baptism of Christ.

Toledo was conquered by Muslims in 712, in the same year as Seville. The revival of the city and its development began with the reign of Alphonse of Castile. Even then, Toledo became famous for the art of manufacturing steel products, especially in the manufacture of valued swords. The Cathedral of Saint Mary, the main cathedral of the country, which was under construction for 267 years, is also a museum and an architectural monument. This cathedral contains many masterpieces, including paintings by El Greco and Titian. Among the many chapels of the Temple, I was most astounded by its beauty and the unusually complex performance of Capella Transparante, created by Narcisco Tome. I stopped, attracted by the exceptionally soft and at the same time bright lighting of the entire baroque hall. I could not move for a long time until I felt Larisa's hand taking me away from this beauty.

The church of San Juan de Los Reyes with traces of architecture, in which the influence of Arab culture felt, is beautifully preserved to our time.

Our visit to the Alcazar fortress once again reminded us of the Spain events in 1936. About a thousand supporters of Franco, including women and children, took refuge in the walls of this fortress. They defended themselves for 70 days from the attacks by republicans who bombarded the fort with guns and bombed from the air, almost destroying it. The help of the troops of General Varela saved the captives from destruction.

With interest and sorrow, we walked around the Del Transito Synagogue, commissioned by Samuel Levy, treasurer, lawyer, and diplomat in the service of King Pedro Castile. Later, part of the synagogue bought by El Greco, where now is his museum. After the expulsion of Jews from Spain in 1492, the synagogue ceased to exist. The building occupied by the monastery.

We have heard so much about Granada that it would be unforgivable not to visit it. This city was the last stronghold of Islam on the peninsula. In January 1492, Mohammed the Twelfth capitulated to the army of King Ferdinand and the Arabs were driven out to North Africa, where they accepted in Morocco. On March 31, 1492, in the Grenada Palace of Al Amber, King Ferdinand and Queen Isabella signed the famous decree on the expulsion of Jews from the territory of Spain. The descendants of Jews expelled from Spain and Portugal began to be called Sephardic because of the closeness of their everyday language, Ladino, to Spanish. Seven years later, in 1499, ten thousand treatises on Islamic theology and ancient manuscripts were burned on the central square in Granada at the decree of the archbishop. The Jewish quarter of La Hurdia in the city destroyed.

We visited the castle of Al Ambra, the infamous decree of the expulsion of Jews. Now it is a museum of Islamic architecture. Here among the fountains and water channels, the play of light in the spray of fountains and blooming flower beds, in the silence of the inner courtyards, the fate of the Spanish Jewish population was decided with a stroke of a pen.

The last tour of our trip to Spain brought us to Barcelona. Barcelona - the capital of Catalonia, was rebuilt by Hannibal. Yes, the most famous Hannibal whose name I have already mentioned. The second-largest city in Spain enjoys the attention of tourists for a good reason.

In Barcelona, lived and worked Pablo Picasso, Jean Miro, Salvador Dali and the eminent architect Antoni Gaudi; his extraordinary architectural complexity of the project - the Temple of the Holy Family. He spent 40 years on its construction which he could not finish before the end of his life. We saw it only outside because during our visit it was closed under reconstruction.

In the "Quarter of the Disagreement" we were able to get acquainted with his world-famous "Casa Balló" - the House of Bones, as they call it, and saw near his other building - "Casa Mila," or - the Quarry. In Barcelona, there are many old quarters with narrow dark streets, one of which we visited the Picasso

Museum, which located in an ancient palace of the 15th century. Of the 20 thousandth collection works by Picasso, in this small museum was a private collection, which he presented to his friend Haime Sabates.

After narrow streets and houses smelling of antiquity, we again found ourselves on the boulevards and streets of this merry city, resembling Europe rather than Spain. By the way, singer Jose Carreras lives in this city.

In the string of tourists and local citizens, we walked along the boulevard Rambla. In the middle of the avenue, in the alley, people of the town sat on the benches and rested. Some of them had conversations or dozed. We paid attention to many artists of all genres in the form of fixed statues.

The next busy street called Princess, with many shops in the quarter of La Ribera, stretched to the sea.

We climbed Manjuik Hill overlooking the city and the port. Unexpectedly, we saw on the hill a well preserved ancient Jewish cemetery. It was a contrast to the Jewish cemeteries in our former country, which were destroyed and desecrated, and on the graves of the victims of the Holocaust, no mentioning that they were Jews.

Jews appeared in Barcelona after the destruction of the Temple by the Romans, and they became a vibrant community, making a significant contribution to the science and education of Spain. Subsequent rulers of Catholic Spain subjected the Jewish population to extermination. Jews were burned on the bonfires, forcibly subjected to baptism. The Christian mob destroyed the Jewish ghetto.

We traveled through many cities, and we saw the traces of the Jewish presence, but we did not see a single active synagogue.

Before leaving, we decided to buy a few items to have a tangible memory of our trip. In the Picasso Museum, we purchased a porcelain set of coffee cups with a series of nude drawings by Picasso. And as a gift to our Lena, we got a copy of one of his works - beautiful picture. Then we went to the ceramic shop in the main street. We liked the ceramic plates, vases, and candlesticks. We inspected all the windows and shelves, trying to find something reminiscent of the Jewish past of Spain. To our question, the shop owner, the young man replied unintuitively -

"We have nothing for Jews in our store for sale."

Going to Spain, we did not pursue our goal to find traces of the Jewish population. We went to see Spain, but what we saw by chance, showed us the fate of our people and the tragedy that they had to experience, starting from ancient times.

After 467 years after the expulsion from Spain, the Jews who settled in Europe and Russia were again subjected unknown by the scale and cruelty extermination by Hitler's Germany. Millions of Jews killed, burned, strangled and murdered in concentration camps of death and the ghettos created in Europe in the occupied territory of the Soviet Union. Seventy years have passed since the end of the war and the defeat of fascist Germany; tens of millions of lives perished. The horrors of the Inquisition and the victims of the Holocaust would forever remind about the unfair fate of the Jewish people. In spite of repression and humiliation, Jews gave the world their best people and made an immeasurable contribution to the better future of humanity.

In 1948, on the ancestral land of the Jews was created their State - Israel. Jews have found their homeland.

We were so busy traveling and getting acquainted with the history of Spain, that we did not think at all about ourselves. We did not take warm things with us, hoping for sunny weather. Cold and harsh winds led to severe colds, and we were leaving home with high fever and downright sick. Larisa lost her voice and could not talk. At the Chicago airport, she aroused suspicion when checking documents. Because she could not answer questions of the person checking our passports, I had to intervene and explain the reason.

After arrival, we have been ill for quite a long time, but the reward was the unforgotten monuments of antiquity and unforgettable beauty of the country that managed to preserve them. Four albums of photographs taken in the cities we visited and several copies of paintings from the Prado Museum remind us of our trip through Spain.

Our treatment of the cold took time, and we still were coming to our senses after the trip, when Ami and his childhood friend arrived. They spent whole days on trips around the city and organized excursions, and managed to see quite a lot, even more than Larisa and I could show them. I looked at the young couple and thought about how fortunate they are. Staying true to school friendship and mutual desire – what could be more reliable for a future family.

But the development of their relationship was not consistent with the wishes of her parents. After visiting us, Ami spent several months in Florida in the family of his girlfriend and returned to Cape Town. The girl's parents decided to interrupt their relationship. In their opinion, Ami's profession could not give their daughter the level of life they wanted for her. I was offended by this statement. The girlfriend's mother dared to tell me that my son does not have any profession needed. I was not upset.

On the contrary, I realized that my son had avoided possible future humiliations in the family of millionaires. I believed in my son professional abilities to build the future he deserve as a decent and honest man – the unacceptable qualities in the family of his now ex-girlfriend's, envious and greedy parents.

Lena found a job in California, but she was missing her mother, and she found a way out of this situation. Working at Stanford University as a programmer, she found a job for her programmer mom. At the same university, only in a different department and with a wage higher than the one Larisa had. I liked the California climate and agreed with the move. Larisa lived temporary at daughter's apartment, as it was not far from work, and I started preparing our house for sale. A few months later, after selling the home, I arrived in California. Larisa at this time, alreadybought an apartment. Bright, all sun-drenched, brand new apartment in the small cozy town of Los Gatos, I liked. The new furniture on a snow-white carpet, equipped a kitchen and a bathroom, transformed our home and I found that we made a successful purchase.
To obtain a license to work in California, I had to re-take exams. It was not easy, but I passed the exam and started to work in one of the local companies. The property market was at its high - homes sold for unbelievable for me prices.

I, as a beginner, did not have any contacts and understood that it would take a lot of time to enter the market, which was conquered by agents for a long time. But I did not lose hope that having previous experience, I would succeed.

I noticed some potential sellers and buyers often ignore me. One, an obvious chauvinist, even declared that he was not satisfied with my English. Snobbery was particularly evident among buyers of multi-million dollar homes. They could not afford to give business to a person whose name in the market is unknown to them. In my previous practice of selling houses in the Chicago areas, I have not seen anything like this.

Gradually, among the emigrants, I was able to see the attention to myself and began to work with them. They appreciated my help. A year later, I started selling and had a few sales of expensive houses. But it was not easy for me to compete with agents who entered the market decades ago and did not allow anyone to their conquered territories. One of the successful agents of our company in the conversation with me said. "Boris, at your age, I would not try to become an agent for the sale of houses. It takes years of work and contacts among the population to have customers. I was born here, studied and my family is in the same business. You waste your time here."

Besides my age, with the rest of his speech, I did not agree. I liked the work, and I felt that I could achieve success.

Suddenly, the unexpected collapse of the real estate market shook my confidence and deprived me of working with clients for six months. Clients have disappeared. To go on with their lives was no problem to those agents whose pockets tightly packed from the previous sales.

Larisa worked hard and, after returning from work, she often worked at home after midnight, solving programming problems. In the morning, it was taking her an hour and a half on the way to work. She was the only programmer who did twice the amount of the programs compare to other people in her department, and better than others.

Such intensive working environment lasted for a year and a half. Larisa was proud of her success and continued to work hard, evoking the envy of other employees, who corrected her English in retaliation.

Quite unexpectedly, when the project came to an end, the department was closed. The loss of work was unanticipated and frightening against the background of the financial instability of the market. Larisa, terrified of the situation in which we both found ourselves, suddenly lost ground and confidence in the future. But most of all, what hurt her, were the lies and deceptions of the Stanford administration. They attracted her with a high salary, the promises of the permanent job and secure environment; even paid the transfer from Chicago.

The depression severely damaged her health. Our budget has suffered immensely.

It was necessary to pay off a loan from a bank to secure our home and pay all other expenses that we easily managed before she lost her job. I had income from the sale of houses, but it was not constant, although it helped.

Our family thought about how to return Larisa health and confidence in her capabilities. It was the time of the worst financial market in the country. The property market was down. Thousands of programmers looked for employment in the different fields of industry. Taking into consideration the high unemployment in the country, her return to programming was improbable, and out of the question.

We came to the conclusion that it was necessary to use her other talents and qualities, in which she had no shortage - one of these talents – the ability to bake. Not only our family but also many friends and acquaintances got pleasure from her delicious cakes.

Larisa agreed. According to her recipe, she made a product that was not on the market. It looked like a small ball and included a lot of ingredients, including chocolate and nuts. Making was not an easy process. The unusually delicious ball could deliver a lot of pleasure to lovers of coffee or wine.

Larisa's daughter gave the name, Orb, to a new product. I started introducing our product to cafe owners. The name of the product was puzzling. Some of the cafe owners did not want to taste it. But those who dared were surprised and asked what it was off and took for sale. We received regular orders because the customers liked the delicious Orb. Because I was the only one in the family who could freely use the time, I began to distribute this product. I had to combine trips to sell the product with my functions of selling houses. I also helped with the purchase of the necessary ingredients and assisted in the process of making the product. Also, I was doing the delivery and receiving payments. As a result, my property sales suffered a lot. But I wanted to help my wife, seeing how hard she works and how happy she is, knowing how popular her product. Some time passed, and the cafe owners started asking if we had other products for sale. There was no problem at all. Cakes and bakery products had no less success. Larisa rented a professional kitchen, hired an assistant, and bought necessary equipment. We began to think about special packaging, but could not afford because of the high cost. Three years have passed. People were buying our products. But due to the high price of primary components and unproductive manual labor, incomes were meager. We just paid off the expenses and were busy. Some cafes were closed, or owners changed, and our orders decreased, and some business owners demanded lower our prices when buying our products. When we saw that our time and efforts do not bring income, we closed the business. Tried to sell the remaining equipment, but failed. Then we donated most of it to a charitable organization.

The most important achievement, in spite of the failure, was Larisa ability to overcome the loss of her beloved programming work. Soon she returned to another occupation that she had before arriving to America - the profession of an economist.

I did not lose contact with my son, and we regularly talked. He was pleased with his work as a journal editor, and I was glad that he had a girlfriend with whom he had a mutual and happy relationship. Therefore, the invitation to a wedding in Cape Town did not surprise me. Before my flight to South Africa, my son told me.

"Dad, I'm sure you will like Michelle. He was right. Tall, strong built, with smiling blue eyes on her freckled face, she hugged me at our meeting, and I felt her sincere joy and kindness. I was incredibly glad that my son made the right choice in his life. Her rather poor parents had a small farm, on which their son helped them. Three daughters lived separately. Two of them came to the wedding from abroad, where they worked under the contract.

My son had already prepared a room for me in one of the private houses near Cape Town and left me there, saying he would come for me on the wedding day.

After a total of 32 hours travel, I slept well. In the morning, the hosts, retired intelligent couple who after retirement settled in a quiet, green and beautiful village, invited me to have breakfast. I stayed in the outhouse, standing separately, which they used on occasion to have additional income. Wanting to know me better and spend time together, they offered a walk to the winery. It was on an old farm which had the museum, showing the stages of a two-hundred-year-old history of wine production on the farm.

For the first time, I had to see the process of winemaking. Having bought several bottles of rare varieties of wine, we returned home.

After dinner, we set with the glass of wine, discussed the situation in Africa and the prospects for the country future. I wanted to know what the original Africaanas inhabitants think about the subject.

After Mandela's ten-year rule, nothing changed in the lives of South Africans. Hungry and unemployed, they always were a danger to those who were well off, be it the white population or their brothers and sisters, as they called themselves.

The next day, invited to the morning walk, I noticed a metal rod in the hands of my companion. When I asked why he needed this, he said that with it he feels more confident. I read that Pushkin also walked with a metal bar in his hands, and even sometimes, he used it against his offenders.

After lunch, the host offered to show me the ocean from a steep bank - his favorite place. We left in his car. The road was in good condition, and we quietly spun along the serpentines of the hills, where oncoming traffic rarely came across and soon drove up to the precipice.

In the distance, the sky was indistinguished from the surface of the water. The coast below the cliff was not visible. We only heard the resounding splash of the surf and the rustling sound of rolling away wave. We sat down on a flat boulder, sighing the fresh ocean air and looking at the invisible thread of the horizon.

The pacifying solitude on the shores of the ocean led me to the thoughts that in my work, I never felt the nature around.

Almost every day I was in the car checking the properties for sale. But apart the address of the house I need to sell, I did not see anything else on my way. I drove through a beautiful alley covered with a tent of mighty trees standing on both sides of the road and walked on the bridge over the murmuring brook. But I never paid attention to the beauty of nature. Then, returning to my office, I sat at the computer until late, looking for the information needed before meeting with the client.

Reluctantly, we got up and went to the car. We left the place where I felt close to nature. And I was grateful to my companion for such an unexpected opportunity.

On the third day, my son came and, explaining that he had paid in advance for my overnight stay and services, took me directly to the wedding ceremony. He introduced me to his bride's parents, sisters, and brother, and leaving me in their care, returned to his friends invited to the wedding.

The ceremony conducted rabbi and priest alternately skillfully combining both religions. This idea touched me with its warmth performance and friendliness.

I looked at my son, and my eyes filled with tears of joy and pride. Many bitter years brought me his mom, but I was happy that on this day I could attend his wedding.

Seeing Michelle and Ami together, I immediately felt that together they would be fine. It will not always be easy, but I was sure that together they would cope with all the difficulties which they would meet in their life. From now, they have a shared destiny and everyday joy. And this is the essential thing in real family life.

After the wedding ceremony, I refused to sit at the same table with his mom and sat among the guests.

The next day I flew to visit my daughter in Johannesburg. Seven years have passed since our last meeting in Israel and eleven years since I left South Africa.

At the airport, seeing the happy face of my daughter, I realized how much this visit meant for her. When I left Africa, I did not doubt that I would visit them often. Unfortunately,

America did not bring me success. My financial options were limited.

I sat in the front seat of the car and peered at the vaguely familiar places that flashed past the window. I did not believe that I had already forgotten the road and the surroundings that I knew so well.

Finally, the streets seemed familiar to me. The gates in the barbed wire fence opened, and we enter the area where live only religious Jews.

We drove up to the house, then into the garage. Walked to the metal front door with the lock, then opened the wooden door and found ourselves in the hallway. Here my granddaughters and grandson meet me. The eldest, Simi, lives in Israel, where, after graduating from university she works as a teacher in elementary school. My visit coincided with her visit to the parents. Eitan is 20 years old, and the youngest Ayala is 17. I was shown to Eitan's room, saying that it would now be my room.

I have not seen their house, yet. In one of the rooms, the maid recognizes me and excited about seeing me. She helped raise all the children; she puts things in order and knows better than the owners where and what to do. In the house, everyone obeys her.

Behind a closed glass door at the exit to the backyard, a dog scratches its paws on the glass. The lovely creature does not understand why such an event occurs in the house without its participation.

My daughter can not wait to show their business. A few years after my departure, Zion bought a house for a small sum from a family leaving Africa and built a two-story extension with separate rooms. The house converted into a restaurant with a fully equipped kitchen and a bar with liqueur drinks. The restaurant is kosher. Zion hired a chef, waiters, and manager. All of them dressed in uniforms.

In the two-story addition to the house, the rooms have all the facilities and intended to accommodate religious Jewish people in business coming to Johannesburg, mainly from Europe. Zion made an advertisement for his only one kosher restaurant in Johannesburg and visitors appeared.

We drove up to a high fence with the metal sliding gates, entered a spacious asphalt yard with covered parking lots. Next to one of the walls surrounding the courtyard was a swimming pool with a fountain and a flower bed. Not far, on elevation with railings and a roof, I saw an open terrace for those who wanted service outside the restaurant. We went inside. Two halls. One large and spacious, the other smaller, in a separate room. The manager came to meet us. Her husband is the chef of this restaurant — both of them from Portugal. Zion ordered for himself and me the plate of fish made per Portuguese style. Then he called the waiter and ordered me a glass of wine. My daughter chose a vegetable dish. The decor was cozy; the tables beautifully served. In principle, my daughter was in charge of the business. She opened it in the morning, made all necessary purchases of products other than meat products, which only Zion bought, monitored kashrut. The rest was the responsibility of the manager. The fish dish was delicious, and I believed that visitors were satisfied with this restaurant. Then I was shown rooms for guests, and we left the fortress-restaurant. In this Jewish "ghetto," as I saw this area, we went to the shopping area and refueled the car. Then Zion decided to present me to the owners of the stores located near the gas station. We went to the bakery and bought fresh bread and buns.

I remember the owner of the bakery long before they moved to this area. In the following stores - all familiar acquaintances. The life circumstances gathered them all in the same area where they now lived close to each other.

It was Friday eve, and I sat at the table with my family. After the ritual of blessing the food, I enjoyed my daughter's Moroccan cuisine. I sat at the table with my family like it was before my departure to Israel.

On Saturday morning, Zion took me to the synagogue, where after the service we sat at the table and talked. The life behind barbed wire was no matter of concern. It looked that the security car, driving along the fence 24 hours a day make them feel comfortable.

I thought of the settlements in Israel - the same security measures. I was depressed

The next day Zion decided to introduce me to the Diamond Stock Exchange, his place of the work. I was surprised to see him wearing old clothes. To my surprise, he explained that the stock exchange area is the most dangerous in the city. Such camouflage helps him not to attract attention. In the past, I had to drive past the stock exchange, and I knew that Zion had his office there, where the diamond deals with clients took place, but I had never been at his workplace. We drove in his old car. Before entering the territory, the guard checked the documents, asked about me, and only after let us in. We drove into the parking place assigned to Zion.

The elevator took us to the last floor. At the end of a long corridor, we came to a metal door. Turning off the alarm, Zion opened the door, and we walked into his office, consisting of two small rooms. Next to his desk, I saw embedded large safe. Opening the thick heavy door of the safe, he took out small boxes with diamonds. His job was to check all the diamonds and indicate the quantity and quality of the material. He receives a commission only during the transaction.

Without his checking and approval, there is no question of buying. This work isvery responsible, and not everyone has the right to do it; only the person with an exclusive license. Then he showed me various appliances in another room. He is going to buy scales with exceptional accuracy and sensitivity that he ordered and delivered to him from abroad.

I was surprised seeing all kind of specific instruments in his office. I did not have any idea what kind of tools he is using and what his work on the Diamond Stock Exchange includes.

Zion's dream to transfer his knowledge to his son and teach him to work with the diamonds, was not successful. Eitan did not show any desire for the father's business.

It reminded me of the story of my first employer, who wanted to transfer business to his son, who wanted to be a chef in the restaurant.

During dinner time we went to the stock exchange kosher cafeteria where almost everyone spoke Hebrew. Zion said people here had known each other for many years. On the day of my visit, Zion finished his work earlier than usual.

Leaving the gates of the exchange, I notice many blacks standing at the crossroads with scrutiny staring at me.

"Sit quietly," said Zion, "and don't look at them; otherwise, they might be interested in us."

The next day I was taken to the local fair market. The day was Sunday. We listened to the singers. Watched the African dances performed by a group of very young girls, and went around numerous tents. The talented African artists demonstrated woodwork and jewelry products. I liked the work in the ebony wood and purchased a whole set of figures and a little elephant. They are in my home on the shelf until today.

For a long time, I did not hear from my grandchildren the word "grandpa" and gladly responded to all their desires. I was happy that I could buy them whatever they liked. For many years I have been deprived of this pleasure.

Later this day, Orit took me along to the grocery store, where she usually buys products for her restaurant.

At the entrance to the garage, she paid for parking and drove inside. As we parked the car, next to the car appeared a black African. My daughter took out a coin and put in his outstretched hand.

"You've already paid for parking," I said. "It doesn't matter. If I don't give anything, I can then find my car with a damaged wheel or its body badly scratched."

Recently driving in her Mercedes, we stopped at a red traffic light. Seeing black people crossing the street in front of our car, I asked why she does not close the next to her window. "It does not matter," she replied, "If they want to grab my bag, they can break the window glass."

While Orit was going through her shopping list, I slowly moved around, looking at the products and compare the prices. The difference in the costs of the goods, from the time I left Africa and now, was incomprehensible.

Now I understood what Orit was telling me about the hardship the working families experience in South Africa.

We delivered the products to the restaurant, and I had my tasty fish dish again. I noticed that only a few tables had attendants. "These are local wealthy people who from time to time, treat their wives in the restaurant," smiled my daughter. "We have them almost every Sunday, and they sit for hours. These people our main income because they also buy a lot of all sorts of drinks. Today is a weekday; as you see, there are only a few families."

Among those sitting at a large crowded table, I recognized the son of Maurice Siff, who replaced his father in the business. In that year, when I worked at their enterprise, he returned from America, graduated from university.

I did not want to leave without buying a gift for my daughter and asked to show me some good clothing stores, realizing that I had no better chance than now. In addition to the diamond pendant around her neck, made by Zion, she did not wear any jewelry, especially since it became dangerous. The whole family dressed modestly. Judging by the clothing, it seems to me that Zion has been wearing the same costume for a long time.

I understood that their financial situation was not great. All the savings went to the restaurant, which does not bring them income due to the lack of customers. I saw it, being there almost every day. Diamond dealers from abroad, on whom Zion was counting on opening his business, began to come to South Africa rarely because of the decline in demand for diamonds on the world market. Moreover, the life of the white population under constant threat of robbery and violence, could not contribute to the desire of diamond dealers to be in fear of their life.

The first years of the opening, the restaurant brought a good income. All rooms for visitors occupied. Former diamond transactions on decent amounts of money carried stable commission income. Zion was satisfied.

Now the visits of the dealers became a random occurrence. The education of children at the synagogue school was expensive. However, Zion, as always, was calm and relaxed. "Be ezrat ha Shem," he always said, which meant in Hebrew, "With God's help."

That is why, before leaving, I wanted to give my daughter something out of clothes, knowing that she would not allow herself to buy anything. We spent hours in clothing stores, where she refused to try on, seeing the price on the label. Another problem, like all religious women, she wore long skirts. If the quality and the color she liked - the style was wrong.

I still managed to persuade her and bought her a few beautiful tops.

I flew back to America with a split feeling. Happy that I had such a long-awaited opportunity to see my daughter's family and very sad by what I saw. I worried about their life behind barbed wire and the lack of necessary income; besides me, neither my daughter nor Zion had anyone else in Africa. And I was on another continent.

The circustances that separated Orit from her half-brother never left me. Between them stood a barrier of his mother's hatred since the first days. I did not see the solution. My son was not guilty of that. When he was small, he did not understand this. When he became an adult, having no previous contacts with his sister, this disunity became for him an already accepted state. Perhaps that is why he never had the desire to see Orit or learn about his nieces and nephew. It's a pity. They both were only siblings in South Africa.

Zion, as I understand, because of religious considerations, did not consider their contacts to be desirable, although he never touched on this issue in conversation.

The brother and sister, having one father whom they love and respect, remain strangers to each other, having no reason for this.

After my departure, Simi returned to Israel. Later, Eitan came to Israel and drafted into the army, where he served for three years. After finishing school, Ayala went to Israel but served only one year. Simi accepted them all in her apartment, which she rented near the school where she worked. I saw them through Facebook. After serving in the army, Eitan and Ayala returned to their parents. Ayala entered the university, and Eitan was appointed the head of the security service with a decent salary. Payment for Ayala's studies again fell on Dad's shoulders, who didn't have any positive changes in income.

After many years of living together with James, our Lena finally agreed to marry him. For a long time, they were not sure that they had a future, despite their mutual feelings. James has had his business for thirteen years, fulfilling the orders of some companies of Silicon Valley. After these companies became liquidated as a result of the collapse of the American market, James closed his company, too.

An enterprising man and having the skills in filming, he decided to make short films on cooking that are popular on many channels of American television. One of his acquaintances was a chef and agreed to take part in filming episodes. Many inserts of cognitive content were introduced by James into this program and made the series of his films exciting and informative. In addition to the recipes for making vegetarian dishes, his film episodes gave people information about achievements in technology and computer science; famous people and inventors, festivals and parades; many beautiful scenic places which not easy to reach.

I liked his films and watched them with interest. He even managed to publish a recipe book of the dishes which people saw in the short movie episodes.

His films were on many local television station channels. Since these stations existed at the expense of public and philanthropic donations, James did not receive payment for his film's demonstrations. Getting to cable channels across the country without connections and money was impossible. But the inventive mind did not stop looking for alternatives, and James has found a way to advertise airline companies. Establishing contacts with the owners of hotels and restaurants in the countries he visited, he started making advertising films for them. It allowed him to have free flights for him and his working group, as well as free accommodation and meals in the most fashionable hotels. For several years, his crew visited many European countries, visited Canada, South America, and New Zealand. For two months, they traveled around Italy. James, during these trips, worked very hard. Coming back home, he had to work on materials and perform the whole process of making the film - a job that a whole group of specialists usually performs.

After making the film, James sent it to the company that paid for the trip. I never take part in these trips. But from those pictures that Larisa made, and from the films I saw later, I had a clear idea of those fantastic places that they were able to visit. Repeatedly, James tried again to return to the business. The attempts did not bring the desired results. Either because of the wrong choice of partners or because of lack of funds. But enterprising James all the time found the possibility of random earnings, allowing to support his family. Being sociable, James and Ellen had many friends. On constant trips, filming, looking for work, years passed, and they suddenly saw that they needed a family.

The wedding ceremony was in the Beit David synagogue, which Larisa and I regularly attended for several years.

Then a little boy appeared in our family - Louie. He filled our whole lives with joy and happiness. Lena left her job and devoted all her time to her long-awaited son. James found a well-paying job at Stanford. The house they rent located in Palo Alto near his place of work, which allows him to save time on the road and pay more attention to the family.

The arrival of my granddaughter Simi from Israel was a pleasant surprise. Invited by her friend, with whom she served in the army, to New York, she made an additional stop for a few days in San Francisco. We gladly welcomed her and fulfilled all her requirements in terms of kosher food. We introduced her to Lena and James, showed her several neighboring cities, and took her to Stanford, where Lena had worked before. The next day I decided to show her an oceanfront town, Carmel. Arriving there, we unexpectedly found ourselves in a different climate. In the middle of the summer, it was windy and cold. We did not have warm clothes, and I decided to buy warm jackets for both of us to continue exploring the city.

Of all three of my daughter's children, only Simi was the most independent, persevering, and energetic. I considered her desire to immigrate to Israel positively. While teaching at school, she simultaneously supplemented her salary, giving lessons in English; and became interested in photography at a professional level.

At her age, it was time to start a family. Being a religious person,   Israel was the right place to find a partner in life. She said that she met one man a few years ago. When she saw his interest only in the amount of money her father would give him for their wedding, she immediately stopped seeing him.

To my cautious question about her intentions about building a family, Simi smiled. "Do not worry, Saba, everything will be fine."

Her confidence and mysterious smile calmed me. A year later, she married. Her husband, Maor, from a religious and intellectual

Jerusalem family, was a student of the last year studies at the university.

Zion took an active part in organizing the wedding of his eldest daughter. Unfortunately, Larisa and I could not come. We were retired and lived on a limited income. Later, talking to Orit, I found out that they had to take money from the bank to travel and attend the wedding and now they want to sell the restaurant to pay off debt.

My granddaughter Simi is already a mother of two children - a daughter and a son. I became a great-grandfather. They live in one of the settlements and dream of their own home. Simi works as a teacher in the same settlement.

After graduating from the university, Maor works, teaches and continues to improve his educational level.

From my daughter, I received sad news. The restaurant closed. It is impossible to sell it. After graduation, Ayala has not been able to find work for more than a year, because she refused to work on Saturday. Zion is still paying off the money borrowed for the daughter's wedding. According to my daughter, the situation in the city has hardly changed. Jews treated the same as the rest of the white population. There are synagogues, yeshiva, schools for teaching Jewish children. Jews are accepted without problems at universities and for work in their specialty if they can find one.

My son's family brings me much joy. He successfully defended his Master's thesis in business (MBA), which allows him to always and everywhere, if necessary, find a job. He continues to work as an editor for one of the magazines and finds time to write some short stories. After reading a few of them, I admired the richness and perfection of the language. I liked that he managed to develop his particular style, by which writers differ in their works. Recently, he wrote an article that received public feedback. I read it carefully and saw how deeply he touched on the political situation in the country. He has two sons, Cameron and Maxim.

Unfortunately, we separated by a vast distance.

Here in America, our only joy is a little boy Louie. We are such great friends with him that if grandma Larisa comes to visit him without me, his first question - "Where is a grandpa?" Together with his grandmother and with me, he walks in the park. The grandma is reading him books. Last night, saying goodbye, he kissed me three times, and when the Babuska asked: "Louie, why didn't you kiss me too?" He threw up his hands and said:

"I have no more kisses left!" Then his mother asked him: "Do you like grandmother's pancakes?"

"Yes," he replied. "Then you have to kiss your grandmother too." He did it.

The first two years, it was impossible to feed him. He so smartly avoided the spoon that the feeding turned his mother into a sufferer. Now, we have no such problem. When he sees plates being set up on the table, he is the first to sit in his chair. His favorite vegetables are cucumber and broccoli.

My career as an agent for the sale of the residential property began soon after my arrival in America. It lasted, with varying success, until my retirement. I was sorry to part with the profession of design engineer, to which I dedicated 35 years of my life. After many failures to find a job, I stopped all attempts, and from the engineer became a salesman. It was not quite easy, as I imagined. Given the scope of activities and the knowledge of the economic and legal structure of the sale of the property, this job required a lot of working hours. These requirements were strict and if violated or not complied with, could cause the agent trouble and even material loss.

When I started working, it seemed to me that the sale procedure was equivalent to walking through a minefield. At the same time, these warnings, as I understood later, were useful. They taught me to be attentive in a conversation. To conduct business professionally and helping clients go through an acquisition or sale procedure, where hundreds of thousands of dollars are received or paid, successfully.

Working in California was different from working in Chicago. I began to realize that the property market is influenced by many factors that govern the entire economy of a country.

As far as I know, the housing boom reached its apogee and made the sale agents, regardless of work experience, quite wealthy. They looked like fishers who did not have to sit all day long and look at the float, often returning without a catch. Clients went to agents in "jambs," like fish in the fishing season. The complacent agents excitedly reported a sale of expensive property. The mood in the office resembled the time of "gold rush" in America.

There was another problem - it was not easy to buy because between buyers there was a "war" for every house on the market. I could not comprehend how an old, crumbling house, which, in my opinion, supposed to go for demolition, and which should cost no more than 300 thousand, only because of a piece of land, was sold for a million and a half. It was more like groundless speculation than a fair sale. When I asked my boss, "How it is possible to sell a wreck for that kind of money?" He replied: "This is now the market works."

I was sure real estate companies and their agents artificially raised the property prices guided only by the goal of personal gain. The dot-com rush contributed to the success of the property market too. Like mushrooms after rain, appeared a mass of small companies connected with the popular demands of the Internet.

Without making any products but with large sums of money from investors and all kinds of funds, these companies paid their employee with the company shares. The cost of the shares had grown incredibly at the Stokes Exchange. Becoming rich at the expense of the shares, which the company awarded them, this paper millionaires flooded the property market.

There were many offers for every home from buyers who could not even think about buying the property before.

But there were companies, which were able to sell their ideas or products. Employees of these companies also became wealthy and were buying houses for cash they had in the bank.

My wife and I came from another state where apartment prices were five times lower. We were purchasers too, but with the only difference that, having sold our two-story house for two hundred thousand, we left with only twenty thousand from the sale. With this amount, we could buy nothing in the area where we wanted. When my wife wanted to buy an apartment near the place of her work at the price of 250 thousand, the buyer came and offered cash for 75 thousand more.

I received buyer's calls from different states with a desire to move to Silicon Valley. I got a buyer, and I still remember his name - Shandrakar. He looked with me a house worth more than two million but did not buy. Then, his query grew, and he looked at homes with prices of more than four million. He traveled with me through almost all the elite areas in the surrounding cities, but in two years working with this customer, I lost the time - he bought nothing. And he was not alone.

When the real value on the stock market revealed, the companies went bankrupt. The bubble in which they lived, deceiving themselves and others, burst. The unexpected collapse of the dot-com companies led their shares rapidly down. The shares of such famous company as Amazon dot-com dropped from 107 dollars to 7. Shares of all companies on the Exchange lost $ 5 trillion. It was a heavy blow to the country's economy.

The market froze, not knowing how to react to it. But the property prices remained high. The National Association of the Real Estate has reported that the property market is not affected by the bankruptcy of the dot-com companies and remains at the same level.

Greenspan, the chief economist at the Federal Bank, denied the existence of bloated prices in the housing market. He did not consider the possibility to lower the costs of the property. In his opinion, because the country has low unemployment, an increase in housing requirements is expected. And the chief economist of the Association of Real Estates of America accused the press and local critics, saying that they are responsible for the allegations that market prices deliberately increased. In short, we, the agents, were kept assure that the market is booming.

The reality I witnessed, spoke of the opposite. Many former programmers who have lost their jobs, came to our agency applying for a job as a property salesman. They believed that by selling the properties, they could make a lot of money. I understood them because I was also one of them. Houses did continue to be sold, but only with one difference - the number of buyers has dropped dramatically.

The newly-grown millionaires, who managed to sell their Internet companies on time, became the main buyers. But to get such clients could only agents established on the property market for many years. From my list of the potential buyers, after the collapse of the dot-com, no one was left. Agents, who had successfully used the opportunity to fill their pockets with commissions over the previous years, quietly observed the market situation. They secured themselves for years. Unfortunately, I did not have time to make a single sale - my employment coincided with the crash of the market.

The terrorist attack on the World Trade Center in New York, made the hearts of people, not only in America but all over the world, turn cold from horror. It caused heavy losses on the Stock Exchange, and the prices on the property market have gone down. The market was in favor of buyers. During this period, I managed to make several large purchases of homes for my buyers. For example, a house bought during the period of the Dot-Com madness for 5 million 500 thousand, I managed to buy for my client for 2 million 700 thousand dollars.

America's invasion of Iraq in 2003, despite the splendid military operation, as it reported by media in America, harmed the property market again. But the request for housing did not disappear, because prices continued to creep down.

The competition between agents for the buyer has become hardened. In the same period, race broke out between banks. They introduced new rules for issuing loans to customers.

One of these programs was the most immoral and cruel. It consisted of attracting clients with low initial interest on loans issued to buy houses. A year later, the loan's percentage increased significantly. Many low-income families dreaming to have a roof over their heads, agreed to these deceptive conditions.
They believed that over time, they would be able to pay off the increased rate. The reality of the American economy did not confirm the hopes, and people began to lose property - they could not pay off the loan. Buyers not only lost money, which they already paid to the bank, but the bank also took their houses. Banks continued to apply additional cruel measures to their clients in distress.

The next trick of the brightest minds of the financial industry - to give loans to the owners of houses, the price of which was the highest during the market boom.
Compare to the price paid for their house years ago; bank gave people loan equal to the difference in value.
After all, people always want to believe in the stability of the American economy. The opportunity to get an amount of money to travel abroad or buy a new car, or rebuild a house, or even pay off debts, was very tempting.
When the economy crashed the value of the houses went down.

Banking stunts led borrowers to part with houses for which they could not make monthly payments. Their houses became the property of banks, which in turn began selling them to cover the owners' debts. About 6 million families have lost their homes. The real estate market fell into decay and rolled down so fast that many experts believed that the American economy was experiencing the second-largest crisis after the Great Depression of 1929. The decline of the trillionth's market has affected all relevant industries related to the purchase and construction of houses.

But this difficult time for the American economy became a "gold rush" for those who had money - investors.
Private individuals and large companies began frantically to buy property from banks at half price for resale later when prices on the market go up.
All, mentioned above investors created whole complexes for renting. And, no matter how bitter it is, to rent out the houses to the same owners who lost them. Many agents and companies, including law firms, concentrated their activities on selling homes that were in bankruptcy or became bank property.

As an agent, I had to meet the owners of houses that, having lost their jobs, could not pay them. I remember the sad faces of two young programmers - a husband and a wife - who at the same time, lost their jobs.
They sat in the house that no longer belonged to them, which they bought from the builder two years ago. Mom, sitting on one of the suitcases, was feeding two small children, before the door will be slam-shut forever. Farewell to what was their joy and belief in a happy life, gave me such a deep feeling of sympathy

that I could not say a word. After all, all the words, consolations or promises to help and return the loss to them, would be a lie. The grief of each family that lost ground under their feet cause me a sense of solidarity with them, and I abandoned the idea of selling the requisitioned property.

My last earnings coincided with the worst market conditions in 2006. The predictions of the financial-guru Greenspan, authority not only in America but throughout the world, were not justified. I remember his recent declaration that the country's economy "has achieved brilliant achievements in recent years."

Since the second half of 2007, the country's economy has already been in one of the worst crises since 1930. The entire structure of the country's economy collapsed and affected the economy of the whole world.

During this period, I was not able to sell a single house. Our family was in dire financial straits. My attempts to find clients did not give results.

My wife accidentally met a woman who invited us to celebrate the New Year. We were glad to have a new acquaintance with the Russian-speaking family in our city, where we lived for seven years. I noticed that the husband, Vladimir, looked much older and shorter than his attractive and welcoming wife. He was laconic. After dinner, he invited me to his office, where I saw two computers.

I asked about his occupation, assuming that maintaining a home and a family in one of the most expensive districts of the city requires considerable funds, and therefore he has them. He replied that he was engaged in various project developments. I did not insist on clarification and said that I am a real estate agent.

A day later he called and said that he would like to talk to me. I came to his house. This time he was guest-friendly and smiling. Vladimir offered a cup of tea and then said that he would like to talk with me about a business matter. He began by saying that in the past, he was engaged in building houses in Europe, and now he wants to find a piece of land and start developing it here. Therefore, he decided to discuss with me the possibility of buying a significant plot of land, but not for residential, but commercial use. I could not believe my luck. Finding a client in the worst period of the real estate market was not easy.

Exploring the market in all the surrounding suburbs, I found several sites, and the next day, we went to see them. From his remarks, I began to realize what he needs. The next trip was more successful. The plot was ten times larger in size and price. Completely smooth and ready for development. He reacted calmly to the cost of twelve million dollars for a parcel of land, explaining that he had to discuss this amount with a partner from New York. I waited for six months to hear about their decision.

Meantime, I made a lot of trips at his request looking for potential additional property their company is interested in buying, as he said.

During our trips he talked a lot about his life, starting with school years and ending with his arrival in America. According to him, in Krasnoyarsk, where he was from, he left a considerable fortune. When conversations about buying and useless trips became suspicious to me, I was going to stop wasting time and return to working with clients. Suddenly, his partner from New York flew in and, having familiarized himself with a piece of land, agreed to the purchase. The partners made a preliminary deposit of two hundred thousand dollars and undertook to pay an additional ten thousand dollars to the owner each month during the year. The remaining amount of more than eleven million, to be paid one year later.

When I signed the contract document, I believed that my clients were interested, and the project has a future. I can get my commission money only when the seller receives the full amount of the contract.

My client did not know English. From the first days, I had to conduct all business talks and meetings in his silent presence. That caused even greater respect for the person making the multi-million dollar deal. His attitude towards me, on the contrary, became rude and humiliating. His constant reminder that thanks to him, I would get a large commission, was unpleasant to hear. I refused to meet with him and did not answer his calls. He appeared on the threshold of my apartment with an apology and a request to continue cooperation. Believing in the sincerity of his words, I agreed.

Because of his communication inability, I managed to find an architect who took up the conceptual layout of the proposed shopping center. Then I went to the Developments department in the City Hall and applied for the construction permit to the parcel of land which was under contract. The buyer was next to me all the time. I was also monitoring the monthly payment to the owner of the land.

My passion for the project went far beyond my function as a sales agent. But I got carried away and wanted to help a person who did not have contacts and knowledge of the language. I was his translator, consultant on all matters relating to the project. I gave all my time to project in the hope of recovering all expenses after the closing of the sale.

His business partner, Ilya, came from New York, wanting to make sure that the information that Vladimir gives him is real. Despite my participation in all the developments of the project, the partners never invited me to discuss such a massive development as a shopping center. On my question, "How are you going to develop a project of such a large scale, where the services of large construction companies needed?"

The answer was simple - "This is not your business. We have contacts, and hundreds of contributors are waiting for the opportunity to participate in this project."

Ilya had his own financial company in New York, and this gave the project reliability. About a year has passed. I was busy finding additional non-large parcels of land that my client told they were going to buy too.

Quite unexpectedly for me, when the time came to pay the rest amount of eleven million, my clients refused to keep the contract. The partners lost the entire amount of the initial payments in the favor to the owner.

I was busy with this project for one year and a half. I have not received a penny from my clients, counting on commissions. In addition to the moral damage inflicted on me by two rogues, the financial situation of our family was critical. I was already 72. I lost all contact with customers, and recovery was not possible in a short time. Given the circumstances mentioned above, which coincided with the collapse of the market and the massive unemployment, continuing to work as an agent did not make sense.

Vladimir Mathisik, as I learned later, turned out to be a swindler. My wife and I parted with the apartment that we tried to pay off from our modest savings.

After many unsuccessful attempts to find a job, my wife agreed to retire. I kept looking for work. But after unsuccessful attempts during the year, I also had to retire.

Many years have passed since we reconciled with the fact that we can no longer work. I am grateful that, in my declining years, I am one of those lucky ones who, thanks to the state support program, have a roof over our heads and food.

My wife, Larisa, and I always support and take care of each other. We are two different people with our interests and hobbies. We do not always agree on various matters, but nothing can separate us even for a moment. It is a comfort in our life we can afford. The joy and happiness bring in our life our grandson Louie.

To my surprise, I began to pay attention to what I had not had time before. I don't need to hurry anywhere. My train is gone. Now, I can look at sunrise and sunset. I love to wander in the park and inhale the fragrant smell of sun-heated pines, or stand on the bridge and look at the murmuring water in the creek, that trying to keep its run in a hot, rainless, California climate. I like to listen to music. I take a book and, as it was during my childhood and youth, with the first page, I forget about everything around.

The need to perform the most necessary household duties gives me pleasure. At home, I find myself helpful. For example, my wife does not need a ladder when she cannot get anything from the high shelf in the kitchen. I unscrew the caps on the glass jars. I catch beetles in the apartment, the sight of which horrifies my wife. Professionally wash the dishes. Every morning make a bed. Help in the preparation of food, for example, such as peeling potatoes. I am placing the plates, knives, and forks on the table. I bring home from the car the purchased products. My wife also appreciates my ability to hold a hammer; when we moved to a new apartment, all furniture assembly, and placement, I did to my scatches. I do everything required of me.

We are always together and as by the dictum of Epicurus: "There is nothing more beautiful than happy poverty."

Farewell to Israel

Understanding the future left me much less than passed; I had a desire to visit the country where I left my heart forever -Israel.

Quite unexpectedly, we had this opportunity. I knew what Israel presents today. I was aware of its achievements in economics, science, and military power. I understood the pride of the citizens, who turned the country into one most developed in the Middle East and have been protecting her existence.

I saw how governments in Europe, Asia, and America, poisoned by the lies of unbridled propaganda by Arab extremists, encourage the inherent evil of humanity - anti-Semitism.

Overcome by a fanatical hatred of the Jews, the radical Arabs do not want peace with Israel. They speak about its destruction. It is hard to imagine that Europe, now ready to sacrifice Israel, believing that by doing so they will save themselves from Islamization.

We flew to Israel to see the family of my granddaughter Simi; to see relatives, among which the most desired visit to Oleg, Ida's elder brother. I wanted to see my friends, see and feel how the people of Israel live. Larisa had a few plans too.

My granddaughter's family lives in a settlement called Dolev. I wanted to stay with her family to have a clear idea of their life in Samaria - the ancient land of Israel.

The world supports Arabs claim that Jews build them on the land, allegedly belonging to the Palestinians. President Obama holds the Arab point of view. Nothing is surprising. America, a country that considers itself a friend of Israel, still refuses to recognize Jerusalem as the capital of Israel and maintains its embassy in Tel Aviv.

But what is surprising that the President's of America point view supported by left-wing Jewish organizations, which, together with Arabs, believe that Israel has no right to exist.

At the airport, Simi already waited for us. On the way to the settlement, we stopped at her husband parent's home, who looked after the children while she was driving to pick us up. Our stay there was short, and we continued our journey to the settlement in order not to miss the ritual to meet Friday Eve Shabath ritual. When we arrived at their home, I was excited to see my great-granddaughter Nitsan and my little great-grandson Inon. He still didn't quite understand why his mother calls a man who appeared at their home, grandpa.

Maor, Simi's husband, a calm man with a friendly manner of speech, greeted us very warmly.

I was pleased to see their friends who came to meet us and, as I understood, these visits were a habit among the settlers. As I saw later, they were in a matter of supporting and helping each other, which, in community, distant from the big cities, was sometimes necessary.

The next day, we went with Larisa to Jerusalem. The ride by bus and transfers took a lot of time. The purpose of the trip was to find a synagogue whose address was known to us.

For twenty-five years, Larisa sent a small amount of money to the Kupat Reubay Meer synagogue on Straus Street. This "mitzvah" (benevolent help) Larisa did to the advice of a religious woman named Hadassah, who helped Larisa on her arrival in America. Now Larisa had the opportunity to see the people whom she regularly helped with her small contribution.

We walked for a long time through the streets of the religious part of the city in search of the right address. Young women in long dresses and a head covered with a scarf or a fashionable hat pushed in front of them prams with small kids. Men of different ages in black suits hurried home, fleeing the heat. We walked passing cafes, bakeries, a multitude of magazines, clothes, jewelry, various workshops, occasionally stopping and looking at shop windows. Finally, we reached the Ostrich Street and did not immediately manage to figure out the numbering of houses. Then it was not easy to find the signboard of the synagogue. It was impossible to see the entrance from the street because it simply did not exist. We had no desire to retreat. When we managed to get into it from a neighboring yard, we were in front of a locked door. Distressed, we were about to leave when we heard the steps and saw an older person coming up the stairs. He opened the door and invited us inside.

Saying that there is no service in the synagogue today, he asked about the matter we came in and how he can help us. Larisa told him about her reason to visit the place and, since we were in Israel, she wanted not to miss this opportunity.

Realizing our interest, he nodded his head and invited us to one of the rooms. All the walls of the room had shelves on which there were thick folders in hardcover.

Each folder had a number and the date of the month and year. In the middle of the room stood a table and several chairs. Rabbi asked us to sit down.

"Our synagogue is one hundred and forty years old," he began, realizing that these visitors needed to know what the synagogue does with their money.

"It exists through donations from people like you. All the money that we receive immediately recorded and transferred to our budget in the bank. To get money from a bank is possible only with the signature of five members of the synagogue board. As you can see, these shelves and chairs are almost as old as a synagogue. We have here only the most necessary. And the payment of our work is also minimal. Our main goal is to help those in need. Many people come to us with different requests, which are considered by our council, which here meets and decides to whom and how much money we can allocate."

He interrupted his explanation, went to one of the nearest shelves, took the folder, and laid it on the table in front of us. Opening it, he began to show neatly numbered and sealed documents asking for help. There was an attached document about the decision on each request and the amount of assistance.

We saw- one family needed money for son's bar mitzvah; a yeshiva student did not have money to buy clothes. The poor lonely woman could not buy a stroller for a newborn. A young couple asked money for a wedding. People needed help to buy clothes, medicine, food, kitchen appliances. There were hundreds of such pages in the book.

He continued to leaf through the documents, but we already knew. The synagogue helped people in need and extended a helping hand and human participation.

We thanked for the attention given to us, wrote out another check and left. This visit helped Larisa feel that with her donations, she also helped the destitute. Living on our two pensions, we never refused to donate to war veterans, the disabled, and the homeless. We understood that without state support, having lost our house, we could be in the same desperate situation.

On the same day, at midnight, Larisa was leaving for the planned trip to see her friend in London. After taking Larisa to the Airport, Simi and I returned home.

In the morning, I felt unwell - throat, nose. I decided to rest in bed. I had tea with lemon and honey, and was in bed for three days, not leaving the settlement. The door was closed, and I did not allow children to come to my room, keeping them away from my fever. When everyone left the house, I, having made myself a big cup of tea, sat down in front of the house under a shed with my computer to check the email. Every day I hoped for recovery, but the virus did not want to part with me. My planned meetings thwarted. But these days of indisposition allowed me to get acquainted with the everyday life of a little village. I saw my great-grandchildren go to kindergarten, the granddaughter teaches at school, and Maor every morning on the passing transport goes to work in Jerusalem.

The had only one old car in the family, helping Simi to take children to the nursery school and pick them up, as well as go to work. It is the reason Maor went to work with occasional transport.

Two tiers on the hillside, on which about a dozen mobile units installed, were the part of the village where my granddaughter's family lived. In each unit block, there were three bedrooms, a family room with a kitchen, one toilet, and a bathroom. I noticed that all families were religious, but not Orthodox. The people of the community were almost of the same age; each family had several small children; all men had the necessary professions and were employed. They also united by the future neighborhood in the new apartment complex, which was under construction.

At the very top of the hill were several hundred families of old-timers. Their homes built many years ago. There was also a synagogue, a school for five hundred children, a club and a food shop. At the base of the hill at the entrance was a guard post. When Simi brought us home from the airport, she drove through this post without stopping, her phone rang, and the guard asked who was in her car he does not know. She explained that her grandfather came to visit. Later, I saw a daily check up on the streets of the settlement by guard's patrol car.

In this small piece of Israel, among numerous Arab settlements, I felt peace and tranquility. Early in the morning dark, the sound of prayer in a mosque located on a nearby hill woke me up. Through the window's mesh, I felt the fresh airflow. In the distance, the flickering lights of the Israeli cities were visible, and around - utter silence, broken by the sounds of the cars of the neighbors leaving for work. And silence again.

At sunrise, the surrounding hillsides lit up, and I saw the planted vines where the Jewish settlements located. The slopes of the hills of the Arab villages without the gnarled trunks of olive trees looked deserted. In the distance, like yellow beetles, buses crawling along the slope, taking children from two neighboring settlements to the school, here in Dolev.
The washed and fed children Simi takes to the kindergarten and goes to work.

I have nowhere to hurry - due to the flu I was not going to visit anyone. After a few days spent in bed, I attempted to climb a steep uphill road to the top of the hill. Despite the fast pulse, I continued to go with stops to rest. On the wat to the top, the road led me along a wire fence with an alarm device. Through the mesh fence, I saw the top of a nearby hill with another Jewish settlement. Passing a little more, I saw, down in the valley, an Arab village and the minaret of a mosque.

Having reached the top of the hill, the first thing I saw was a local store. On the shelves are familiar goods and necessities. I bought a jar of honey, bread, and some fruits. Leaving the store, I noticed a flat piece of ground on the outskirts of the hill and out of curiosity headed towards it. A panorama of many hills opened before me, and on the nearest one I saw not a small settlement, but a whole city of high-rise buildings of modern architecture.

Many houses were in the final stages of construction. Several minarets made me understand that this new city was built for the Arabs by the Arabs.

I read about these urban towns that the billionaire from Saudi Arabia built and financed for the Palestinian Arabs. Now I saw one of them. Compared with the single-story houses of Jewish settlers, high-rise houses in the Arab city, most of them were six or ten floors high, decorated with white stone, like in Jerusalem, looked impressive and built on a territory that in the dispute to this day.

It was much easier to go down the hill, but I didn't make such trips anymore. I thought of those who every Saturday went upstairs on foot on the way to the synagogue, but among them were only young people for whom it was no problem.
When my condition allowed me to leave the settlement, my granddaughter decided to introduce me to the nearest town called Modiin.

The trip took about an hour. A completely new asphalt road with ascents, descents and sparse, straight sections runs along with numerous Arab and Jewish settlements. Most Jewish settlements are religious communities with sturdy houses, synagogues, and yeshivas.

Arab settlements usually easily defined by numerous pointed towers of minarets and Jewish settlements by orthodoxal religious composition and fencing with guards. Arab settlements never needed protection. It continued to remind me of the unjust fate of the Jews living in the ancient land of their ancestors behind the barbed wire.

The town of Modiin-Makabiim is on the main road connecting Tel Aviv with Jerusalem. Founded in 1996, its population currently numbers over 70,000. It is a European city with modern architecture, wide streets, green spaces and a railway connecting it with the main cities of Israel.

We arrived at the Shopping Center, near the railway station. I walked along the long shopping mall; browse through the shop windows. I concluded that goods I saw were no different from American ones, and in some cases, I would even prefer the quality and style of Israeli firms. After a long walk through the floors, we sat in a café, the choice of Simi, because it was kosher, and ordered a large bowl of salad with meat, the two of us barely coped with. After a cup of coffee, we returned to the car and went home - it was necessary to pick up the children from the kindergarten.

It should mention that the bus service from our settlement gave people the ability to get to any place in Israel. The disadvantage was that after four in the afternoon, there was no bus service. Therefore, when Larissa returned from London at midnight, we had to return to Dolev by taxi and pay tenfold charge.

Larisa also had meetings with her relatives. The first on the list was Misha Kaplun, her cousin, whose two daughters lived in Israel. One daughter lived in Bat Yam, the other in Katsrin, where Misha himself lived. By occupation, a military doctor, in his youth a boxer and the international category judge, despite his eighties, he was actively involved in social work. His pride was the section of boxing, created by him in the sports club, where he coached little boys and youngsters.

Misha met us on the train platform at Bat Yam and, taking a suitcase from me, led us to the bus stop. The bus slowly, with frequent stops, made its way through the narrow streets of old Bat Yam. It could hardly cope with the traffic of cars and pedestrians in this many-fold increased by population suburb of Tel Aviv.

Larisa's relatives have been waiting for us. Misha's daughter, Tanya, began to put plates of food on the table. Tanya and her husband did not have professions that could give them a well-paid job. Tanya worked on cleaning the premises in one of the city institutions, while her husband washed private yachts in the seaport of Tel Aviv. Physically strong, the husband earned well. The eldest son also worked, but he lived separately, and the youngest, grandfather's favorite, was a schoolboy.

The next day we went to see Geta Riger, who lived right in Bat Yam. Before leaving America, we wrote to her about our trip to Israel, and she was expecting our visit. I mentioned that she was Ida's closest friend, and we never lost contact. The years have changed us all. But the disease has altered Geta so that it was painful to see this woman fighting for her life. A tube of oxygen and intermittent breathing were evidence that every day of her life is a gift.

A plentiful table with food prepared by her and her daughter Alla testified how much they were pleased with our visit. Geta was interested in everything about the life of my daughter's family in Africa, asked about my son in Cape Town, and the family of my granddaughter in Israel. Her participation in my life was rooted in the distant past of our two families warm and close relationships. This participation in my fate was preserved with her forever. Therefore, she accepted Larisa and became her friend too, realizing how we need each other and how our destinies are alike.

At parting, Geta asked to visit her before our departure. We promised.

After returning to Dolev, we decided to devote the whole day to Jerusalem and the Wailing Wall. I have been there more than once, but this time, I stood with my forehead pressed against the ancient stones and wept because I knew that this was my last visit. I felt that my state of health and my old age would not allow me to touch them again.

Hundreds of generations have been here before us, and hundreds of generations will come here after us. These ancient stones remind the whole world - the people of Israel will live. And this faith is strong as the stones of the Wall itself.

I wanted to refresh the memory of the streets of the old city, and we wandered along the way of De La Rosa and other law-streets. We joined the excursions, looked into the shops of the Arabs-merchants that were along our way. Then we walked through the area of religious Jews in the old town, and tired sat at the cafe for a snack. Before leaving, we handed out the last remaining coins to the women who were sitting on the stone steps. My wife told me that, in her opinion, those beggars making more money than we have.

Tired of many hours of walking, we met with Maor, waiting for us at the building of his work. He warned us before we left to Jerusalem that, due to the lack of buses in the direction of the settlement, he would help us to get home. During the daily trips early in the morning to work with passing transport and returning late at night, he had no problem — many already knew him.

Therefore, he wanted to help us, fearing that by mistake, we could get into a car with an Arab driver. When the vehicle of one of his acquaintances from the settlement approached, he asked him to take us first while he remained to wait for the next one. He appeared at home a few minutes after our arrival. So we got to know his daily commuting. Pursuing his after graduation study and additionally lecturing to students, he often had to return home almost at midnight, and go to work again at six in the morning. He rested only on Saturday, but this rest was relative because Maor was a voluntary lecturer in the synagogue explaining the material of the Torah, which he knew perfectly well.

The Jewish holidays of the New Year were coming. Simi with her husband and children were leaving for a planned visit to her mother in South Africa.

The public transport will not work for four days, and we decided to move to Beit Shemesh where the niece of Larisa, Vita lived. She agreed to accept us.

Saying goodbye to Simi, we took the bus, which from the village brought us to Modiin. Vita drove from Jerusalem, where she worked, to pick us up

When I saw her little car, I doubted whether our luggage could fit in it. But we found a solution. Larisa, I and Vita's daughter managed to squeeze into the back seat, and part of our luggage we put on the front passenger seat.

On the way, Vita told us about her city, its remarkable sights, archeological excavations, and historical sites visited by tourists.

I've never been there before. I knew that the city began to develop significantly after the Aliya of the 50s. One of the ancient cities of Israel, it was mentioned in the Old Testament (Tanach) BC as a city belonging to the tribe of Yehuda. He was then turned over to the tribe of Cohens. Perhaps this is why this city has a predominantly religious part of the population. Nowadays Beit Shemesh (in translation - the City of the Sun), has more than 80 thousand inhabitants. Nearly a quarter of the population repatriated from the former Soviet Union.

Even before entering the city on a hill, we saw a lot of new high-rise buildings. Pointing to these houses, Vita said that they were entirely inhabited by "penguins," explaining that by this she means orthodox Jews. I liked this comparison - clothes consisting of black and white colors, like those of penguins. It had a lot of humor and, unfortunately, bitterness. The orthodox community headed by the mayor of the city introduced many decrees, disregarding the needs of the rest, the population of the city, not religious.

We passed the railway station, next to which the bus station located. Our overloaded mini-car confidently began to take all the ascents and sharp turns of the road — paying tribute to Vita's driving experience. I would have difficulty driving a car in the labyrinth of endless turns, climbs, descents, and narrow streets of the old city. I saw that two cars could hardly miss each other. When I lived in Israel, it was not difficult, but living abroad, I had already lost the habit of narrow streets and cars parked on the sidewalk.

We drove up to a four-story complex built in the period of my Aliya of the early 70s. The climb to the fourth floor with two suitcases was not easy for me, especially after the illness, and I had to stop a few times. Inside the apartment, I sat down on the sofa, trying to take my breath. I looked around — a similar-sized apartment I had in Kiryat Yam. Outside the window, the city lights were flickering in the dark.

Vita gave us a separate room. Having unpacked the suitcases, we immediately fell asleep, tired of the long journey.
In the morning, the breakfast, and Vita had already left for work. We were taken care of by her daughter Michele. A pretty, beautiful, thin girl for her age, the girl stayed with us at home, as she had summer vacations.

It was time for Larisa to go to Germany, where she was invited to by her school friend Alexander Zatuchny, who at present was visiting his son in Jerusalem. Knowing when he was leaving Israel for Germany, Larisa, before we left America, ordered a ticket for the same flight.

She had only one day before the trip to Europe, and we again devoted this day to Jerusalem. We arrived right in the center of the city, booked an excursion. For several hours, sitting in the comfortable chairs, l we listened about the places we were passing by and learned a lot of historical details. The bus stopped frequently, and we hurried to take pictures of the amazingly beautiful city.

After completing the tour, we went to a cafe for a snack and a bottle of cold beer. After a short rest, we continued to stroll slowly without a definite goal, wanting to feel the atmosphere of the ordinary life of the citizens, which is inherent in this particular city of legend.

It was time to return to Beit Shemesh. I went to buy tickets and Larisa, tired of prolong walking around the city, was sitting on the benches outside of the central bus station.

The one who had to visit the central bus station in Jerusalem knows how this full and endless line of passengers in transitions, escalators, elevators and ticket offices, looks. Returning with tickets, I did not find my wife. In a panicked state, I quickly walked through the several similar stops, then began searching in the next street, thinking that, tired of the long wait, she decided to walk a bit. I saw her nowhere and was terrified of what could happen because when we left home, she forgot to take her phone. I could not imagine how to find her. Before asking the police for help, I decided to walk through all the stops for the last time. On one of them, I saw Larisa. She sat in the same place where I left her. I regained my composure. She was scared of my long absence. Not for a minute did she leave her seat. It was my fault - I did not remember the place where I left her. On the bus, I held her hand, as if wanting to make sure that we were together again. We were frightened but relaxed.

With the departure of Larisa to Germany, my plans to visit friends and relatives, whom I could not see because of the disease, were resumed.

Travel to see friends I often used trains because I could reach any big city. Sitting by the window and passing Tel Aviv, I looked at the skyscrapers, at the unique and talented architecture of residential, commercial, and public buildings, the city I hardly could recognize.

The endless streams of cars on wide highways did not interfere with the smooth movement of the train. With amazement and joy, I looked at the country built and how it has changed in the past sixteen years since my last visit. There were so many changes that I could not recognize the places which I often visited in those early years of my life in Israel.

Everywhere, at bus stops and on the platforms of the stations, one could see Israeli soldiers - a sign that the country is not only being built but also protected.

There are checkpoints on all major bus routes. Convinced by bitter experience, Israelis decided - it is better to lose time than human life.

Finally, I had the time to meet with Garik Schultz. He was one at the meeting in Minsk in 1970 where I first time received information about the group of people who started the movement to get permission to emigrate to Israel. Since then, we became close friends. He was in touch with me until my final immigration to South Africa. We had lost contact sixteen years ago. In Israel, he changed his name to Azgar, but I continued to call him out of old habit Garik. When I phoned him from America, I realized that he had lost his wife from lung cancer. Now he was diagnosed with brain cancer.

When I arrived in Israel, I immediately called him but being ill with the flu and knowing his condition; I decided to cancel the visit until my recovery. Then I tried to call him at home my but could not get through.

Concerned, I was able to find the phone of his daughter Karni, and she told me that her father was not at home, but in the hospital. There were allowed visits only at a specific time, and it was impossible to rely on public transport. Therefore, I was grateful to Geta's daughter, Alla and her husband Alexander for offering to help me to come to the hospital on time.

It was a sad meeting. Garik recognized me, and a smile appeared on his face. His speech was disturbed by the disease; therefore, I was talking, and he listened. I was hugging his shoulders and felt bitter that our meeting took place in such an environment. I spent nearly two hours with him, realizing that this was our last meeting. We recalled our first acquaintance forty-five years ago in Minsk, our struggle for immigration to Israel and the hard life in the early years in our long-awaited homeland. He knew more about my personal life than anyone else. He sheltered me in his apartment when I arrived in Israel.

He repeatedly took me to his home. He immediately came to my house when he learned that my daughter has disappeared before leaving for Africa. Seeing my condition, he insisted on my trip to the hospital. He always met me at the airport when I was arriving from Africa. He was one of the first creators of the Ariel settlement, where the families of his three daughters now live and where his descendants will live forever. He could not even imagine a better memory of himself.

He was excited and pleased to meet me.

Saying goodbye, we hugged for the last time. For a short instant, his eyes sparkled, and I again saw my former friend. Coming out of the room and turning around, I saw his extinct look.

The next trip was to Haifa, to meet my school days friend, Lenya Ledvich. We have not seen each other for twenty-five years. It seemed to me, except that he had gray hair and grown stout, he remained the same energetic person, I knew - the same voice, the same smile. We sat at a small table where Bella, his wife, had already arranged a tasty snack to the glasses of cognac. We came back to the events we remembered since our school days. We recalled our teachers, our friends, we recalled those who are alive and those who passed away. I stayed with them overnight, and in the morning he went with me to the bus stop. Before leaving the house, his wife reminded him of taking medicine (needed after heart surgery).

After parting with Lenya, I went to meet with Oleg - Ida's elder brother. He also lived in Haifa.

Arriving in Israel, I repeatedly tried to call him. I did not succeed. But Matvei's wife Rita told me that she gave the right phone number. Finally, I was delighted when I heard his voice. Sixteen years ago, I arrived at the Bar Mitzvah of my grandson Eitan. Oleg, learning that I was in Israel and did not visit him, was upset.

For many years I have failed to fulfill my cherished desire to come to Israel and to see Oleg.

And here I am standing in front of the door of his apartment on the tenth floor. The door opened Mara, his wife. She has changed beyond recognition. I walked over to Oleg, who was sitting on the couch, and we hugged each other. Only now I noticed two small tubes in his nose and an oxygen cylinder near the floor. I knew about the tragic death of his son Leonid in Minsk. The irreversible loss of his son, who was his pride and the joy of his life, immediately affected his health.

Oleg went through a lot of medical procedures that saved his life, but they left a trail of suffering that I saw on his emaciated face and body. "I don't understand how I can live so long when I almost died ten years ago," he said.

We sat together and recalled the distant past. We remember Ida. His devotion to his younger sister was unlimited. He reminded me how she, in the morning, before going to work, stood in the winter by the open window and cooled the hot porridge she had prepared for my breakfast. He brought only one case of her care for me, and I can never forget every day of our life, those days when we were happy.

I told Oleg about my life after my departure to Israel, about my mistake, which crippled my life and made me go to Africa. I told him about my endless worries about the bread and a roof over the heads of the family, about the loss of work and numerous failures to achieve financial stability. I told him that I am guilty, not finding an opportunity to see him before.

Rising from the couch, he led me to the wall next to his bedroom. There was a frame with photos. Among them, I saw a picture of their entire family. This photo was taken by my father in a photo studio when Ida and I got married. Ida was so beautiful and happy in this photo. Now Oleg and I, two of us, whom she had in her life, stood together and looked at her smiling face. Who could not imagine in the past what is waiting for us in the future? We looked at the photo, embraced by shared grief.

Oleg, a man who did so much for his sister and me, and whom I immensely respected and loved, could not even imagine how he was always dear to me.

Moving with difficulty and leaning on a cane, he went to accompany me to the bus. Always extraordinarily energetic and cheerful, as I knew him, and now, half-blind and old, he said goodbye, hugged me and said, "I forgive you."

I left reassured by his word that the guilt which tormented me for many years, was forgiven.

Before leaving Haifa, I called Oleg's son Volodya intending to visit, but he said that he had no time to meet with me. I remembered his meeting with me in Ra'anana when I was staying at Naomi's place. He refused to come into the house and, having talked with me for ten minutes, outside of the building, left with his wife and daughter back to Haifa. In 1998, when I arrived at Eitan's Bar Mitzvah and learned that Vova had a daughter, we bought a gift and asked Matvei to give it to Vova. Matvey refused. Then we left a box with a gift with Geta, giving her Vova's phone in Haifa. A few months later, Geta called and told us that Vova had refused the gift. We asked Geta to provide the contents of the box to those in need.

The remaining two days before Larisa's return from Germany I spent on exciting trips around the Beit Shemesh area. Vita and her daughter decided to show me the famous Stalactitic caves. A long line of cars surprised me. Visitors had to leave their cars a mile before entering the territory of the cave. We walked down the slope of the road, then stood in line for tickets. The guide led us through a semi-illuminated underground chain of caves.

Moving on the wooden flooring with a railing, we saw countless stalactites of different colors and shapes. They hung from the top of the cave like icicles. Others, on the contrary, were pointing up from the base of the grotto. There were such stalactites, which were already able to connect and they looked like two vertical carrots, which touched their sharp noses, like an hourglass. The variety of configurations was admiring, and I did not stop clicking the camera.

After leaving the cave, Vita showed me a local Christian monastery, famous for its vineyard, wine, and honey.

Not far from the monastery was a beer bar. I imagined a mug of cold beer and headed towards the enticing entrance. Vita and her daughter followed me.

At the counter with bottles, completely unknown names of beer, there was a friendly, older woman. It turns out that besides the bar, she and her husband were the owners of their brewing industry. Having explained how beer varieties differ, she poured me a large tall glass of my choice.

Having ordered a plate with several varieties of cheese, olives, bread, and a bottle of water for Vita (she did not want a beer), we sat down at a table in the shade. While Michelle and I were cracking down on our snack, I would not call it a food; Vita went to look at the Sunday market of jewelers.

When we found her, she attentively examined the silver ring and offered her daughter to try it on, saying that it was her birthday present. I was ashamed, unable to pay even for a cheap little ring. The tickets to the cave and beer at the cafe turned out to be expensive, and I only had a couple of shekels in my pocket left.

After Larisa's return from Germany, we started the scheduled visits to her relatives. Misha Kaplun mentioned above, invited us to Katsrin. We decided to stop on the road to him in Nazareth, which was halfway through, and thus visit another family of my wife's relatives.

Keeping our suitcases, we just opened the door to leave Vita's apartment when I got a phone call. It was Geta's daughter. She said that her mother had passed away last night and that there would be a funeral today. Then she added. Because of our remote location, and the traffic problems we would not be at the funeral on time. "We will meet later," she said.

This sad message took away our enthusiastic mood. We left the flat and proceeded with our plans and took the bus going to the train station. Having paid for the tickets, I found that my wallet with documents and money was gone. I got up from my place and began to check all my pockets and bag - to no avail. Larisa was depressed. Without documents and money, our trip was impossible.

The passengers looked at me with sympathy. At that time, a woman walked into the bus. One passenger, sitting next to me on the other side of the aisle, showed in the direction of the driver and said: "Look this woman found a wallet on the floor and handed it to the driver." Looking at my ID in the wallet, the driver immediately returned it to me. I sighed with relief, but for all-day, I could not recover from my carelessness.

Straight from Beit Shemesh train took us to Haifa, from where we arrived by bus to Nazareth in the afternoon. The relatives knew about our arrival.

In the big room, we saw the table laid with a lot of salads, meat dishes and, of course, alcohol. We added our bottle of good cognac and sat during the conversation until late evening. When I woke up in the morning, I looked at rooms with many porcelain, glass, crystal, vases, toys, and garlands of artificial flowers, with surprise. The furniture did not leave enough space for easy access. I was not going to make any comments about this to our hospitable hosts.

After all, each of us has its interests in life, and we must respect it.

Our trip went on. The bus brought us to Tiberias, one of the oldest cities in Israel. There, at the final stop, Oleg, the husband of Ira, Larisa's niece, was already waiting for us. Sitting in the car, he saw two older people wandering in the parking lot, pulling along a small suitcase, and came out to meet us. It turns out that he had been waiting for us for more than an hour, and with a sigh of relieve, he started the engine of the car.

The road led us up to the steep mountainous ridge, revealing a view of Lake Kinneret, on the water of which, according to legends, walked Jesus. He lived in the north of Tiberias in the Jewish city of Kfar Nachum, renamed Kaper-naum. In this city 2000 years ago, he preached his ideas and was engaged in healing. Later, in the same place, settled his followers and disciples. In the time of Jesus, the Jewish population densely populated the western shore of the lake.

It was among them that he found his faithful followers. In place of the house where Jesus lived, there is now a church.

Lake Kinneret also called the Sea of Galilee, is 213 meters below sea level. In terms of its volume, it is the largest source of drinking water in Israel, from which the Jordan River flows. It supplies the surrounding territories with water, and also serves as the border between Israel and the State of Jordan. The lake is rich in various species of fish, the most popular of which, thanks to the taste of juicy white meat, is tilapia.

In Tiberias, founded in 17 AD and named in honor of the Roman emperor Tiberius, there are holy sites for the Jews of Rabbi Rambam Maimonides, Rabbi Ben-Zakai and Rabbi Akiva. To this day, these sacred places are the subject of pilgrimage for religious Jews.

After the expulsion of the Jews from Jerusalem, Tiberias became the spiritual center of the Jewish people. As known from the Talmud, this city was the residence of the patriarch Jacob. Jerusalem's Talmud was also written there in the 5th century.

Tiberias is also known as hot mineral springs and mud sanatoriums. It is because of the presence of curative properties of the springs, the ruler of Galilee, Herod Antipas, chose it as the place of his residence. He built his palace and temple in Tiberias and made a synagogue for the Jews since it was the only city of the Roman Empire in which the majority of the population were Jews.

At present, archaeological excavations are continuing in Tiberias and its suburbs, reminiscent of the past greatness of two religions - Jewish and Christian.

Leaving Tiberias and Lake Kinneret behind, we drove along the flat plateau of Golan, which is approximately 1000 meters above sea level.

Occasionally we saw the settlements. Driving past the moshavs, we admired the fresh greens of crops and fruit trees, most of which were apple or cherry. The few oncoming vehicles testified to the evidence of sparsely populated settlements in the Golan. The development of Samaria began with the advent of Aliya from the Soviet Union, and in the 70s the settlement and irrigation of waterless land began.

Golan was the kingdom of Judah in the days of King David.

Syria became an independent state in 1946, and in the same year received the Golan from France, which until then had been decided by the League of Nations as a French Mandated Territory since 1923.

After the formation of the Jewish state of Israel, Syria began to use the Golan Heights as a springboard for attacking Israel, creating numerous military bases and fortifications there.

The war of 1967 was provoked by the Soviet Union, which wanted to strengthen its position in the Middle East and supplied a large number of the most modern arms to Egypt and Syria. Provoking the conflict, the USSR informed Egypt that, based on secret reports, Israel was collecting a large number of troops on the border with Syria. It was a lie. Invited UN observers confirmed the inconsistency of Soviet messages. Soviet Ambassador of the USSR refused an invitation from the Israeli government to visit the Israeli border with Syria and make sure that there is no concentration of Israeli troops there. Prepared by Soviet propaganda, Nasser raised his army and large formations of Egyptian forces concentrated near the Israeli border in Sinai. Then Nasser demanded from UN Secretary U Thant to remove the peacekeeping forces from the border with Israel, which had been there since 1956 by agreement of both parties.

Israel could not ignore the threat of attack, because Egypt closed the Tyrant's strait to ships carrying supplies to Eilat.

Nasser, who lost popularity in his country and neighboring countries, decided to restore his prestige. The king of Jordan, Hussein, confident in the power of the Egyptian army and Israel's defeat, decided to take the side of Egypt and concluded an alliance with it about joint actions in the attack.

Egypt did not stop there and drew Syria, Iraq, and Algeria to its side. Nasser did not conceal his plans and spoke publicly before the assembly of Arab countries about the need to destroy the state of Israel.

The Government of Israel, in dismay overseeing the coalition of five Arab countries, after Nasser's speech, made the only decision - in the name of preserving the lives of the population and soldiers - to deliver a preemptive strike. The war began on June 5, 1967, and lasted six days. It went down in history as the Six-Day War.

During the first two days of the war, Syria did not launch ground attacks. They verbally condemned the Israeli aggression, and their aircraft, attacking Haifa on the first day of the war, shot down several Israeli airplanes over their territory. After that, Israel destroyed the aviation of Syria. Then Syria began shelling Israel from guns mounted on the Golan Heights. They were well fortified, and most of the Syrian army was in the area of Quneitra, defending the road to Damascus, the capital of Syria.

Only on June 9, the Israeli army captured the Golan, and on June 10, Syrian troops fled the city heavily bombarded by Israelis.

When the UN officially declared a cease-fire, the Golan Heights were already under the control of the Israeli forces, and Quneitra occupied.

Egypt, Syria, and Jordan were defeated entirely, suffering considerable losses in man and equipment. The decision of the Soviet Union and America to stop the Israeli offensive and declare a truce saved Arabs from further defeat.

Half a century passed since that day, and now we are riding on the earth, where peace and silence reigns.

I mentioned the Six-Day War because we were on the Golan Heights. Hundreds of Israeli soldiers died here, defending the farms and cities of Israel from the shells of Syrian guns.

The Soviet Union could not forgive Israel's victory in 1967. Egypt and Syria lost almost the entire supply of the best Soviet aircraft, tanks, and other weapons. The Russians began to prepare the Arab countries for a new war, supplying them with even more modern weapons, airplanes, and tanks.

The hardest, sudden war, called the Yom Kippur War (Judgment Day), when Jews fought for their existence, was won by Israel again. Arab countries participated in the evil attack on Israel during the Holiest Day for the Jews, were again defeated. The Soviet Union and America united again, demanding that Israel stop the defeat of the Arab armies.

Israel paid for this victory at the cost of many thousands of its soldiers, died in the Judgment Day war in 1973. Despite the defeat, Syria during the peace negotiations demanded from Israel the return of the Golan Heights, which had never been a land of Syria. Syria received the Golan as a gift from France, which ignored the Jewish past of this land. For twenty-one year of ownership of this land, Syria has done nothing for its development and has built only military bases there to attack Israel. Years have passed. Syria continued to demand the return of the Golan Heights.

The Presidents of the USA showed the greatest zeal during these negotiations - Bush and Clinton - demanding that Israel agree to the terms of Syria, which owned the Golan Heights from 1946 to 1967.

Only one of the Presidents of the United States, Gerald Ford, once said that "Any peace agreement with Syria must provide for Israel to remain on Golan Heights."

Golan was the land of Jews. Wandering for 40 years in the Sinai desert, they came to the area of Canaan, which, according to the Torah, was given to settle people of Menashe. Under King David, the lands of Golan and Damascus were part of the northern kingdom of Israel.

Golda Meir warned future leaders of Israel.

"If ever there would be a government that wants to remove the Jews from Golan, the people of Israel will not forgive."

It is a pity that those rulers of Israel who ordered to remove Jewish settlements from Gaza, forcing all the inhabitants of the country to sit in bomb shelters.

Never, in the entire history of the existence of the Jewish state, was peace on its land. Unfortunately, those countries that believed in Israel right to exist, sacrifice Jews in favor of those who want to destroy Israel. Sadly, the policies of these countries shared by Israel's best friend, America. How friends differ from those who wish to destroy the Jewish state?

Coming into Katsrin, I was surprised to look at the neat and clean streets of the city, which is not on the Wikipedia map. However, why be surprised - on the maps of Arab neighbors and Palestinians - there is no Israel either. Israel does not exist in the Arab school textbooks. The majority of the Arab population has never had contact with the Israelis, and children even more so, but Arab children have developed hatred for Jews since childhood.

Archaeologists found the ancient city of Katsrin and its existence as a Jewish city dates back to the reign of Herod I. The new city was founded forty years ago and currently has a population of 15,000 people.

Katsrin is called the "capital of Golan." Today's Katsrin is a city built by Aliya settlers.

The house of Larisa's hospitable relatives was right in the center of the city. The apartment struck me with cleanliness and quality of finish. Everywhere felt the professional skill of the owner, who made his apartment comfortable for their small family of two. With the arrival of Misha Kaplun, Ira's father, we sat together at the table. During lunch, I enjoyed the smoked salmon, cultivated in artificial ponds near Katsrin. Oleg told me about his frequent fishing trips to Kinneret - they always have fresh fish at home.

Having two artificial knees, Oleg could not walk for a long time, and he drove us through the entire city in his car. We saw the first settlement houses. Then high-rise buildings of new construction, amazingly beautiful private residences, beautiful parks and several snow-white high-rise buildings for the elderly and disabled people, who lived there on the government subsidy. But our trip did not end there - he suggested to go to the border with Syria, from where we can see the city of Kuneitra, or rather what left of it.

On the highway rarely we could see incoming vehicles. More often began to appear large areas of crops and moshavs. Tree branches sagged under the weight of apples, pears, and cherries. Then we saw many long, covered with awnings, greenhouse buildings, and vineyards.

The closer we approached the border, along the road, we could see the military units. On the flat surface of the plateau, we saw high cone hills of natural origin.

One of these hills of several hundred meters high arose in front of us as we arrived at the border. A narrow road climbed straight to the top of the mountain, with many towers and antennas. Oleg, who has been here more than once, explained that this is an important observation and defense post of the Israeli army. Having passed several hundred meters, we were on the observation deck with a parking lot. Below we have a double wire fence. On the viewing platform stood a telescope, around which crowded the children of several Arab families. They looked towards Syria. With the naked eye, we could see dark gray clouds of explosions from shelling and bombing behind a ridge of low hills, to the right of Quneitra. We saw the war in reality - what usually shown on the TV screen. At this distance, nothing was visible, even with the binoculars that I took with me. We could only see the movement of the border guard of UN troop's vehicles. Their camp was in the valley on a stretch of territory serving as a dividing line between Israel and Syria.

The city of Quneitra was the main military base of the Syrian army on the border with Israel. After the defeat of Syria during the Six-Day War, when Israeli troops occupied it, the Syrian government did not allow its population to return to the city. Syria built an entirely new city next to Quneitra.
Despite the truce, Syria continued to bombard Quneitra repeatedly. It had no population. Turning it into ruins Syria at the same time often shot at Jewish settlements in the Golan Heights. After the six-day war, Israel left Quneitra, reassigning it to Syria. These ruins, for propaganda purposes, Syria showed to foreign delegations, trying to convince them of Israel's cruelty towards the city they did not occupy.

We returned home impressed by what we saw on both sides of the border.

The next day, Misha took over the patronage. Starting from his pride - the city sports club, he opened the entrance to the club with his key and led us in a vast hall.
Here, as he explained, many public events of the city and sports competitions take place. Then he brought us to the hall of his boxing section, recognized as one of the best in Israel.

Nearby there was a separate building of the city pool and a sports ground. Pointing to the wasteland next to the club, Misha said that he has plans to expand the sports complex. One could only wonder at the efforts and energy of this man, whose age was not a hindrance in such intensive social activities.

Our presence in Katsrin coincided with Yom Kippur day - the most important day for all Jews - the day when the fate of their lives decided for the next year. Transport does not work - Jews pray in synagogues. But the kids and school children on that day enjoyed themselves, riding the bikes on the streets of the city, free from traffic.

On the last day of our stay in Katsrin, Oleg and Ira decided to spend a day with us at the well-known mineral springs from Roman times. Hamat Gader – as called this place - was located in the south of the Golan Heights near the border of Jordan. The Israelis built a large swimming pool with a canopy and recreation areas at the site of these healing springs with constant water temperature. Some vacationers liked massaging the entire body with hot water streams on horizontal stone slabs hidden underwater. Others wanted to stand under the overthrowing jets of water of various shapes, as in a shower, or stand under a solid wall of water, like a waterfall. We tried all kinds of water massage.

When we returned home, was dark and bright stars glittered in the sky.

On the day of departure, we got up early at five o'clock in the morning. Soaring from the cold, we were at the bus station waiting for a direct journey to Jerusalem. It was still dark. The bus route passed through the southern part of Golan and continued along the eastern side of Lake Kinneret. I did not know this part of Israel, and therefore, was interested in everything visible outside the bus window.

At dawn, we could see Lake Kinneret. On both sides of the bus were visible settlements, moshavs, and kibbutzes on the Golan territory. One of them, Ein Gev, a small kibbutz located directly on the Kinneret River, was founded in 1937 by European immigrants who had escaped from the looming threat of fascism. This kibbutz, located on the border with Syria, was the first to endure a Syrian attack. These days the kibbutz has its fishing, based on which they opened a well-known and popular in Israel fish restaurant. There is also a vast banana plantation. The former mayor of Jerusalem, Teddy Kollek, was one of the founders of this kibbutz.

Having passed the lake, we were already driving along a narrow border strip, beyond which were visible Jordanian villages. Then we left behind the first Jewish kibbutz Degania, founded back in 1909. Degania was the next kibbutz attacked by the Syrians. The legendary commander of the Israeli army Moshe Dayan was born in this kibbutz. In 1948, he was appointed the commander of all combat units, providing resistance to the Syrian troops which were much more significant in the number of soldiers and weapons.

A Syrian tank stood at the entrance to Degania. I read about this tank, which one of the kibbutzniks stopped with an anti-tank projectile when they beat off the attack of the Syrians.

A further trip along the Jordan border along the Jordan River and the desert highlands of the West Bank was unremarkable.

The bus made a stop at a lonely cafe house next to the high way where the passengers went out to treat soar legs or to have a snack in a cafe.

The rest of the road was more pleasant. We found ourselves in the Dead Sea area, and two hours later, entered Jerusalem. Six hours on the road brought new impressions and opened to us another page in the country's life.

When we arrived at Beit Shemesh, our main base, it was already afternoon.

On the same day, we managed to go to the local grocery store, buy cake, drinks, sweets, some products, and celebrated Michelle's, Vita's daughter, birthday

My gift to Michele was an Apple iPad, a former gift to me from Ilya Bass. I used iPad only to check my mail and to be in contact with Larisa during her two trips abroad. This model did not have a photo camera, but I thought that it would be useful to her at school.

Our stay in Israel ended. Tired, tormented by constant moving from place to place and carrying suitcases behind us, we were finally going to spend the remaining three days on the Dead Sea. Simi, before her departure to Africa, when we lived in her settlement, ordered for us the hotel there.

On the day of the trip to the Dead Sea, Karni, Garik Schultz's, daughter called us to inform of his death. The loss of one of my best friends overclouded the planned vacation.

A strange coincidence - in both cases, I did not have the opportunity to pay the last debt to people so dear to me. In a sad mood, I arrived at the Dead Sea. The hotel finally allowed us to sleep and forget about the need to go somewhere. Above all expectations, the full service that accompanied us during the holidays was of high quality. After breakfast, Larisa took a course of medical procedures, and I spent this time in the open-air freshwater pool. Then, in the same building where Larisa took the healing procedures, we cautiously entered the pool connected to the constant flow of water from the Dead Sea.

From the pool, we went to our room to rest. In the hotel room, I began to look for my watch and remembered that I had left it by the pool on the couch. When I checked, it was not there. I asked the workers in the pool hall and talked with the administration. Nobody knew, and I submit to the loss. The next day, a pool worker approaches me and hands me my watch, which was on the floor under a towel next to the couch.

Naturally, we also spent several hours on the beach, swimming in the saltwater of the sea. Then, smearing ourself with mud that we bought in the store, we dried out on the sun and went to wash it off with water right there on the shore.

That was the routine of our holiday- daily visits to the pool, medical procedures, breakfasts and dinners in the restaurant, where we could choose any dish. Then it was a good sleep at the end of the day. This short vacation was the salvation of our exhausted souls after numerous trips and carrying suitcases. Three days of rest refreshed our tired bodies, and we were ready to leave.

Our plane flew off at midnight. On the day of departure, we returned from Dad See to Beit Shemesh, packed our bags, and in the evening, Vita and her daughter took us to Ben Gurion Airport.

On the plane, flying back to our new homeland, I thought about the trip and accomplishment of my cherished desire — to see Israel and my friends, to touch the Wailing Wall. My heart I left there, in Israel.

I saw what the Israelis had achieved in their small country. Inside and outside were Arabs, poisoned from an early age with hatred towards Jews.

I saw that many Jewish families find it hard to make ends meet. I saw the sad faces of those who lost their sons, daughters, and fathers. I saw the tired soldier's faces and those who returned to their homes after a hard day at work. People understood that a country surrounded by enemies was in constant danger.

I envied them all. No matter how hard life was, they were at home in their own country.

The foes are furious and inciting hate to Israel, but the Jews will never give up their land, bequeathed by God and poured over with the blood of thousands of Israeli soldiers. They defended it in four wars against five and even seven, united by a common hatred, of the Arab coalition countries, tens of times surpassing

Israel in population and armament. Arab hatred has not been able and can never defeat the people fighting for their existence.

Afterword

This book concludes the trilogy of my story - the era of the life of four generations.

My grandchildren and great-grandchildren are about as old as I remember myself before the start of the war. They will live in a different world that could seem to us as a fairy tale, but for them, it will be the world of extraordinary technological progress. The things that we see today as a fantasy; for them, it will be a reality.

My grandchildren use a computer without seeing anything surprising in it. But the natural environment that I got to know in my childhood, in their mature age, probably will be rare.

In my post-war years, there were no refrigerators. There were cellars dug in the ground, usually in barns. In the house, there was no running water. Food cooked on the gas stove (primus). The main transport in the village was a horse-drawn cart. I still remember cars which fuel was firewood.

And today we see self-driving cars and fly into space. In the countries of the civilized world, hundreds of thousands of scientists and engineers solve complex technical problems to make life better and free people from unnecessary labor and time. Advances in medicine help people deal with serious illnesses, prolonging the lifespan.

Progress cannot stop, just as none can stop thinking. The Internet has revolutionized all spheres of human life. It made it possible for the people on earth to participate in the events everywhere they desire.

Unfortunately, the high level of industry and the use of fuel have got a negative effect on our planet. Disappearing gas and oil reserves can damage all human activities. If thousands of years ago, people could do without oil and gas, and nothing would happen to them, then the current generation could hardly survive. Lack of drinking water on the planet is the most critical problem that cannot postpone for the future.

Climate change causes unprecedented floods, hurricanes, and typhoons. They destroy the lives of people, destroy the residential properties, transport, and public communications.

The destroyed nuclear power plants of Chernobyl and the Fukushima caused immeasurable harm by polluting the atmosphere, the soil, and the oceans with life-threatening to the entire living world on earth by radioactive radiation.

I think about the changes to our small planet because I'm worried about the future of my children, grandchildren and great-grandchildren, and all children on earth. Surrounded by the care and affection of the parents, I see in their eyes a joy of absorbing the beautiful world around them. And I cannot help but think about those threats to the existence of the planet's population they know nothing.

No wealth will save humanity from destruction by the forces of nature unless the most developed countries on the planet start planning the defensive measures.

Unimaginable funds spent during the endless wars, while these funds could be used to rescue from the destructive forces caused by climate change and radioactive radiation.

Now I will touch on the topic of another threat to humanity - an unexpected threat to the civilized world from the sinister forces of extremist Islam. It set a task to create an Islamic caliphate on earth and force the whole world to live according to Sharia law - to bring us back to the medieval era.

For decades, Muslims of the Middle East countries settled in all countries of the world. Millions of Arab refugees occupied the nations of Europe. Some of them became citizens, received education, worked and served in all spheres of public and private organizations, evoking respect and recognition. Unfortunately, most of them remained alien to the culture, customs, and laws of countries where they live. Mosques have become a place of incitement to hatred towards all who are not Muslim.

Imams conduct the most poisonous anti-Semitic propaganda in mosques. The small Jewish state created on the land of their ancestors is the only democratic and well-developed country in the Middle East. The Israelis defended it in four wars against countries united by common hatred of the Arab coalition.

The monstrous Holocaust of Jews by Hitler's fascism not forgotten. But this time the Jews again threatened by Islamic fascism. The world is looking at this Islamic madness with indifference as if it is not their concern. The world turned away from the Jews extermination during World War II.

German fascism wanted to destroy only Jews and communists, Islamic fascism will ruin all the rest of the world that does not accept Islam.